PRAISE FOR LINCOLN AND CHIEF JUSTICE TANEY

"In this splendidly written book, Mr. Simon . . . has given us an excellent dual biography of these two giants in American history who clashed directly on the issue of presidential power in pressing times. Thus, we are reminded that the current tension between executive power and the rule of law has a precedent from the Civil War era that merits our attention . . . an excellent history and fine biography. But it also causes us to focus on one of the critical issues of our time."

—William E. Hellerstein, *New York Law Journal*

"Fascinating. . . . An enthralling, clear and fast-moving account of Lincoln and Taney's battles from the time of the *Dred Scott* decision until Taney's death in 1864. . . . Places the Lincoln-Taney disputes into the context of the broader sweep of U.S. history, providing nourishing food for thought. . . . A fine book."

—J. Michael Parker, *San Antonio Express-News*

"*Lincoln and Chief Justice Taney* is a forceful reminder that the Civil War was more than a conflict of soldiers and that, under the rule of law, the decisions of courts could make fully as much difference—and be fully as much of a struggle—as the results of battles."

—Allen C. Guelzo, *The Wall Street Journal*

"Excellent. . . . A fresh take on who Lincoln was and how he became American history's indispensable man. . . . *Lincoln and Chief Justice Taney* is a good example of the recent renaissance of constitutional history. It preserves a sense of suspense while conveying the nuances of legal arguments."

—David Waldstreicher, *The Boston Globe*

"Simon describes this epic struggle over the Constitution in dramatic fashion, by skillfully weaving together biographical detail, political intrigue, and constitutional history. . . . As pure, old-fashioned historical narrative, the story of these two titans of the Civil War era is hard to beat."

— . . . *The Weekly Standard*

"As new books on Abraham Lincoln arrive in a seemingly relentless stream, we expect each one to disclose distinctive aspects or accomplishments of his life and presidency and to do so convincingly. Some satisfy that expectation. . . . *Lincoln and Chief Justice Taney* exceed[s] it. . . . A well-crafted dual biography. . . . Simon's analysis of the constitutionality of Lincoln's conduct is still relevant."

—Myron A. Marty, *St. Louis Post-Dispatch*

"Fair and judicious. . . . Simon is especially clear on the legal principles involved in *Dred Scott* and in a variety of other issues that came to the Taney Court. Mr. Simon is well versed in explaining Lincoln's emergence as a wartime president and his controversial decisions as commander in chief."

—Michael P. Riccards, *The Washington Times*

"Roger Taney's strained relationship with Lincoln is the subject of James Simon's brilliant exposition, *Lincoln and Chief Justice Taney*. . . . As questions of presidential power during wartime echo today, this most readable look at the events of an earlier century seems most relevant."

—Charles Stephen, *Lincoln Journal Star* (Nebraska)

"Informative, thought-provoking."

—Robert Ruth, *The Columbus Dispatch*

"Taut and gripping. . . . Simon's focus on Lincoln and Taney makes for a dramatic, charged narrative—and the focus on presidential war powers makes this historical study extremely timely."

—*Publishers Weekly* (starred review)

"Simon skillfully charts the battles that pitted Taney's acute legal mind against Lincoln's transcendent one. . . . This story is as timely as it is well-written."

—*Kirkus Reviews*

"Simon considers Lincoln's presidential actions, such as the suspension of habeas corpus and the trial of civilians in military courts—actions

Taney attempted to thwart. Their topicality to current debate is a self-evident recommendation of Simon's book; yet its jargon-free discussion of constitutional matters and the biographical angle on Taney would commend it to libraries' attention even in less acrimonious times."

—*Booklist*

"The United States has faced a number of national emergencies, fake or real, but indisputably the greatest national emergency came with the Civil War. James F. Simon has written an exciting and notable book where Abraham Lincoln and Roger B. Taney, the president and the chief justice, two men of the highest intelligence and passionate judgment, argued the future of this democratic republic."

—Arthur Schlesinger, Jr.

"Here—with apologies to Doris Kearns Goodwin—is the story of rivals who never played on the same team. Yet, as Simon skillfully shows, their mutual antipathy had a dramatic impact on the nation. Taney's infamous 1857 *Dred Scott* decision stripped African Americans of their scant rights, inspiring Lincoln's outrage—and in turn spurred his rise to the presidency. Four years later, in one of history's great ironies, Taney presided over the future emancipator's inauguration. Lincoln had the last word—and so does Simon, with a book that sheds new light on a 're-lationship' that in a way hastened the end of slavery."

—Harold Holzer, author of *Lincoln at Cooper Union* and cochairman of the U.S. Lincoln Bicentennial Commission

"The tug of war between the executive and the chief justice during the Civil War reverberates to our own days. James Simon tells the tale with insight and verve."

—Gabor Boritt, author of *The Gettysburg Gospel: The Lincoln SpeechThat Nobody Knows* and director of the Civil War Institute at Gettysburg College

"The United States suffers an unexpected attack. The president deploys the armed forces and assumes extraordinary powers that go well beyond the Constitution. Hundreds of persons suspected of aiding the enemy are arrested and held without charge. James F. Simon discusses these tensions between the president and the Supreme Court, created not by 9/11, but those between President Abraham Lincoln and Chief Justice Roger Taney during the Civil War. This well-written and engaging narrative is a primer for today's challenge of balancing national security and civil liberties."

—Frank J. Williams, chief justice, Supreme Court of Rhode Island, and
Chair, The Lincoln Forum

"In a clear, declarative style, and with balanced, fair analysis, James Simon combines legal history and grand narrative to tell the compelling story of Lincoln's epic battles with Taney. Simon does not blink on Lincoln's over-reach on the suspension of habeas corpus, nor does he shy away from Taney's retrograde racial judgments. This is a good, provocative read, and a reminder of why the constitutional separation of powers is so important, in war or peace."

—David W. Blight, Yale University, author of *Race and Reunion: The
Civil War in American Memory*

"Abraham Lincoln and Roger B. Taney, so far apart for so long, have been brought together in James F. Simon's insightful story. The aged Chief Justice Taney, known chiefly for the *Dred Scott* decision, is brought back to life in all of his rich complexity and context."

—Ronald C. White, Jr., author of *Lincoln's Greatest Speech*

Lincoln

and
Chief Justice

Taney

Slavery, Secession, and the
President's War Powers

James F. Simon

Simon & Schuster Paperbacks

NEW YORK LONDON TORONTO SYDNEY

To Marcia
and our wonderful family

SIMON & SCHUSTER PAPERBACKS
A Division of Simon & Schuster, Inc.
1230 Avenue of the Americas
New York, NY 10020

First Simon & Schuster trade paperback edition November 2007

SIMON & SCHUSTER PAPERBACKS and colophon are registered trademarks
of Simon & Schuster, Inc.

For information about special discounts for bulk purchases,
please contact Simon & Schuster Special Sales at
1-800-456-6798 or business@simonandschuster.com.

Designed by Paul Dippolito

Manufactured in the United States of America

1   3   5   7   9   10   8   6   4   2

Library of Congress Cataloging-in-Publication Data
Simon, James F.
Lincoln and Chief Justice Taney : slavery, secession,
and the president's war powers / James F. Simon.
p.   cm.
Includes bibliographical references and index.
1. Slavery—Law and legislation—United States—History.
2. Executive power—United States—History.   3. War and emergency powers—
United States—History.   4. Secession—United States—History.   5. Lincoln,
Abraham, 1809–1865.   6. Taney, Roger Brooke, 1777–1864.   I. Title.

KF4545.S5S55   2006

342.7308'7—dc22   2006044399

ISBN-13: 978-0-7432-5032-0
ISBN-10:   0-7432-5032-X
ISBN-13: 978-0-7432-5033-7 (pbk)
ISBN-10:   0-7432-5033-8 (pbk)

CONTENTS

INTRODUCTION

President Abraham Lincoln and Chief Justice Roger Brooke Taney bitterly disagreed on three fundamental issues—slavery, secession, and Lincoln's constitutional authority during the Civil War. But had they known each other in less perilous times, they might have been friends, or at least respectful adversaries. In fact, they had much in common.

Lincoln and Taney were homely physical specimens—tall, gaunt, slightly cadaverous figures, usually attired in drab, ill-fitting clothes. Each man believed in a divine design that guided him, though Lincoln shirked organized religion while Taney was a devout Catholic. Both men were known for their personal integrity, fairness, and compassion for those less fortunate than themselves. Self-effacing in public, they possessed an unrelenting will to succeed.

In their prime, Taney and Lincoln were among the best litigators in their respective states of Maryland and Illinois. Without flourish, Taney demonstrated the extraordinary ability to lay the facts and law of a case bare before a judge or jury. Lincoln often embroidered his major legal points with folksy stories, but he never lost sight of the argument that would win the case for his client.

Both men disapproved of the institution of slavery. As a young lawyer, Taney freed his slaves and pronounced slavery immoral in a Frederick, Maryland, courtroom. Since childhood, Lincoln had considered slavery wrong and never wavered in his conviction. Taney and Lincoln were actively involved in colonization societies whose purpose was to remove free blacks (including, they hoped, an increasing number of eman-

I

cipated slaves) from the United States to be resettled in a self-governing colony in Africa. But as lawyers, they defended the property rights of slaveowners under state laws that protected slavery.

Taney and Lincoln agreed on the need for a strong Union. Each was active in state politics and was considered a moderate, though they followed national leaders with very different philosophies. Taney campaigned vigorously for the populist Democrat Andrew Jackson in 1828. Like Jackson, Taney was suspicious of vested corporate interests. After Jackson was elected president, he appointed Taney to be his Attorney General and, later, Secretary of the Treasury. Together, Jackson and Taney fought the Second Bank of the United States, which they believed symbolized autocratic corporate power. When Chief Justice John Marshall died, Taney was Jackson's choice to replace him.

Lincoln's political hero, Kentucky's Henry Clay, challenged Jackson in his reelection bid for the presidency in 1832. The twenty-three-year-old Lincoln (who was a generation younger than Taney) supported Clay's American System, which defended the Bank of the United States as essential to the economic prosperity of the country. After Clay lost the 1832 election, Lincoln served four terms in the Illinois legislature and became a successful Springfield lawyer. Throughout those years, he remained loyal to Clay, supporting him in two more losing efforts to win the presidency.

The issue of slavery did not dominate the national political debate during the 1840s, as it would the next decade. Taney and Lincoln took cautious public positions on slavery in the forties. As Chief Justice, Taney carefully steered the Court away from expansive decisions when slavery was an issue, insisting that the relevant state law governed. In his single term in the House of Representatives in the late forties, Lincoln did not take a leadership role on the slavery issue. His only initiative on the subject was to propose a referendum for the District of Columbia that abolished slavery, but enforced the Fugitive Slave Law and compensated slaveowners who freed their slaves. His compromise proposal did not satisfy either abolitionists or pro-slavery members of Congress and was never formally introduced.

During the 1850s, Taney and Lincoln moved to center stage in the increasingly rancorous national debate over slavery. In his *Dred Scott* opinion, Taney declared that the U.S. Constitution did not grant the black man any rights that the white man was bound to honor. Taney also held that Congress could not prohibit the spread of slavery in the western territories. Shortly after Taney announced the Court's *Dred Scott* decision in 1857, Lincoln attacked it as a warped judicial interpretation of the framers' intent. Lincoln made his opposition to the Court's decision a major theme in his campaign for the Senate in 1858. In the famous Lincoln-Douglas debates, Lincoln denounced the *Dred Scott* decision and accused Douglas and Taney of being members of a pro-slavery national conspiracy.

In his presidential inaugural address in 1861, Lincoln insisted that the South had no legal right to secede. Chief Justice Taney disagreed. He not only believed that secession was legal, but also that a peaceful separation of North and South, with each section forming an independent republic, was preferable to civil war. Once eleven states in the South had seceded, Lincoln broadly interpreted his constitutional powers as commander in chief to prosecute the war. Chief Justice Taney vociferously dissented, accusing Lincoln of assuming dictatorial powers in violation of the Constitution.

This book will trace the long, sometimes tortuous journeys that brought Lincoln and Taney to their final judgments, and actions, on the issues that threatened the survival of the United States.

Chapter One

"A MOONLIGHT MIND"

R oger Brooke Taney* was born on St. Patrick's Day, 1777, in a three-story white clapboard house set on the crest of a gentle hill overlooking the Patuxent River in southern Maryland. Taney's birthplace had served as home to five generations of Taneys, beginning with the first Michael Taney, who had immigrated from England in 1660. Michael I, as he was known in Taney family lore, initially worked the land as an indentured servant. After paying off his debt, he acquired a small plot of land and gradually expanded his holdings to several thousand acres. The land was fertile and particularly conducive to the growth of tobacco, which found an eager market in Great Britain. Michael I prospered, befriended other leaders in the colony, including Lord Baltimore, and was pleased to be referred to as "Michael Taney, Gentleman."

The flourishing tobacco economy of southern Maryland transformed the Taneys into members of that region's landed aristocracy. Slaves labored in their fields and served them in their plantation home. Succeeding generations of Taneys rode to hounds, entertained neighbors on a grand scale, and married other members in their high social class. Michael II inherited the estate overlooking the Patuxent and married Dorothy Brooke, a descendant of Robert Brooke, who traced his family roots to William the Conqueror. Sometime between the first and fourth

---

* The name is pronounced "Taw-ney."

generation, the Taneys, who were originally members of the Church of England, converted to Catholicism.

Michael V, the future Chief Justice's father, was educated at a Catholic English school at Saint-Omer in France before assuming his position as gentleman planter and leader of the prominent Taney family. But Michael V's boisterous personality and restless nature were not well suited to his designated aristocratic station. He was a loud, hard-drinking sportsman who was happiest fishing, shooting wild geese, and fox-hunting. And he had a volcanic temper. In 1819, Michael stabbed another man to death in an argument over the honor of a woman. He fled to Virginia; a year later, he was thrown from a horse and died.

It was said that Roger Taney inherited his father's temper but little else. He was a frail, bookish boy, who appeared to be greatly influenced by his mother, Monica Brooke Taney. She possessed a kind, sensitive nature, which her son lovingly recalled. "She was pious, gentle, and affectionate, retiring and domestic in her tastes," he wrote. "I never in my life heard her say an angry or unkind word to any of her children or servants, nor speak ill of any one." As an adult, Roger would emulate his mother in his compassionate treatment of his own children and the family's slaves.

Roger's older brother, Michael VI, was destined to inherit the family estate. Education, therefore, became particularly important for Roger, so that he might acquire the knowledge and skills necessary to fulfill his father's ambition that he should become a lawyer. As small boys, Roger and his older brother walked three miles to a tutor whose qualifications were limited to a modest ability to read and write. Later, the two boys boarded at a grammar school ten miles from the Taney estate. But the teacher was delusional and drowned in the Patuxent River after acting upon his misguided belief that he could walk on water. Finally, Roger came under the excellent tutelage of Princeton-educated David English, who instructed the boy until he was sent away at the age of fifteen to Dickinson College in Carlisle, Pennsylvania. For the next three years, Roger took classes in ethics, metaphysics, logic, and criticism with the brilliant head of the college, Dr. Charles Nisbet, a Presbyterian minister from Montrose, Scotland. He also studied languages, mathematics, and geography with other members of the faculty. At graduation, Roger was chosen to make the valedictory address, an honor that he modestly devalued, pointing out that his selection was based neither on grades nor the faculty's judgment, but rather on the vote of his fellow students.

Taney returned to the family estate in 1796 and spent the winter days fox-hunting and eating lavishly. In the evenings the Taney men and their male neighbors gathered around the fireside to swap stories, frequently about the courtroom triumphs of two of the state's legendary trial lawyers, Luther Martin and William Pinckney. These anecdotes were particularly welcomed by Michael V, who made no secret of his desire to have his intense, intellectually gifted son, Roger, study law. Later that year, at the age of nineteen, Roger was dispatched to Annapolis to read law in the chambers of Jeremiah Chase, one of the three judges of the General Court. For the next three years, Taney pored over law books for twelve hours a day. And when he was not studying, he sat in court taking notes on the techniques and arguments of the leading trial lawyers.

After Taney was admitted to the bar in 1799, he anxiously prepared to try his first case in Annapolis's Mayor's Court. His client was a man charged with assault and battery in a fistfight in which neither combatant was severely hurt. For Taney, the details of his legal argument were the least of his problems. He was paralyzed with terror at the thought of his first courtroom argument, his fright compounded by consuming concern over his fragile health. His hands shook uncontrollably and his knees trembled throughout the ordeal of the trial. Taney, nonetheless, won the case.

Even as an experienced litigator, Taney never completely overcame a chronic panic when he rose to speak in court. "[M]y system was put out of order by slight exposure," he recalled, "and I could not go through the excitement and mental exertion of a court, which lasted two or three weeks, without feeling, at the end of it, that my strength was impaired and I needed repose." His worries about his health were unrelenting, and so were his courtroom successes.

After a brief time in Annapolis, Taney moved to Frederick, Maryland, where he built a thriving law practice. He married Anne Key, the sister of Taney's close friend Frank Key (who became famous later as Francis Scott Key, the composer of the national anthem). Anne Key Taney embodied many of the attributes of Roger's adored mother. She was gentle and kind, and appeared, over the years, to moderate her husband's dark moods and quick temper. Together, they raised six daughters, all in Anne's Episcopal faith. Once, when a local priest visited the Taneys to press his case for Catholicism on the Taney children, Roger abruptly interrupted, informing the clergyman that religious debate was not allowed in his home.

Michael V expected Roger to distinguish himself in state politics as well as law. Toward this end, he persuaded his son to become a candidate for the Maryland House of Delegates shortly after he had settled in Frederick. Roger ran as a member of the Federalist Party, to which the Taneys as well as virtually all other members of the landed aristocracy in southern Maryland belonged. He won the election, primarily because of his father's influential contacts—and despite his own lack of the natural politician's rapport with a crowd. He was defeated for reelection two years later.

The election defeat did not discourage Taney from taking an active role in Federalist politics, and he soon became a state leader of the party. Taney took forceful positions on controversial issues, none more important than his dramatic split with Federalist Party regulars over the War of 1812. No sooner had the bankers and merchants in the northeastern states, the backbone of the Federalist Party, denounced the war than Taney declared his support for it. After he was viciously attacked by Federalist Party regulars in Maryland for his position, Taney unleashed a blistering rebuttal, suggesting that his critics had placed their property interests above the nation's honor.

Taney's attack on the mercantile class was not so radical as it first might appear. The Taneys and other members of the planter aristocracy in southern Maryland had always been suspicious of the merchants and bankers who had served as middlemen between the tobacco planters and their foreign markets. Taney's support for the War of 1812, and, implicitly, Republican president James Madison, allowed him to vent his hostility toward the Federalists' mercantile class that opposed it. In so doing, Taney sounded more like a Jeffersonian Republican than a Federalist in his support for the masses against the vested commercial interests of urban America. It was a theme that Taney would strike again and again, first as a member of President Andrew Jackson's cabinet and later as Chief Justice of the United States.

In 1816, Taney ran successfully for a five-year term in the state senate. During his legislative term, Taney acted publicly on behalf of free blacks and privately to improve the lives of his slaves. He supported state legislation to protect free blacks from unscrupulous whites who seized them for sale as slaves. He also became voluntary counsel to an organization that fought the kidnapping of free blacks and their imprisonment for lack of papers to prove their freedom. With his friend Frank Key, Taney served as an officer of a colonization society that worked to send free blacks to a colony in Africa. And Taney quietly manumitted most of his own slaves and took personal financial responsibility for supporting his older slaves, giving them wallets for small silver pieces that he replenished every month.

As a practicing attorney in Frederick, Taney was opposed to slavery and made his views known most dramatically in 1819 in his successful defense of an abolitionist preacher, the Reverend Jacob Gruber. At an early age, Gruber had left his family in Bucks County, Pennsylvania, to preach the Methodist gospel throughout the countryside of the mid-Atlantic states, from New York to North Carolina. Dressed in a somber gray suit and broad-brimmed hat, Gruber exhorted the faithful to fear God and lead a righteous life. He detested alcohol, cigars, and high fashion, taking special exception to men's walking sticks and women's exposed petticoats. But he saved his harshest judgments for those who strayed from basic Methodist tenets, among them, the church's belief that the institution of slavery was immoral.

On August 16, 1818, Gruber preached to three thousand men and women, including several hundred blacks, at an evening camp meeting of the Methodist Society in Hagerstown, Maryland, located in the western part of the state near the Pennsylvania border. Gruber spoke for slightly more than an hour on the subject of national sin, enumerating the obstacles to a righteous life, which included intemperance, profanity, and infidelity. Finally, he devoted the last fifteen minutes of his sermon to what he called the national sin of slavery and oppression.

"Is it not a reproach to a man to hold articles of liberty and independence in one hand and a bloody whip in the other, while a negro stands and trembles before him with his back cut and bleeding?" Gruber asked. What he termed "this inhuman traffic and cruel trade [in slaves]" had torn apart the most tender familial bonds. "That which God has joined together," the preacher thundered, "let not man put asunder." He condemned the slaveowners in his audience who had disregarded this divine injunction, and asked, "Will not God be avenged on such a nation as this?"

There was much grumbling among the slaveowners who attended Gruber's sermon, and rumors quickly spread that the preacher would be jailed for his inflammatory ideas. A few weeks later, a grand jury returned a true bill charging that Gruber "unlawfully, wickedly, and maliciously intended to instigate and incite diverse negro slaves, the property of diverse citizens of the said state [of Maryland], to mutiny and rebellion." After the indictment, Gruber was assured by a fellow Methodist clergyman that he would be represented by the finest legal counsel available in western Maryland—"Lawyer Taney, the most influential and eminent barrister in Washington and Frederick [counties]."

Taney's first official act as Gruber's attorney was to successfully petition to have the trial moved to a courtroom in his hometown of Frederick, away from Hagerstown, where, according to Taney, "great pains had been taken to inflame the public mind against him." In his opening statement at the trial, which took place in March 1819, Taney reminded the three-judge panel that freedom of expression was protected by the Maryland Constitution, even a discussion of that most controversial subject, slavery. "No man can be prosecuted for preaching the articles of his religious creed," said Taney, "unless his doctrine is immoral, and calculated to disturb the peace and order of society." With that simple opening, Taney suggested to the judges the high legal standard they should apply to find his client guilty: the Reverend Gruber could only be convicted if his words were "immoral," and *calculated* to disturb the peace.

With sure, lethal blows, Taney then proceeded to destroy the prosecutor's case, first noting that the indictment had not accused Gruber of "immoral" speech. That left the single charge that the preacher had intended to incite the slaves to riot. But his client was no calculating incendiary, Taney insisted. No one in the crowd, he maintained, could have been surprised that Gruber, a member of a religious sect that believed slavery was a sin, would preach on the evil of the institution. If a slaveholder feared the effect that the Reverend Gruber's words would have on his slaves, he could have kept them on the plantation. "Mr. Gruber did not go to the slaves; they came to him. They could not have come if their masters had chosen to prevent them." Based on the facts, the judges were bound to conclude, as Taney did, that the intentions of the Reverend Gruber were pure and entirely consistent with both his religious calling and the laws of Maryland.

Had Taney rested his case there, his presentation would have been no more remarkable than that of scores of his other superb courtroom arguments. He had laid out his case to the judges in a spare, direct narrative that clung tightly to the facts and relevant law. But in this case, unlike any other that Taney tried during his distinguished career, the future author of the Supreme Court's *Dred Scott* opinion chose to speak with uncharacteristic passion about the institution of slavery:

> A hard necessity, indeed, compels us to endure the evil of slavery for a time. It was imposed upon us by another nation, while we were yet in a state of colonial vassalage. It cannot be easily or suddenly removed. Yet, while it continues, it is a blot on our national character, and every real lover of freedom confidently hopes that it will be effectually, though it must be gradually, wiped away; and earnestly

looks for the means by which this necessary object may be best attained. And until it shall be accomplished, until the time shall come when we can point without a blush to the language held in the Declaration of Independence, every friend of humanity will seek to lighten the galling chain of slavery, and better, to the utmost of his power, the wretched condition of the slave.

Despite his peroration at the Gruber trial, Taney remained true to his heritage as a member of the planter aristocracy of southern Maryland. While he deplored slavery at the abolitionist's trial in 1819, he never advocated forcible elimination of the institution. For Taney, the evil of slavery could only be eliminated gradually through state laws that were supported by the voters, presumably including some of the slaveowners who had perpetuated the system. Though the record is not conclusive, Taney appeared to have opposed the Missouri Compromise in 1820 because he did not believe Congress had the authority to determine whether future states carved out of the Louisiana Territory would be slave or free.

Taney left Frederick in 1823 to establish a law office in Baltimore, and his reputation as an outstanding advocate rapidly expanded beyond Maryland's borders. With Massachusetts senator Daniel Webster as his co-counsel, Taney made an important argument before the U.S. Supreme Court in 1826, representing Solomon Etting, a prominent Baltimore merchant. Etting had endorsed a security bond of the Baltimore branch of the Bank of the United States, unaware that the branch's cashier, James McCulloch, had been systematically plundering the bank's reserves. When Etting learned about McCulloch's illegal practices, he indignantly refused to pay, declaring that the bank had effectively voided the contract by concealing the fact of McCulloch's fraudulent conduct until the security was provided. The bank sued Etting and won in the lower courts.

Taney and Webster appealed to the Supreme Court, where Associate Justice Joseph Story eagerly anticipated their oral argument. The case promised relief for the justices who, according to Story, "have had but little of that refreshing eloquence which makes the labors of the law light." Story expected Taney and Webster to illuminate the complex issues of what he called "a great case of legal morality." Webster was well known to the justices, but Story wrote that his co-counsel, Taney, was also "a man of fine talents." Taney and Webster's arguments persuaded three members of the Court, including Story, that the bank had engaged in "a positive deceit by acts though not by words." But unfortunately for Solomon Etting, an equal number of justices, led by Chief Justice John Marshall, refused to hold the bank legally responsible for its cashier's acts. The lower court judgment, therefore, remained in effect.

While practicing law in Baltimore, Taney reached middle age, and his frayed appearance reflected the wear and responsibility of the years. His tall frame and loosely fitting clothes would later invite comparisons with Abraham Lincoln. But Taney lacked Lincoln's physical energy. His broad, stooping shoulders seemed to support his lank body tenuously. And yet when Taney spoke to judge or jury, he commanded their complete attention, an improbable feat given the fact that he spoke in a low, hollow voice, without gesture, literary illusion, or highly charged oratory.

William Pinckney, a superb trial lawyer himself, said that he could match the logic of Taney's arguments, but there was no adequate response to "that infernal apostolic manner of his." With grudging admiration, Pinckney concluded that Taney, above all other members of the Maryland bar, made the most difficult legal problems seem clear. Taney was a man with "a moonlight mind," said Willard Wirt, who would later serve as U.S. Attorney General, explaining that "like moonlight of the arctics," Taney "gave all the light of day without its glare."

In 1827, Taney was appointed Attorney General of Maryland, a position that offered meager remuneration but enormous prestige—implicit recognition by the state of the officeholder's superior achievements in the legal profession. Taney acknowledged that a large measure of his satisfaction in serving as state attorney general derived from the fact that his predecessors included Luther Martin and William Pinckney, giants of the state bar whom Taney had attempted to emulate all of his professional life.

Taney began to take admiring notice of General Andrew Jackson after Jackson became a candidate for president of the United States in 1824. The crowded field of presidential aspirants included not only Jackson, the military hero of the Battle of New Orleans in the War of 1812, but also Massachusetts's John Quincy Adams and Henry Clay of Kentucky. Jackson impressed Taney as honest and independent, qualities that Taney believed would allow Jackson, if elected, to make decisions free of sectional prejudices or pressures from powerful commercial interests. During the campaign, Jackson clinched Taney's support when he denounced the Federalist regulars who had opposed the War of 1812, a position that Taney himself had publicly taken many years earlier.

Jackson won the popular vote, but that did not make him president. When no candidate could claim a majority of the electoral votes, the contest was sent to the House of Representatives for resolution. There a deal was reputedly made between representatives of Adams and Clay. The result was that Clay electors switched their support to Adams and, subsequently, President-elect Adams appointed Clay Secretary of State. This left Jackson's supporters, including Taney, feeling helpless and bitter, but resolved to win the presidency for Jackson outright in 1828.

The nation was divided along sectional lines in the presidential campaign of 1828. The incumbent, Adams, was unbeatable in the northern and eastern states. But Jackson, the Democrat, was wildly popular in the western and southern states. Taney took a leadership role in Jackson's campaign in Maryland, which, as a border state, was the scene of furious activity by both presidential camps. Although Maryland's electors split almost equally between the candidates, Taney's strong efforts helped neutralize Adams's advantage of incumbency and the spoils of office. He was elated when returns across the country gave Jackson a decisive victory in both the popular and electoral vote.

President-elect Andrew Jackson arrived in Washington on a giddy wave of populist enthusiasm. The white-maned, ramrod-straight Jackson promised to decide issues of national policy fearlessly and without favor to any special interest. His pledge delighted the rank-and-file farmers and small-town merchants in the West and South, but made the large banking and corporate interests in the East exceedingly nervous, an anxiety that would intensify throughout Jackson's presidency.

Midway through his first presidential term, Jackson appointed Taney Attorney General of the United States. Jackson's selection of Taney, like so many fateful political appointments in American history, owed as much to happenstance as to Taney's obvious talents as a lawyer. From the very first days of the Jackson administration, the president presided over a dysfunctional cabinet whose most prominent members displayed both personal and professional animosity toward each other. Finally, Jackson demanded the resignations of his original cabinet, including Attorney General John Berrien, who was replaced by Taney.

Over the next three years, Taney became Jackson's indispensable ally in the president's monumental fight with the powerful Bank of the United States. But before that confrontation between Jackson and the bank erupted, Taney was asked to provide a wide range of legal opinions to the administration. Taney's reasoning in one of these early unpublished advisory opinions, on states' rights and slavery, would be stored like a time bomb, to be detonated more than a quarter century later in *Dred Scott v. Sandford*.

Taney's opinion was written in response to a request from Secretary of State Edward Livingston for a legal opinion on the apparent conflict between U.S. treaty obligations with Great Britain and state laws, with particular attention to a South Carolina statute protecting slavery. Taney was also asked by Livingston to determine if slaves on colonial vessels flying the British flag were protected by the flag while in northern ports of the United States, or whether, upon disembarking, they became free under abolitionist laws of the states.

The South Carolina law provided that free blacks employed on foreign vessels that entered the ports of the state should be seized and held in prison while the vessel was in port. Upon the departure of the vessel, the blacks were released if the master of the vessel paid the costs of their imprisonment; otherwise, they were sold to recover these costs. A British diplomatic officer in the United States had objected to South Carolina's seizure of members of a British crew, who were free blacks and subjects of the king, as a violation of U.S. treaty obligations with Great Britain.

In his response to Livingston's inquiries, Taney contended that neither U.S. treaty obligations nor federal law could interfere with laws of the individual states. A slave state like South Carolina had the legal right to enforce its laws, Taney wrote, even if those laws deprived British subjects who happened to be free blacks of their freedom. Applying the same states' rights interpretation in the northern case, Taney suggested that neither an international treaty nor a federal statute could protect the property interests of slaveowners. If their slaves disembarked in a free state, they became free under the relevant state law.

In an analysis later repeated in his *Dred Scott* opinion, Taney insisted that the southern states had not surrendered their right to protect slavery when the Constitution was adopted. Nor could this right be abrogated by federal laws or treaties. The Constitution made treaties the law of the land, Taney conceded, but no treaty could undermine the reserve rights of the states under the Tenth Amendment.* He denied that African Americans, whether free or slave, had any constitutional rights. The framers, according to Taney, never intended for blacks of any status to have rights protected by the document. "They were not looked upon as citizens by the contracting parties who formed the Constitution," he wrote, and "evidently not supposed to be included by the term *citizens*."

In blunt, uncompromising language, the future Chief Justice relegated African Americans to the status of a permanent underclass in the United States: "The African race in the United States even when free, are every where a degraded class, and exercise no political influence. The privileges they are allowed to enjoy, are accorded to them as a matter of

---

* The Tenth Amendment provides: "The powers not delegated to the United States by the Constitution, nor prohibited by it to the States, are reserved to the States respectively, or to the people."

kindness and benevolence rather than of right. They are the only class of persons who can be held as mere property, as slaves. And where they are nominally admitted by law to the privileges of citizenship, they have no effectual power to defend them, and are permitted to be citizens by the sufferance of the white population and hold whatever rights they enjoy at their mercy."

Had Attorney General Taney's opinion been made public, it would undoubtedly have inflamed opponents of slavery in the North. That was surely a reason that the opinion was left unpublished. But on another divisive issue, the federal government's challenge to the authority of the Bank of the United States, Taney's opinions were both public and controversial and would place him at the epicenter of the greatest political storm of Jackson's presidency.

The Bank of the United States had been the original idea of Alexander Hamilton, who had envisioned the institution to be a mutually beneficial alliance between the private business community and the federal government. As Secretary of the Treasury in President George Washington's first cabinet, Hamilton had recommended the creation of the National Bank, modeled on the Bank of England, that would instantly provide fiscal credibility and economic might to the fledgling republic. Under Hamilton's plan, the government could borrow large sums from the bank, which would also serve as the exclusive depository of federal funds.

Even in 1791, the concept of a national bank was controversial and the subject of an intense debate within President Washington's cabinet. Secretary of State Thomas Jefferson adamantly opposed the creation of the bank for both political and constitutional reasons. Jefferson feared that the bank would become Hamilton's ready instrument to centralize power in the federal government, sapping the authority of the individual states. On the constitutional level, Jefferson argued that nothing in the Constitution authorized Congress to charter a national bank. He conceded that Congress, under Article I, could use all "necessary and proper" means to achieve legitimate constitutional goals.* But Jefferson insisted that the framers meant the "necessary and proper" clause to be interpreted narrowly to preserve the rights of the states. The bank could only be deemed "necessary," he argued, if it were indispensable to achieve an express congressional objective. Since the bank was not essential to any of the nation's basic objectives, Jefferson maintained, its creation by Congress was unconstitutional.

Hamilton countered that the bank was vital to ensure the nation's economic growth. He argued further that the framers intended the Constitution's "necessary and proper" clause to be interpreted much more broadly that Jefferson had suggested. So long as the bank was a "convenient" or "useful" means to achieve Congress's express goals under Article I, Hamilton contended, it must be considered constitutional. And Hamilton had no doubt that the bank would facilitate several of Congress's goals, including raising and collecting taxes, borrowing money, and regulating commerce.

President Washington sided with Hamilton in his debate with Jefferson, and the Bank of the United States was born. Jefferson never overcame his hostility to the bank, nor was he ever convinced that, under his strict interpretation, it was constitutional. The bank, nonetheless, became an integral part of the nation's economic life, so much so that Jefferson's successor and close Republican ally, James Madison, supported the creation of the Second Bank of the United States in 1816. Three years later, Hamilton's argument in favor of the bank's constitutionality became the law of the land when Chief Justice Marshall, in his opinion in *McCulloch v. Maryland*, adopted the first Treasury Secretary's broad interpretation of the "necessary and proper" clause to justify the establishment of the bank.

Only eleven years after the Court's *McCulloch* decision, President Andrew Jackson challenged the authority of the bank, which he viewed

---

* Under Article I, section 8, Congress is given the authority to tax, regulate commerce, borrow money, and raise and support armies, among other powers, and "to make all laws which shall be necessary and proper" to implement those powers.

as a symbol of concentrated and unaccountable economic power. In an address to Congress, Jackson fired the first shot in what would be known as the Bank War. He proposed that a new Bank of the United States be established with strictly limited responsibilities. Under Jackson's plan, the bank would operate as a branch of the Treasury Department and would no longer be able to make loans or issue notes.

The Jackson proposal held obvious appeal to the president's states' rights supporters in the West and South as well as for state banks throughout the nation. But it chagrined Nicholas Biddle, the urbane, supremely confident president of the Bank of the United States. Under Biddle's shrewd, autocratic leadership, the bank had developed into a formidable national political and economic powerhouse that no office-holder, not even the president of the United States, could afford to ignore. From his well-appointed office on Chestnut Street in Philadelphia, Biddle ran his institution as a private corporation completely independent of the federal government, even though government deposits represented one fourth of its capital and federal officials composed one fifth of its directors.

Since Biddle had become president of the bank in 1823, he had assiduously courted the most powerful politicians in Congress. After Jackson announced his proposal to curb the bank's authority, Biddle demanded that his congressional supporters meet the president's challenge head-on. Pro-bank members of Congress were instructed by Biddle to support a bill to renew the charter of the bank with its existing authority intact, even though the charter was not due to expire for several years. To champion the bank's cause, Biddle enlisted the services of Henry Clay and Daniel Webster, two of the Senate's most influential members, who also served as private counsel to the bank. And when Biddle learned that President Jackson's Secretary of the Treasury, Louis McLean, might favor the bank's position, he arranged for bank officials to open confidential discussions with McLean to gain his support with the ultimate objective of discouraging the president from opposing the recharter bill.

On the basis of early cabinet discussions on the bank controversy, Taney had the impression that he alone opposed the renewal of the bank's charter. He, nonetheless, did not hesitate to attack the bank's bill. And later, in the privacy of his office, he wrote a memorandum to Jackson urging him to veto the bill if Congress passed it, boldly arguing that the president should declare the legislation unconstitutional. Even if the bank was once "necessary" to conduct the nation's business, as Chief Justice Marshall had concluded in his 1819 *McCulloch* decision, Taney contended that the institution run by Nicolas Biddle in 1832 could no longer sustain that constitutional argument.

In addition to challenging the constitutional orthodoxy of Chief Justice Marshall, Taney expressed his long-standing hostility to concentrated economic power. There was no justification, wrote Taney, for "subjecting the people of this country to the evils and abuses which great moneyed monopolies have always occasioned." The president should declare the bank legislation unconstitutional, regardless of the opinion of Congress or the Supreme Court. That was Jackson's constitutional prerogative as the nation's chief executive, he concluded.

A week after the bank's recharter bill was passed by Congress, Jackson sent a veto message condemning the bank's concentration of economic power in the hands of a few men unresponsive to the people. In declaring the legislation unconstitutional, the president's words reflected the audacious opinion of his attorney general. "The opinion of the judges [of the Supreme Court] has no more authority over Congress than the opinion of Congress has over the judges, and on that point the President is independent of both," Jackson wrote. "The authority of the Supreme Court must not, therefore, be permitted to control the Congress or the Executive when acting in their legislative capacities, but to have only such influence as the force of their reasoning may deserve."

After delivering his veto message, Jackson returned to his Tennessee home. "The veto works well everywhere," he reported. "[I]t has put down the Bank instead of prostrating me." But Jackson's opponents disagreed with his assessment, and immediately acted to turn the president's defiant veto message to their advantage. Daniel Webster, stately and severe in appearance, rose on the floor of the Senate to denounce Jackson's action. In his booming baritone voice, he charged that the president's veto message was dangerous demagoguery, which "wantonly attacks whole classes of the people, for the purpose of turning against them the prejudices and resentments of other classes."

Webster also scorned Jackson's constitutional argument, which he recognized as Taney's legal handiwork. He ridiculed the notion that the bank, whose constitutionality had been proclaimed by the great Chief Justice Marshall, could later be challenged. Since the Marshall Court had declared the bank constitutional, Webster maintained that all of the features that might normally belong to it were constitutional. Later, in a private letter to Justice Joseph Story, Webster dismissed Taney's constitutional argument as "trash."

Webster's Senate speech attacking Jackson was quickly converted into a widely distributed campaign document for Henry Clay, the presidential nominee of the National Republicans (later known as Whigs) who opposed Jackson in the 1832 election. Clay, fifty-five years old, had commanded a national following for two decades and had already made one serious run for the presidency. He was tall and thin, with twinkling gray eyes, and could dazzle a crowd with his casual charm or oratorical brilliance. Clay's platform for election was his American System, a three-pronged commitment to a strong federal government: high tariffs, internal improvements, and an unwavering endorsement of the Bank of the United States.

The Clay-Jackson presidential campaign in the fall of 1832 was tense and bitter, with each man's supporters conjuring up apocalyptic visions of the consequences of the victory of their opponent. Clay was portrayed by the Democrats as a tool of the National Bank and other vested corporate interests, while Jackson was seen by the National Republicans as an unprincipled demagogue pandering to the masses. Though the election in many states was tightly contested, in the end Jackson won by a decisive electoral vote margin, 219–49.

Attorney General Taney rejoiced when he heard the news of the president's reelection, not only because the victory was vindication for

Jackson's Democratic principles, but also for his own resolute opposition to the Bank of the United States. Taney now rivaled the ambitious Treasury Secretary, Louis McLean, as the president's most influential cabinet member. McLean hoped to enhance his standing in the cabinet as well as his presidential credentials by becoming Secretary of State, replacing the scholarly but passive Edward Livingston. He discussed his plan with Vice President Martin Van Buren, who pledged his support. But McLean recoiled at Van Buren's suggestion that Taney should succeed him at Treasury. The president acceded to McLean's wishes, agreeing to appoint McLean Secretary of State and replace him at Treasury with McLean's friend, William Duane, rather than Taney. The new appointments appeared to diminish Taney's role in the cabinet. But Jackson's renewed challenge to the Bank of the United States once again made Taney a crucial presidential adviser.

Soon after his second inauguration, Jackson met with Taney to discuss several possible assaults on the bank, including the removal of government's deposits and opposition to the recharter. Taney responded in a memorandum to the president opposing the recharter of the bank under any circumstances. He accused the bank of a breach of the public trust, citing statistics showing that Biddle had consciously manipulated its loan policy to curry political support during the fight over the recharter bill. He also reminded the president that the bank had been a powerful supporter of Jackson's presidential opponent, Henry Clay. On constitutional grounds, he repeated his earlier argument that the bank was not an institution that could be justified as "necessary" for the nation's economic health. Far from being an indispensable national institution, he contended that the bank was a menace to democratic government.

With Taney's strong support, Jackson attacked the bank's economic base by removing all federal government deposits and having them redistributed to selected state banks. The president instructed his new Treasury Secretary, William Duane, to implement the new policy. But Duane, a friend of Biddle, first equivocated and then balked at Jackson's order. Jackson was astonished at Duane's stubborn refusal to obey. The president issued an ultimatum: Either obey my order or resign. When Duane refused to act, Jackson fired him.

The president immediately appointed Taney to replace Duane. His new Treasury Secretary "unites with me heart in hand to meet the crisis," Jackson wrote Vice President Van Buren "Mr. Taney is commissioned, sworn into office, and the business of the Treasury is progressing as though Mr. Duane had never been born."

In October 1833, only three days after he had been sworn in as acting Secretary of the Treasury, Taney carried out the president's order, announcing that federal government deposits would no longer be made in the Bank of the United States. Effective immediately, he said, all federal funds would be distributed in selected state banks. He anticipated, and relished, the coming battle with Biddle's bank. "We have a fiery contest before us," he wrote Andrew Stevenson, the Speaker of the House of Representatives, "but we shall conquer the mammoth, with all of the allies that are coming to its aid." In his report to Congress, Taney denounced the bank in uncompromising terms. "It is a fixed principle of our political institutions," he declared, "to guard against the unnecessary accumulation of power over persons and property in any hands. And no hands are less worthy to be trusted with it than those of a moneyed corporation."

Biddle was eager for the showdown with the president and his Treasury Secretary. Even before Taney had withdrawn the federal government's deposits from the bank, Biddle had begun to flex the bank's muscle, demanding that vulnerable state banks present their notes for redemption, reducing their discounts and calling in their loans. While demonstrating the economic might at the bank's disposal, Biddle also deployed his heaviest political guns to attack the president.

Before a packed gallery in the Senate, Henry Clay, mellifluous and passionate, castigated Jackson's decision to withdraw government deposits from the bank as a brazen step toward dictatorship. "We are in the midst of a revolution," Clay warned, "hitherto bloodless, but rapidly tending towards a total change of the pure republican character of the Government, and to the concentration of all power in the hands of one man." Only Congress stood between the American people and tyranny. "If Congress do not apply an instantaneous and effective remedy," Clay declared, "the fatal collapse will soon come on, and we shall die— ignobly die—base, mean, and abject slaves; the scorn and contempt of mankind; unpitied, unwept, unmourned."

Despite Clay's protestations, it was Biddle rather than Jackson who appeared consumed with the power of his office during the Bank War. After reducing the bank's loans by more than $18 million between August 1, 1833, and November 1, 1834, in an obvious attempt to manipulate the nation's economy, Biddle reversed course and, over the next five months, increased its loans by more than $14 million. Ultimately, Biddle's efforts were self-defeating. His heavy-handed policies alienated many of his traditional allies in the mercantile community who became increasingly uneasy with his unbridled efforts to control the nation's financial markets.

Having failed to reverse the president's policy to withdraw funds from the Bank of the United States, Biddle's political allies in Congress were determined to exact some measure of revenge against the administration. Their target was Jackson's tough, combative Treasury Secretary. Although Taney had shown vigor and decisiveness in his new cabinet position, his recess appointment still required confirmation by the Senate. Bank forces in the Senate, led by Clay and Webster, vowed that Taney would pay for his aggressive opposition to the bank with the loss of his office.

Aware of the threat to Taney, Jackson tried to protect him by withholding his nomination from the Senate until the last week of the session. But to no avail. On June 24, 1834, the Senate, without debate, defeated Taney's nomination, 28–18. A disgusted President Jackson wrote Edward Livingston, "Nicholas Biddle now rules the Senate, as a showman does his puppets."

Taney's rejection as Secretary of the Treasury did not end the president's efforts to appoint his trusted adviser to high public office. Jackson's next opportunity occurred after Associate Justice Gabriel Duvall of the U.S. Supreme Court, eighty-two years old, decrepit and virtually deaf, resigned. Jackson sent Taney's nomination to the Senate on January 15, 1835, as Duvall's replacement. But Taney and Jackson's Senate enemies were ready, once again, to punish them. Even though Taney had support among respected conservatives, including Chief Justice Marshall, his nomination languished. By midnight on the last day of the Senate session, still no action had been taken on the nomination. With silky efficiency, Webster moved that it be postponed indefinitely, a motion tantamount to defeat. A vote was taken, and again Taney was rejected.

Taney's career of public service appeared to be finished. Within the space of a year, Jackson's nominations of Taney to be Secretary of the Treasury and Associate Justice of the U.S. Supreme Court had been defeated by the Whig-Bank coalition in the Senate. If the defeats weren't humiliating enough, those who led the opposition to Taney gloated over their victory. At a public dinner in Salem, Massachusetts, shortly after the Senate had rejected Taney as Secretary of the Treasury, Senator Webster excoriated Taney as "a pliant instrument" of President Jackson, suggesting that he lacked both integrity and sound judgment.

At the time of Webster's attack, Taney had returned to Maryland to resume the private practice of law. He was usually content to absorb insults from his enemies in silence, but Webster's assault stirred him to retaliation. The occasion was a dinner in Taney's honor in Elkton, Maryland. In his remarks, Taney not only delivered a spirited defense of Jackson's bank policy, but also took Webster's taunt that he was a "pliant instrument" of the president and hurled the phrase back at his assailant: "Neither my habits nor my principles lead me to bandy terms of reproach with Mr. Webster or any one else. But it is well known that he has found the bank a profitable client, and I submit to the public whether the facts I have stated do not furnish grounds for believing that he has become its 'pliant instrument,' and is prepared on all occasions to do its bidding, whenever and wherever it may choose to require him."

Like Taney, the president was enraged over his Senate rejections. But Jackson would have yet a third chance to return Taney to the highest echelons of the federal government. Six months after Chief Justice John Marshall died in office on July 6, 1835, Jackson nominated Roger B. Taney to succeed him. This time, Jackson was confident that the Taney nomination would succeed, largely because the fall congressional elections had given the Democrats a comfortable majority in the Senate. The president was also buoyed by the fact that Taney's appointment would be considered in an open-ended session, which prevented last-minute tactics by opponents, such as Webster, that had doomed Taney's earlier nomination to the Court.

Webster and Clay again led the Senate opposition to the nomination. Clay later recalled that "[t]here was hardly an opprobrious epithet which . . . he failed to use against the nomination." Despite Clay's and Webster's denunciations of the nominee to the very end, Taney was confirmed on March 15, 1836, to be the nation's fifth Chief Justice of the United States.

Associate Justice Joseph Story grimly prepared for the first session of the Taney Court. "I confess my hopes are subdued, my confidence shaken, and my zeal chilled," Story wrote Francis Lieber, the editor of the *Encyclopedia Americana*, to which Story contributed articles on legal topics. "It seems to me that the spirit of party (which is always the spirit of self-ishness) is become irresistible." A devout Whig, Story feared the imminent invasion of Jacksonian democracy into the sacred sanctuary of the Court, where Chief Justice Marshall had written so many unanimous opinions favoring the federal government over the states and protecting private property rights.

The Whig press viewed the ascendancy of Chief Justice Taney with a mixture of apprehension and disgust. "The pure ermine of the Supreme Court is sullied by the appointment of that political hack, Roger B. Taney," sneered the *New York American*. Just as predictably, Democrats celebrated the Taney appointment. "The accomplished Taney has succeeded against the vengeance of his foes and is now Chief Justice of the United States," exulted the *Richmond Enquirer*. Taney himself privately expressed gratitude for his appointment to President Jackson. "I owe this honor to you," he wrote Jackson, "to whom I had rather owe it than any other man in the world."

On January 2, 1837, Chief Justice Taney and his judicial colleagues entered the chamber in the basement of the Capitol Building that served as the official home of the U.S. Supreme Court. For this first term of the Taney Court, a fresh carpet had been laid and new furniture purchased to give the room a stately appearance. Still, nothing could disguise the fact that the Supreme Court's residence was strikingly inferior to that of its two co-equal branches of the federal government. Both houses of Congress, which were located on the first floor of the Capitol Building, as well as the White House at the other end of Pennsylvania Avenue, exhibited a modest grandeur that their subterranean judicial neighbor could not match.

But official appearances were deceiving. Thanks to the magisterial opinions of Chief Justice John Marshall over the thirty-four years he had presided at the Court, the judicial branch had achieved parity with the other co-equal branches in authority, if not in accouterments. The Chief Justice's seminal opinions began in 1803 with *Marbury v. Madison*, the decision in which the Court struck down an act of Congress as unconstitutional. Marshall's opinion for the Court in *McCulloch v. Maryland* recognized the implied powers of Congress to pass far-reaching legislation and, at the same time, insulated the federal government from state taxation. The Marshall Court also established the supremacy of the Supreme Court's appellate authority over state supreme court decisions in interpreting federal laws. And the Chief Justice with his brethren consistently endorsed the sanctity of private contracts, protecting them from intrusive state laws.

When he took the center chair on the Court's bench, Chief Justice Taney created a minor stir by wearing trousers under his black robe rather than the knee breeches favored by his predecessor. Would this sartorial gesture to the common man be followed by a rash of opinions championing Jacksonian democracy? Whigs, like Associate Justice Story, were particularly nervous because Taney would preside over the seven-member Court with four fellow Jackson appointees.

Story, as the senior justice, sat to the right of Taney. At fifty-seven years old, he was two and a half years younger than Taney. He was of medium height, wore rimless spectacles, and carelessly allowed his fair, receding hair to curl over the collar of his robe. Though appointed by Republican president James Madison in 1811, Story had become a loyal adherent of Chief Justice Marshall's nationalistic opinions (and was Marshall's choice to be his successor). He wrote one of the Marshall Court's most important opinions, which rejected the claim of Virginia that its state supreme court's judgment on the interpretation of a federal treaty was final. Story, who had inexhaustible intellectual energy, was not only fully engaged in the Court's work but also taught law at Harvard and wrote a series of legal treatises, ranging from equity pleading to constitutional law.

The seat to Taney's left was occupied by Smith Thompson, who had been appointed to the Court by President James Monroe in 1823. Small in stature and slightly emaciated, the sixty-nine-year-old Thompson had recently taken a much younger wife and gallantly escorted her to parties around the capital. He had served as chief justice of the New York Supreme Court as well as Secretary of the Navy under Monroe before his Court appointment. Thompson's judicial philosophy was not so easily categorized as Story's. He occasionally dissented from Marshall Court opinions but also endorsed broad constitutional authority for the federal government. He was not a Jackson supporter and particularly deplored the president's attack on the Bank of the United States.

The first Jackson appointee was John McLean, an Ohio native with stern, craggy features and a pronounced moral fervor. A former member of the Ohio Supreme Court, McLean was a peculiar choice for Jackson, since he had served as U.S. Postmaster General in the administration of President John Quincy Adams (though he did not support Adams's re-election bid). Once on the Court, McLean bragged that he did not vote for Jackson and quickly gravitated toward the strong nationalistic views of Justice Story. Though he enthusiastically embraced Whig politics, McLean's intense presidential ambitions did not limited him to a single party's policies. Increasingly, he became an outspoken opponent of slavery and expressed his strong views on the subject in his judicial opinions, even when they were not essential to the decision of the Court.

Yale-educated Henry Baldwin of Pennsylvania vigorously supported Jackson for the presidency in 1828 and was appointed to the Court by Jackson in 1830. He possessed a logical mind, but was also emotional, often showing an unpleasant petulance. Addicted to black Spanish cigars, Baldwin became noticeably restless when deprived of them during long Court sessions. Unfortunately for Baldwin, his judicial tenure was marred by mounting financial debts, which led to increasingly irrational behavior. On the bench, Baldwin was neither a doctrinaire states' rights judge nor a follower of Justice Story.

Justice James Wayne of Georgia was equally adept at politics and law. A graduate of Princeton, Wayne practiced law in Savannah, served as the city's mayor and in the state legislature before his election to the House of Representatives. He was a states' rights Democrat, but also a supporter of the Union, who rejected John C. Calhoun's nullification doctrine which insisted states could declare an act of Congress unconstitutional. Perhaps most important, Wayne supported Jackson and Taney in their struggle against the Bank of the United States. He was appointed to the Court in 1835.

The appointment of Phillip Barbour, fifty-three years old, was confirmed in the same congressional session as Taney's. A Virginia country gentleman, Barbour lived on a spacious estate with a large herd of cattle and many slaves. He had served in the Virginia House of Delegates and in the U.S. House of Representatives, where he was Speaker until he lost the office to Henry Clay. He opposed every Whig policy, from internal improvements financed by the federal government to support for the Bank of the United States. His ardent states' rights philosophy put him radically at odds with Story's nationalism.

As if choreographed for judicial history, the Taney Court, in only the third week of its first term, heard oral arguments in a case guaranteed to produce a collision between the old and new Court orders. In the Charles River Bridge case, the justices were forced to choose between two competing constitutional values: protection of private contracts versus promotion of the general welfare. In political terms, the Charles

River Bridge case pitted private corporate interests, defended by the Whigs, against the Jacksonian Democrats' demands that the public's needs superceded private profit. The case, moreover, was freighted with far-reaching economic consequences for the westward development of the nation.

In 1785, the Massachusetts legislature had chartered a company to build the Charles River Bridge, which linked Boston with Charlestown. To entice private investors, the legislature granted the company the right to collect tolls for forty years, which was later extended for an additional thirty years. With the steadily increasing population in the Boston area, the Charles River Bridge prospered. Shares of Charles River Bridge stock having a par value of $333 sold for $1,650 in 1805 and $2,080 in 1814. The original capitalization had been $50,000; in 1823, the company claimed a value of $280,000. Despite complaints from the public and pressure from the state legislature, the company refused to reduce tolls or improve its bridge service.

The state legislature in 1828 responded to mounting public protests over the practices of the proprietors of the Charles River Bridge by chartering another company to build a second bridge less than 100 yards from the older bridge. As soon as tolls on the new bridge, the Warren Bridge, paid for the costs of construction, the bridge would become state property and toll-free. No one doubted that the public would choose the new, eventually toll-free Warren Bridge over the old and expensive Charles River Bridge.

To prevent the public from making that choice, the proprietors of the Charles River Bridge sued in the Supreme Judicial Court of Massachusetts to stop construction of the Warren Bridge. They argued that its charter gave it exclusive rights to operate a bridge over the Charles River. When that argument was rejected in the state court, the company's most prominent legal counsel, Daniel Webster, appealed to the U.S. Supreme Court.

After the case was first argued before the Court in 1831, Chief Justice Marshall and Associate Justices Story and Thompson were ready to reverse the state court decision and rule in favor of Webster and the

Charles River Bridge. But the ailing Justice Gabriel Duvall had been absent from the session and other members of the Court were in sharp disagreement with Marshall, Story, and Thompson. The case was therefore put over to the next term. But, again, one justice was absent, and the other justices were evenly divided on the outcome.

In an effort to persuade a fourth justice to adopt his view, Story drafted an opinion that broadly interpreted obligations under the Constitution's Contract Clause* to protect the Charles River Bridge's charter from later competition. When Story's draft opinion failed to attract the necessary fourth vote for a Court majority, the case was again postponed. By the time of reargument of the case before the Taney Court, the Warren Bridge had been built and was indeed toll-free (the early tolls had paid off construction costs); the public overwhelmingly used it rather than the older Charles River toll bridge.

The justices listened to arguments for a full week, beginning on January 19, 1837. During the three days that Daniel Webster was scheduled to make his argument on behalf of the Charles River Bridge, the Court's visitors' gallery was filled to capacity with fashionable ladies wearing fine plumed hats, members of Congress, and foreign dignitaries. Webster was noticeably moody and uneasy waiting to argue before the new Chief Justice, whom he had labeled "a pliant instrument" of Andrew Jackson. Despite his initial discomfort in appearing before Taney, Webster quickly recovered his composure once he stood to address the justices.

Webster began his argument by describing the scene of the controversy on the Charles River in elegant painterly detail. After providing the Court with his version of the facts, he made the constitutional argument that had been successful for him in past appearances before the Marshall Court. Contracts between private investors and a state legislature were inviolate, Webster maintained, and could not be undercut by later legislation. The charter granted to the proprietors of the Charles River Bridge by the Massachusetts legislature was such a contract and

---

* Article I, section 10, provides that no state shall pass any law "impairing the Obligation of Contracts."

implicitly forbid the state legislature from authorizing the construction of a second bridge that would compete, and drain profits, from the first.

Webster insisted that the terms of the Charles River Bridge charter must be read to give the private company exclusive rights to operate a bridge over the Charles River. Otherwise, private investors would be forever vulnerable to pressures for new legislation from the masses, and the obligation of contract would be meaningless. Without constitutional protection of contract, state legislatures would be free to take money out of the hands of private property owners, as he insisted had been done in the Charles River Bridge case, and give it to the public. Webster's summation, according to Justice Story, was extraordinarily effective, though it exhibited "a little too much of fiérte here and there."

Defense attorney Simon Greenleaf conceded that the Charles River Bridge's charter was a contract. But nowhere in the document, Greenleaf quickly added, did the charter provide for the corporation's exclusive right to build a bridge across the Charles River. Where the public's welfare is at issue, a contract must be construed narrowly, Greenleaf argued, and therefore no rights were granted to the Charles River Bridge that were not explicitly provided for in the charter. If the Charles River Bridge had a legitimate legal grievance, it must be taken to the state courts where the private investors could argue that they had been unjustly (but not unconstitutionally) deprived of future profits.

After arguments in the Charles River Bridge case had been completed, Webster wrote to Jeremiah Mason, a prominent Massachusetts attorney, that he expected the case to be decided wrongly, that is, against his client, the proprietors of the Charles River Bridge. Webster then provided Mason with what turned out to be accurate descriptions of the individual justices' positions, suggesting that one member of the Court—presumably Webster's friend Joseph Story—had provided him with inside information. The Court had been revolutionized, Webster declared, and the justices in the majority, led by Taney, were motivated by crass political considerations. "Taney is smooth and plausible, but cunning and jesuitical, and as thorough going a party judge as ever got onto a bench of justice," Webster noted. "He is a man who wears his robes for the purpose of protecting his friends and punishing his enemies."

Two weeks after Webster had dismissed the Chief Justice as a Democratic Party lackey, Taney entered the courtroom with his colleagues to announce the *Charles River Bridge* decision. Once he had sat down, Taney began to read aloud his opinion for the four-member Court majority (Taney, Baldwin, Barbour, and Wayne). The Chief Justice's conclusion was, as Webster had anticipated, that the Charles River Bridge charter did not grant the company exclusive rights to operate a bridge between Boston and Charlestown.

While the Court must respect the rights of private contract, Taney wrote, it must also be sensitive to the public interest. And where there is an apparent conflict between the general welfare and a private contract, the contract must be interpreted narrowly. In the Charles River Bridge case, this meant that only the express terms of the charter were binding. It was contrary to law and sound public policy, the Chief Justice declared, for a state charter to give implicit monopolistic rights to a company providing services to the public. Such an expansive judicial interpretation of private contract would not only stifle competition but severely constrict the nation's economic development.

Taney's opinion was written in an understated manner reminiscent of his arguments as a trial lawyer. His prose was spare and unemotional, characterized by the "apostolic simplicity" that had maddened, and impressed, his courtroom adversaries. If charters such as that of the Charles River Bridge were interpreted to grant monopolies, Taney warned, then the old turnpike corporations would soon inundate the courts with claims that they, too, could prevent public transportation improvements. "The millions of property which have been invested in railroad and canals, upon lines of travel which have been before occupied by turnpike corporations, will be put in jeopardy," Taney wrote. "We shall be thrown back to the improvements of the last century, and obligated to stand still until the claims of the old turnpike corporations shall be satisfied, and they shall consent to permit these States to avail themselves of the lights of modern science, and to partake of the benefit of those improvements which are now adding to the wealth and prosperity, and the convenience and comfort of every other part of the civilized world."

A distressed Justice Story wrote his wife: "A case of grosser injustice never existed." But Story's opinion not only represented the minority view on the Court, but in the nation at large. The Taney Court's *Charles River Bridge* decision provided an important antidote to the Marshall Court's overly solicitous protection of private property. It was particularly welcomed at a time of unprecedented westward expansion. After the decision, entrepreneurs ready to invest in improved roads, canals, and railroads no longer were inhibited by fear of lawsuits from hidebound monopolistic interests. To be sure, Taney's opinion reflected the Chief Justice's Jacksonian hostility to powerful corporate interests. But it also provided broad constitutional protection for aggressive commercial development at a critical time in the nation's history.

Two other decisions in 1837 further signaled the new constitutional direction of the Taney Court. As in the Charles River Bridge case, both lawsuits had previously been argued before the Marshall Court without resolution. The first, *New York v. Miln*, appeared to challenge one of John Marshall's most important opinions, *Gibbons v. Ogden*. In *Gibbons*, the Chief Justice had written for the Court that Congress had broad authority to regulate interstate commerce. The challenged New York statute in *Miln* required masters of incoming ships to report information on all passengers they brought into the country, including age, health, and their last legal residence. Did the state statute undercut Congress's authority to regulate commerce? Or, as New York claimed, was the law a police measure, fully within the authority of the state to keep out undesirable immigrants?

The Taney Court majority framed the constitutional question as New York had wanted. The control of immigration into New York was within the state's police power, wrote Justice Barbour for a six-member Court majority (Story alone dissented). Since the New York statute could be justified under the state's police power, the Court dismissed the argument that it violated Congress's authority to regulate commerce, and that it conflicted with Marshall's opinion in *Gibbons v. Ogden*.

In a third notable decision by the Taney Court during its first term, the justices rejected a challenge to the constitutionality of a commercial note issued by a Kentucky bank, abandoning a Marshall Court precedent in the process. Justice Story's long dissent accused the majority of judicial gimmickry and the unforgivable sacrilege of defacing the principled earlier opinion by the great Chief Justice Marshall. The name of the late Chief Justice was "never to be pronounced without reverence," Story wrote. Since Chief Justice Marshall could not speak for himself, he continued, "I have felt an earnest desire to vindicate his memory from the imputation of rashness, or want of deep reflection."

Story overestimated the devastation of the Taney Court's rulings, not just in the bank decision but also in *Charles River Bridge* and *Miln*. In truth, the Taney Court, led by the new Chief Justice, had ruled cautiously in all three decisions, though not in the manner favored by Story and the late Chief Justice Marshall. In the *Charles River Bridge* decision, Taney had endorsed the Court's long-standing protection of private contract rights. But he had refused to recognize rights that were not expressly set out in the terms of a private contract, particularly when the claimed implicit rights conflicted with the public interest. In *Miln*, the Court had not challenged Marshall's opinion in *Gibbons v. Ogden* that Congress had broad power to regulate interstate commerce; it had ruled only that a state could act under its police powers where there was no conflict with federal authority. And in the bank decision, the Court could hardly be accused of a reckless states' rights rampage when the opinion supporting the state bank was written by an outspoken nationalist, Justice McLean, and based on the argument made by Henry Clay, the Whig Party's presidential aspirant, who represented the Kentucky bank in the case.

All three decisions foreshadowed much of the later work of the Taney Court, but not in the way that its critics, like Justice Story and Daniel Webster, charged. The majority was more sensitive to states' rights arguments and local community interests than the Marshall Court, which had consistently supported broad federal authority and individual property rights. But the decisions were not, as Webster claimed, the work of revolutionaries. The Court rulings reflected the pragmatic judicial approach of the Chief Justice, who was, at the same time, a Jacksonian Democrat suspicious of vested private interests and centralized government power. Just like the president who appointed him.

The Whigs' initial negative opinion of the Taney Court had, within a remarkably short time, turned benign. Primary credit was due to the Chief Justice's quiet leadership and determined pragmatic approach to constitutional law. No better example could be offered than a Taney commercial law opinion for the Court during the 1839 term. The case involved the issue of whether an out-of-state banking corporation could engage in bills of exchange business in Alabama.

The Court challenge was closely watched by corporations throughout the nation since bills of exchange were a critical means of commercial exchange between regions with no common currency except gold and silver. After the financial Panic of 1837, gold and silver were in short supply. Recently appointed Justice John McKinley,* a states' rights Alabamian, had written the circuit court opinion in the case declaring in unadorned absolutes that out-of-state corporations had no constitutional right to do business in Alabama. McKinley's decision, Justice Story wrote Charles Sumner, a young lawyer and future U.S. senator from Massactusetts, "frightened half the lawyers and all the corporations of the country out of their proprieties."

Two broad themes in McKinley's lower court opinion—a stalwart defense of states' rights and an intense suspicion of large corporate interests—appeared to be perfectly pitched to Taney's Jacksonian Democratic principles. But the Chief Justice, in writing the Supreme Court's opinion reversing the circuit court decision, rejected McKinley's doctrinaire pieties in favor of a practical, carefully reasoned judicial solution. Out-of-state corporations, like foreign corporations under the international

---

* The Supreme Court was expanded to nine members after its 1837 term. President Martin Van Buren appointed two Democrats, McKinley and John Catron of Tennessee, to fill the new seats.

law of comity, Taney wrote, were entitled to do business in other jurisdictions so long as the state (or nation under international law) did not explicitly forbid it by law. Since the Alabama legislature had not passed a law expressly prohibiting the out-of-state banking corporation from doing bills-of-exchange business in the state, its operations in Alabama were constitutional.

Had the Taney Court upheld McKinley's lower court decision, the justices would have effectively erected a "No Trespassing" sign at every state's border, applicable to any bank, manufacturing, or insurance corporation with interstate commercial ambitions. At a time when the nation was still reeling from the Panic of 1837, Justice Story instantly recognized the wisdom of Taney's opinion. He wrote the Chief Justice that his opinion "has given very general satisfaction to the public, and I hope you will allow me to say that I think it does great honor to yourself as well as to the Court." The Whigs' National Gazette also approved of the decision, reassured "that patriotism may still find a tribunal high above the destructive and depraving influence of party."

The Taney Court's growing reputation for non-partisanship made it a natural destination for resolution of the nation's most divisive issue: the institution of slavery. When the framers had met in Philadelphia in 1787, representatives from the northern and southern states knew that no constitution could be ratified if either region dictated the terms concerning "the peculiar institution" of slavery. The document, therefore, made vague but unmistakable references to slaves and the rights of slaveowners in the southern and border states to maintain their human property.*

After the ratification of the Constitution, the first serious political attempt to solve the nation's slavery problem emerged in the form of the Missouri Compromise in 1820. The legislation's chief sponsor, Henry Clay, had successfully proposed that Missouri enter the Union as a slave

---

* Under Article I, section 2, slaves were counted as "three fifths of all other Persons" in determining taxation and apportionment for the House of Representatives; the slave trade could not be prohibited by Congress before 1808. Article IV provided for the recovery of fugitive slaves.

state but that slavery be prohibited from all future states carved from the Louisiana Territory above Missouri's southern boundary.

By 1840, the slavery issue, rather than gradually disappearing from national political debate, had returned with a fresh virulence. The United States under President-elect William Henry Harrison was a very different nation from the one formed when the Constitution was ratified in 1789 or that existed when the Missouri Compromise was enacted. In the founding fathers' time, slave states enjoyed parity with the northern states both in wealth and population. But much had changed in the succeeding fifty years. With rising industrialization and massive westward migration, non-slave states in the North and West far exceeded slave states in both economic power and voters. Where slavery proved ill-suited to the multifaceted economies of the northern and western states, it became the indispensable staple of the southern agrarian economy. Extremists on both sides sharpened the debate and deepened the divide. Abolitionists preached their anti-slavery doctrine with rising fervor. Southern defenders of slavery were no less certain of the moral correctness of their cause as well as its economic necessity.

Within a period of thirteen months in the early 1840s, the Taney Court was confronted with three separate legal challenges that involved the slavery issue. In 1841, the justices were asked to decide what to do with cargo on the Spanish schooner *Amistad,* which had been intercepted by a U.S. naval brig off the coast of Connecticut. What made the case a national *cause célèbre* was the fact that the *Amistad*'s cargo included more than fifty black Africans who had been kidnapped by Spanish merchants and sold in Havana as slaves (in violation of Spanish law). While the blacks were being transported from Havana to another Cuban port, they mutinied, murdered the captain, and ordered their kidnappers to return them to Africa. The Spanish merchants, ostensibly obeying orders, navigated the *Amistad* to the United States.

Pro- and anti-slavery forces quickly aligned themselves on the competing sides of the legal contest. The northern press urged the Court to free the blacks, since they had been illegally seized and forced into slavery in violation of what they considered the laws of humanity and justice. But the *Charleston Courier* deplored the pressure exerted on the Taney Court by the northern abolitionist press, expressing confidence that the justices, unaffected by such fanaticism, would honor U.S. treaty obligations to Spain and return the blacks to their Spanish owners.

The *Amistad* case inspired the seventy-four-year-old former president, Massachusetts congressman John Quincy Adams, to make his first argument before the Court in thirty-two years. A man of ardent abolitionist sentiments, Adams worried that he was too agitated to make a persuasively coherent oral argument to free the blacks. Adams's argument extended for more than twelve hours spread over three days. After hearing it, Justice Story, a fellow abolitionist, suggested that the former president's wide-ranging diatribes against slavery might more effectively have been made on the floor of the House of Representatives than under the stricter limitations imposed by legal argument. Adams's argument had been extraordinary, Story conceded—"extraordinary, I say, for its power, for its bitter sarcasm, and its dealing with topics far beyond the record and points of discussion."

It was left to Joseph Story, writing for the Court majority, to bring together the disparate strands of the arguments of the four lawyers, including Adams, who had presented the case to the justices for eight days. Rejecting Adams's invitation to condemn slavery, Story concentrated on the specific legal issue before the Court: whether the Spanish merchants could, under a treaty between the U.S. and Spain, demand the return of the rebellious blacks. Story answered emphatically that they could not. U.S. treaties with Spain only provided for the return of slaves who had been legally held. The blacks on the *Amistad*, however, had been kidnapped in Africa and claimed as slaves in violation of both Spanish and international law. Once he had decided the case on its strictest legal terms, Story became expansive, declaring that "upon the eternal principles of justice and international law," the United States was forbidden from making a treaty with Spain or any other nation that deprived free blacks of their liberty.

Chief Justice Taney joined Story's opinion, but left no written record of his views on the *Amistad* case. Presumably, he supported the Court's narrow reasoning—that the blacks had been illegally seized and could not, therefore, be claimed by the Spanish merchants as their property. But Taney must have exercised severe self-restraint in not responding to Story's dictum announcing "the eternal principles of justice." As Andrew Jackson's Attorney General, Taney had expressed his conviction that all legal issues concerning slavery were governed by state law, and that there could be no legitimate appeal to federal laws, international treaties, or "eternal principles of justice."

For Taney, the line between morality and constitutional law was carefully delineated. On moral grounds, he freed his slaves and hoped that slavery, which he considered evil, would eventually disappear from the United States. But on constitutional grounds, he was convinced that the framers had accepted slavery as a choice to be made by the individual states, and that it could only be eliminated by the laws of those states.

In a second case involving slavery decided during the 1841 term, Taney again joined a majority opinion that was limited to a judicious analysis of the relevant law, therefore avoiding an open-ended discussion of the volatile race issue. The Court found that a state constitution's prohibition of the importation of slaves was not self-executing, but required a supporting statute. When the decision was announced, Associate Justice John McLean, an outspoken opponent of slavery, unexpectedly pulled a written concurrence from his pocket and read it to his surprised colleagues. Denouncing slavery in emotional terms, McLean declared that every state had a fundamental right to exclude it from its borders.

This time, Taney refused to remain silent. The regulation of the institution of slavery, he emphasized, was the business of the states, not the federal government. Just as McLean's home state of Ohio could exclude slavery under the constitutional compact, the Chief Justice implied, so states in the South could, by law, perpetuate it.

A year later, the Taney Court heard a third case raising the issue of slavery, and this time the justices could not avoid confronting the issue directly. The challenge in *Prigg v. Pennsylvania* focused on the constitutional right of slaveowners to recover their runaway slaves in non-slave states. The Constitution had sanctioned the recovery of fugitive slaves, and Congress in 1793 had passed the Fugitive Slave Law providing statutory support for the constitutional obligation. But as abolitionist sentiment gained force in the northern states, non-slave states, like Pennsylvania, passed laws that required rigorous proof of ownership before blacks could be returned to slaveholders claiming ownership of fugitive slaves. The laws, in part, were passed to protect free blacks from unscrupulous whites trying to force them into slavery. But the laws were also encouraged by abolitionists who, regardless of a slaveowner's claim, wanted to ensure a black's freedom.

Edward Prigg had been hired to pursue a runaway slave, Margaret Morgan, who had crossed Maryland's northern border to reside with her children in the free state of Pennsylvania. After capturing Morgan, Prigg appeared before a state judge to swear that Morgan and her children were fugitive slaves. When the judge balked at granting the required certification, Prigg seized Morgan and her family and returned to Maryland. Law enforcement authorities in Pennsylvania issued a warrant for Prigg's arrest for kidnapping. After much negotiation between high-level officials of the two states, it was decided that Prigg would test the constitutionality of the Pennsylvania law. He agreed to return to Pennsylvania, where he was found guilty of kidnapping, a conviction that was eventually appealed to the U.S. Supreme Court.

The question before the Taney Court in 1842 was whether the Pennsylvania law imposing detailed legal procedures on a slaveowner before he could recover his runaway slaves was an unconstitutional impediment to the enforcement of the federal Fugitive Slave Law. To the consternation of his fellow abolitionists, Justice Story wrote the majority opinion that struck down the Pennsylvania statute. The state law was unconstitutional, Story wrote for a unanimous Court, because its provisions interfered with the mandate of the federal statute that imposed a legal obligation to recover fugitive slaves.

Before he was finished, Story had roiled both pro- and anti-slavery forces by going well beyond the facts of the Pennsylvania case to declare that *all* state fugitive slave laws were unconstitutional. The state laws were void, Story wrote, because the jurisdiction of the federal government in recovering fugitive slaves was exclusive. Abolitionists were furious that Story's opinion deprived them of a ready legal instrument, like Pennsylvania's statute, to protect blacks, both free and slave. But proslavery partisans were no happier with Story's opinion, since it meant that fugitive slave laws in southern states—whose purpose was to assist in the recovery of slaveholders' property—were no longer valid.

For the third time, Chief Justice Taney joined the majority in a decision involving slavery. And in each case he agreed with his abolitionist colleague, Justice Story, on the specific holding of the majority opinion. But in the *Prigg* decision, Taney wrote a concurring opinion challenging Story's view that southern states were forbidden from passing their own laws that actually assisted in the recovery of runaway slaves. For Taney, the issue was states' rights—the statutory authority of a state to protect the institution of slavery. In objecting to Story's general prohibition against state fugitive slave laws, the Chief Justice raised the specter of rampant lawlessness, warning that southern states would involuntarily "become an open pathway for fugitives escaping from other states."

Taney's concurrence was devoted to the need for state laws to protect the property rights of slaveowners; nowhere did he consider the argument of abolitionists that it was morally wrong for one human being to own another. That argument, in Taney's constitutional universe, was irrelevant.

Throughout the 1840s, the Taney Court continued to build its reputation for prudent, restrained decisions on every complicated issue of constitutional law, from corporations to slavery. Chief Justice Taney's understated leadership won belated accolades from his most diehard critics. Several years after Taney's appointment, Henry Clay called at the Chief Justice's residence in Washington, D.C. Clay clasped Taney's hand and, deeply moved, said: "Mr. Chief Justice, there was no man in the land who regretted your appointment to the place you now hold more than I did; there was no member of the Senate who opposed it more than I did ... I am satisfied now that no man in the United States could have been selected more abundantly able to wear the ermine which Chief Justice Marshall honored."

Taney reportedly responded to Clay's conciliatory words with grace and appreciation. Behind Taney's polite demeanor, however, lay a political partisan who did not easily forgive the attacks of opponents of Jacksonian democracy. Only months after he had written the fine, carefully balanced opinion for the Court in the Charles River Bridge case in 1837, for example, Taney expressed to Andrew Jackson his utter disgust with the recharter efforts of the Bank of the United States and its supporters. "The Bank of the United States is nothing more than the concentrated power of the whole class of the moneyed aristocracy who have so long struggled to get possession of the government," Taney wrote, "carried along . . . [by] the numerous army of greedy speculators and ambitious politicians who hope to profit from its aid." In 1842, Taney condemned the Whigs' "disgraceful buffoonery of coonskins and hard cider . . . received under the auspices of Mr. Clay." And he savored the victory of the Democrat, James K. Polk, over Clay in the 1844 presidential election, writing the president-elect: "We have passed through no contest for the presidency more important than the one just over; nor have I seen any one before in which so many dangerous influences were combined together as were united in support of Mr. Clay. Your triumphant success gives me increased confidence in the intelligence, firmness and virtue of the American people; and in the safety and stability of the principles upon which our institutions are founded."

Fortunately for Taney, the Court, and the nation, his highly partisan comments in his private correspondence were not known to the public. During the decade of the 1840s, the Chief Justice of the United States was perceived to represent the interests of all Americans—Democrats and Whigs, southerners and northerners—at a time when the slavery issue had called into question the very notion of Union. In a dissenting opinion written in 1849, Taney gave eloquent testimony to his belief in a strong Union.

The Taney opinion was written in response to a majority decision declaring New York and Massachusetts laws that taxed foreign passengers arriving at ports in the states unconstitutional. Taney challenged the majority's ruling that states were forbidden from excluding undesirable indigents from their borders through taxation. What made Taney's dissent memorable was not his familiar states' rights position, but his declaration that a state could not exclude American citizens, as opposed to non-citizens, from other states or U.S. territories. He wrote: "For all the great purposes for which the federal government was formed, we are one people, with one common country. We are all citizens of the United States; and, as members of the same community, must have the right to pass and repass through every part of it without interruption, as freely as in our own states."

Taney did not intend his words to offer encouragement to free blacks or slaves. The Chief Justice limited his opinion to citizens of the United States, a privileged category from which he believed African Americans were excluded by the Constitution.

Chapter Two

"MY POLITICS ARE SHORT AND SWEET"

Abraham Lincoln did not speak with pride of his family heritage. "My parents were both born in Virginia, of undistinguished families," he told a friend who was seeking more autobiographical information in 1859 to promote Lincoln's nomination for the presidency. Lincoln believed that he was a self-made man whose family made no significant contribution to his success. He knew that his grandfather and namesake, Abraham, had moved from Virginia to Kentucky in the early 1780s, but provided no information on earlier generations of Lincolns who had come to America. Had he done research into his family's records, Lincoln would have had to revise his opinion that his ancestors were singularly "undistinguished."

In 1637, Samuel Lincoln, a weaver, emigrated from England and settled in Hingham, Massachusetts, where he became a prosperous trader and businessman, a leader of his church, and the father of eleven children. Among Samuel Lincoln's descendants were many good citizens and prominent public officers, including Levi Lincoln, who served as President Thomas Jefferson's Attorney General and turned down an appointment to the U.S. Supreme Court. One of Samuel Lincoln's grandsons, Mordecai, achieved noteworthy economic success as an ironmaster and landowner in Pennsylvania. Mordecai was sufficiently wealthy to be able to give his son John more than 200 acres of rich Virginia farmland in the Shenandoah Valley, which Abraham Lincoln's grandfather inherited.

Shortly after the American Revolution, the senior Abraham Lincoln sold his Virginia farm and moved his wife and five children to Kentucky, where his distant relative, Daniel Boone, had reported that the land was vast and fertile. Within a few years, Lincoln had acquired more than 5,000 acres of productive Kentucky's farmland. But hostile Indians in the territory made the Lincolns' life dangerous. In 1786, when Abraham and his three sons were planting corn, Indians attacked. Abraham was killed instantly.

Abraham's youngest son, Thomas, then eight years old, leaned over his fallen father while his two older brothers scurried for help and cover. What happened next became family legend, a harrowing story told and retold by Thomas to his own son. After his father was shot, Thomas's older brother, fifteen-year-old Mordecai, ran to a nearby cabin, peeked cautiously through a crack in the logs, and spotted an Indian moving toward Thomas. With the distraught Thomas still hovering over his father's body, Mordecai picked up a rifle, aimed, and shot the Indian dead.

The future president of the United States never gave his father, Thomas, much credit for ability or initiative. "Uncle Mord had run off with all the talents of the family," Abraham Lincoln once said. And it was true enough that Mordecai Lincoln, Thomas's older brother, became a prosperous landowner, breeder of fine racehorses, and leading citizen of Washington County, Kentucky. But Mordecai, unlike his two younger brothers, was given a considerable boost up the economic ladder by the law of primogeniture still applicable in Kentucky in the late eighteenth century. Under the law, Mordecai inherited his father's estate. Thomas and his other brother, Josiah, were left to fend for themselves.

Thomas Lincoln was pictured by his son, Abraham, as a plodding, somewhat inept farmer and carpenter. Thomas deserved better. He never prospered like his older brother, Mordecai, nor was he intellectually curious and ambitious like his own son, Abraham. But Thomas Lincoln worked hard and steadily on small farms in Kentucky and later in the Indiana wilderness to provide for his family, often under extremely harsh conditions. And on one important subject, slavery, Abraham Lincoln shared his father's values. Like Thomas, Abraham was "naturally anti-slavery." As president in 1864, Lincoln said: "I cannot remember when I did not so think and feel."

Thomas's wife, the former Nancy Hanks, could read but not write and, according to her son, was illegitimate. She was a hardworking housewife and devoted mother who gave her love unselfishly to Abraham and his older sister, Sarah, as well as to her nephew, Dennis Hanks, who lived with them. Tragedy struck the Lincoln family in 1818 when Nancy fell ill, suffering from what was called milk sickness and later diagnosed as brucellosis. She died, leaving Thomas to care for nine-year-old Abraham and his sister, who was twelve.

Within a year of Nancy Hanks Lincoln's death, Thomas dutifully left the family farm in Pigeon Creek, Indiana, to return to Kentucky to find a spouse and stepmother for his children. He came back to his Indiana farm with a new bride, the widow Sarah Bush Johnston, who moved into the spare Lincoln cabin with her own three children. It would have been easy, and predictable, for Sarah to favor her children over Sarah and Abraham Lincoln. But she did not, giving equal attention and affection to all five. Abraham called her "Mama" and was devoted to her, as she was to him. Many years later, Sarah Lincoln declared that "she had been his best Friend in this world and that no Son could love a Mother more than he loved her."

When he was ten years old, Abraham was sent to the first of three schools located near the Lincoln cabin. The lessons were limited to basic reading, writing, and elementary mathematics. All told, Lincoln's formal education "did not amount to one year." His primary education was derived from the books he read, beginning with *Dilworth's Spelling Book* and including those in his stepmother's sparse library brought from Kentucky: a family Bible, *Robinson Crusoe*, *Pilgrim's Progress*, *Aesop's Fables*, and *Lessons in Elocution*. Lincoln committed major passages from these books to memory and freely recited them throughout his political career.

Most of the boy's days were spent helping his father with the chores—chopping down trees, making fences, planting and harvesting corn, tending hogs. And when Abraham had finished his work on the Lincoln farm, Thomas rented out his son's services to nearby neighbors. Whenever he had an idle moment, Abraham could be seen with his feet propped up on a chair or next to a tree absorbed in a book.

Under Indiana law, every penny that Abraham Lincoln earned while a minor belonged to his father. This familial indentured servitude made Abraham bristle and surely contributed to his harsh judgment of his father. Gradually, he ventured farther and farther from the Lincoln cabin to find company and work. He was seen at house raisings, log rollings, selling firewood to steamers on the Ohio River, and floating a flatboat with produce for sale to New Orleans. In 1830, just before he turned twenty-one, Abraham helped his father and stepmother move from their farm in Indiana to a 15-acre tract of land in Macon County, Illinois, on a bluff overlooking the Sangamon River.

That summer he made his first political speech in front of a Decatur, Illinois, general store, after two candidates for the state legislature had addressed the crowd that had gathered. Partly in jest, Lincoln was asked to respond to the candidates—to berate them for failing to offer the customary drink to those in the crowd. Instead of accepting the invitation to ridicule, Lincoln delivered a serious speech, a precursor to many he would make only two years later as a candidate for the state legislature. With barely a hint of nervousness, Lincoln implored the crowd to demand improvements in transportation on the Sangamon River and, more generally, to dream with him of a better future for the state.

As a teenager, Abraham Lincoln had devoured books on American history and biography (Parson Mason Weems's *Life of George Washington* was his favorite), as well as journals and newspapers reporting the politics of the day. The anti-Jackson *Louisville Journal*, which trumpeted the achievements of Kentucky's native son, Henry Clay, was Lincoln's preferred source of political news. He had, by then, developed an abiding allegiance to Clay.

In 1832, when Clay challenged Jackson for the presidency, the twenty-three-year-old Lincoln engaged in his first political campaign for a seat in the Illinois legislature. With less than a year of formal education, no public service, and no influential patrons in his new home, the thriving village of New Salem, Lincoln did not appear to have much chance for success against the twelve other candidates. He had lived in New Salem less than a year, worked as a clerk in a country store, and was best known as a raconteur who could quickly draw a crowd to listen to his folksy anecdotes and tall tales. He stood six feet four inches tall, weighed 180 pounds, and had already earned a reputation among local residents for his prodigious physical strength.

With the self-confidence and ambition that would mark his entire political career, Lincoln campaigned tirelessly for the elective office. At his stump speeches, he wore a straw hat, jeans coat, tow-linen pantaloons, and boots. He introduced himself to voters as "humble Abe Lincoln," who "was born and have ever remained in the most humble walks of life."

Shrewdly, Lincoln seized upon a local issue on which he considered himself an expert, the need to improve the navigable waters of the nearby Sangamon River. Lincoln understood the requirements for successful navigation, he told prospective voters, since he had twice navigated a flatboat down the Ohio and Mississippi Rivers to New Orleans. During the campaign, Lincoln was given the opportunity to impress voters further with his navigational expertise after it was announced that the steamer *Talisman*, bound for Springfield from Cincinnati, would test the Sangamon River's navigability. When the *Talisman* reached Beardstown, just ten miles west of New Salem, Lincoln boarded, helped clear overhanging brush, and finally took charge, piloting the steamer upstream. On the *Talisman's* return voyage, the Sangamon River's water level dipped dangerously low, underscoring Lincoln's point—the need for state funds to improve the river's navigability.

With sly humor and directness, Lincoln also pledged his commitment to Henry Clay's American System. "My politics are short and sweet, like the old woman's dance," he told a crowd at Pappsville. "I am in favor of a national bank. I am in favor of the internal improvements system and a high protective tariff. These are my sentiments and political principles." For Lincoln, Clay's vision offered the best hope for the nation, not just for the tradesmen and large industrial interests in the East, but also the farmers and small businesspeople in the West and South. He believed Clay's leadership would not just benefit the wealthy but also young men from humble backgrounds, like Lincoln himself, who wanted to work for a share of America's prosperity. Lincoln's announcement that he was "a stanch anti-Jackson, or Clay, man" did not appear well calculated to win him votes, since Illinois voters had given Jackson a large electoral majority in the 1828 presidential election and were expected to do so again in 1832. But Clay, too, was popular in Illinois, second only to Jackson in national standing, so Lincoln probably did not lose many votes by endorsing the National Republicans' presidential candidate.

When the votes were tallied, he stood eighth in the field, four shy of success (the four candidates with the most votes were elected). Despite his defeat, Lincoln's performance in his first political contest was impressive. Without any notable credential for public office, Lincoln had not only made a credible showing throughout the voting district, but had won 277 out of the 300 votes cast in New Salem. It was a promising beginning in politics for a young man who by his own admission, could boast no early advantages of pedigree, wealth, education, or professional skill.

After his defeat for election to the Illinois legislature in 1832, Lincoln's career prospects appeared dim indeed. None of the three general stores in New Salem needed his clerical services. He was certainly strong enough to hire himself out as a laborer, but he did not like physical labor. Fortunately, he had already demonstrated an uncommon capacity to make friends in New Salem, and several of them would find ways to help him through a bleak economic period in his life.

One of Lincoln's New Salem friends, Rowan Herndon, owned a half-share in a general store. When Herndon was ready to sell his share, he approached Lincoln, who had boarded in Herndon's house. Lincoln agreed to buy Herndon's share, but no money was exchanged. Lincoln's note was sufficient to close the deal. "I believed he was thoroughly honest," Herndon said, explaining his trust in the young (and impoverished) Lincoln, "and that impression was so strong in me I accepted his note in payment of the whole."

What appeared to be a fine business opportunity turned out, for Lincoln, to be a debacle. Neither Lincoln nor his partner, William Berry (who had bought the other half-share of the store from Rowan Herndon's brother, James), demonstrated any competence, or much interest, in making their store a commercial success. Turning a profit with a general store in New Salem in 1832, under any circumstances, would have been difficult. There was simply not sufficient demand for the tea and coffee, blue calico, brown muslin and straw hats, even the whiskey, that Lincoln and Berry's store offered for sale.

To fill the idle time, Berry reportedly drank heavily. Lincoln's twin addictions were books and conversation with every man, woman, and child he met. He read between sales at his store, walking to and from work, even during his conversations with customers and friends. Lincoln's eclectic reading list included Shakespeare's plays, the poems of Robert Burns, Gibbon's *Rise and Fall of the Roman Empire*, and Thomas Paine's *The Age of Reason*, a rationalist's attack on the literal interpretation of the Bible. And he studied, most intensely, Samuel Kirkham's *English Grammar*, kneading the lessons in his mind, committing large portions to memory. No wonder that within months, Lincoln's first business venture "winked out."

Out of work and money, Lincoln was again rescued by devoted friends who lobbied on his behalf for the position of town postmaster. It was not difficult to push aside the incumbent, a New Salem storeowner who regularly alienated women standing in line to pick up mail by ignoring them in favor of men ready to buy liquor. Although the federal appointment was controlled by the Jackson administration, Lincoln's strong support for Henry Clay did not disqualify him for the office. The office, Lincoln speculated, was "too insignificant to make his politics an objection."

Though his wages were modest for his three years of postal service ($55.70 in one year), Lincoln performed his duties with dedication. When residents failed to pick up their letters in New Salem, he stuffed them under his stovepipe hat and walked, sometimes several miles, to deliver them to their homes. One of the perks of the job, which Lincoln eagerly accepted, was being able to read all of the newspapers that came to the post office.

His income, welcome as it was, still did not pay all the bills. One of Lincoln's friends recommended him to John Calhoun, the county surveyor, who needed an assistant. Lincoln was somewhat reluctant to apply for the job, since he knew that Calhoun was an active Jacksonian Democrat. After he was assured that he would not have to compromise his political principles, he applied and was offered the job.

Lacking even rudimentary knowledge of surveying, Lincoln buried himself in treatises on practical surveying and principles of trigonometry. With a newly purchased compass and chain, he trudged through swamps and hacked through wilderness to make his measurements. The work not only provided him with the opportunity to meet more potential political supporters but also to expand his skills. One impressed county resident recalled: "Mr. Lincoln had the monopoly of finding the lines, and when any dispute arose among the Settlers Mr Lincolns Compass and chain always settled the matter satisfactorily."

In 1834, Lincoln made a second attempt to win a seat in the state legislature. Both political ambition and financial need (the salary was $258 a session) drew him to the campaign. At the time, the Bank War between President Jackson and his pro-bank opponents, now called Whigs, had raised political tempers to white-heat intensity. In Sangamon County, loyalties were almost evenly divided between Whigs in New Salem and Jacksonian Democrats in the rural areas. Lincoln needed votes from both constituencies and wisely chose not to raise the Bank War or any other divisive national issue. Changing tactics from his campaign two years earlier, he did not mention his support for Henry Clay or his American System.

Lincoln was content to put aside any discussion of serious issues in favor of an old-fashioned political campaign—shaking every hand he could reach, trading quips, engaging in any sport or work that might win him votes. When laborers harvesting grain at Rowan Herndon's farm told Lincoln they would never vote for a candidate who could not do their chores, Lincoln knew he had found another 30 votes. Seizing a scythe from a laborer's hands, Lincoln said: "Boys if that is all I am shure [sic] of your votes." He then led them on another round of harvesting. "The boys was satisfied," Herndon recalled, "and I don't think he Lost a vote in the Croud." Overall, Lincoln received 1,376 votes, the second highest in the field, and was elected to his first political office.

After his election Lincoln asked Coleman Smoot, a supporter and one of the wealthiest men in the New Salem area, for a loan to buy his first tailor-made suit of clothes so that he could "make a decent appearance in the legislature." Lincoln also sought the assistance of John Todd Stuart, a lawyer and prominent Whig in the county who had been elected to the legislature. During the campaign, Stuart had encouraged Lincoln to study law, assuring him that most of the lawyers in the state were self-taught. Lincoln borrowed law books from Stuart's Springfield office and, on one of his visits to the town, bought a copy of *Blackstone's Commentaries* at an auction. By his own admission, Lincoln was studying law "in good earnest." In addition to reading and rereading Blackstone, reworking key passages in his mind and copying them on paper, Lincoln studied legal texts on evidence and pleadings, as well as Justice Joseph Story's treatise on *Equity Jurisprudence*.

Lincoln's work in his first legislative term at the state capital of Vandalia was routine. He introduced bills to limit the civil jurisdiction of justices of the peace and to authorize a constituent, Samuel Musick, "to build a toll bridge across Salt creek in Sangamon county." But the mundane legislative tasks that would have bored a more experienced or less eager lawmaker were accepted by Lincoln as important lessons to be mastered in his endless journey to acquire knowledge. Before the session was completed, he had earned a reputation as an outstanding legislative draftsman whom other young lawmakers asked to assist with their own bills.

After he returned to New Salem in the spring of 1835, Lincoln resumed his duties as postmaster and studied his law books. He also pursued the first serious love interest of his life. She was Ann Rutledge, the pert, comely daughter of the tavern owner where Lincoln sometimes roomed and boarded. Lincoln's courtship was complicated by the fact that Ann was betrothed to another suitor, John McNamar, an enterprising merchant and landowner. But McNamar had returned to his native New York to settle some family debts and wrote Ann sporadically during his long absence. Meanwhile, Lincoln, apparently with genial good humor and lively conversation rather than passion, won Ann's heart. Tragically, Ann succumbed to "brain fever"—probably typhoid caused by the relentless rains that flooded the county that summer and contaminated the Rutledges' well. She died in August, sending Lincoln into a profound depression.

In the fall, Lincoln began to work his way back from his depression and sorrow over Ann's death, again taking his compass and chain to survey remote stretches of Sangamon County. He was later called back to a special session of the legislature where he voted against a drastic state reapportionment plan. And he voted in favor of financial support for the building of a canal that would connect the Illinois and Chicago Rivers, though this required him to adjust his previous Whig position that all internal improvements should be financed by the federal government.

In his campaign for reelection to the state legislature, announced in the summer of 1836, Lincoln responded to a request from readers of the *Sangamo Journal* for all candidates to "show their hands." Lincoln declared that he favored the vote for all whites "who pay taxes or bear arms, (by no means excluding females)." Lincoln was not serious in his ostensible support for women's suffrage; he knew that women did not pay taxes or serve in the militia in Illinois. He supported a cooperative effort among the states to distribute the proceeds of the sales of public lands, so that a system of canals and railroads could be built without borrowing and paying interest. And in November, Lincoln said that he would vote for the Whig presidential candidate, Hugh L. White, who opposed President Andrew Jackson's chosen successor, Vice President Martin Van Buren. Lincoln did not mention his anti-slavery views.

In his third campaign for elective office, Lincoln displayed a steely confidence in confronting a hectoring opponent, George Forquer. After Lincoln had treated a crowd to a speech of "great power and originality," the assured Forquer, a Democrat and leading lawyer in the county, announced condescendingly that "the young man would have to be taken down."

When it was his turn for rebuttal, Lincoln took devilish advantage of two well-known facts about his opponent. Forquer had only recently switched from the Whig to the Democratic Party and had been instantly rewarded by the Jackson administration with a lucrative appointment as registrar of the federal land office. He also had erected the county's first lightning rod on his roof. Armed with these disparate pieces of information, Lincoln attacked. "I am not so young in years as I am in the tricks and trades of a politician, but . . . I would rather die now, than, like the gentleman [Forquer], change my politics and simultaneously with the change receive an office worth $3,000 per year, and then have to erect a lightning-rod over my house to protect a guilty conscience from an offended God."

Lincoln received more votes than any of the other fifteen candidates in the field. Only four years after his first run for public office, he had chosen a career for which he demonstrated conspicuous talent. At the same time, he was completing his law studies and would soon take his place among the most effective courtroom advocates in the state of Illinois.

Governor Joseph Duncan of Illinois was an unlikely critic of the Jackson administration. He had been elected to Congress as a Democrat and Jackson man. And when he had successfully run for governor of the state in 1834, he kept whatever anti-administration sentiments he harbored to himself. It was shocking to Democrat and Whig alike, therefore, when Governor Duncan chose in his annual message to the state legislature for the 1836–37 term to unleash a blistering attack on the Jackson administration. The particular object of the governor's wrath was Jackson's war on the Bank of the United States. Unless the president reversed his bank policy, Duncan warned, "we shall . . . have established a despotism more absolute than that of any civilized government in the world."

Democrats in the legislature were outraged by Duncan's attack. A select committee of the Illinois House of Representatives, dominated by Democrats, was convened and promptly issued a report praising Jackson's policies. The committee proposed resolutions approving the policies of the Jackson administration and condemning the governor's remarks. The Whigs countered that the Democratic resolutions should be rejected, so that the legislators could get on with the more pressing business of state internal improvements and debate over whether the state capital should remain in Vandalia or be transferred to another county.

Absolutely not, roared the Democratic majority leader, Stephen A. Douglas. Only twenty-three years old and a mere five feet four, Douglas dazzled his older, taller, and more experienced colleagues with his mental agility and precocious political acumen. In his deep, resonant voice, Douglas passionately defended Jackson's Bank War and dismissed the Whig opposition as pathetic evidence of "the sinking fortunes of a desperate political faction." The first Democratic resolution defending the Jackson administration carried overwhelmingly, 64–18, and the second resolution rebuking Governor Duncan passed by more than a 2-to-1 vote. Representative Abraham Lincoln of Sangamon County voted against both resolutions.

At the age of twenty-eight, Lincoln was a prominent member of the "Long Nine," the nickname given to the preternaturally tall nine-member Sangamon County delegation. As a Whig floor leader for the legislative session, Lincoln badly wanted the legislature to pass an ambitious internal improvements bill that included a central railroad traversing the state from north to south, as well as a canal linking Illinois and Michigan. Even more important, Lincoln was determined to have the state capital moved from Vandalia to his home county's Springfield.

The internal improvements measure turned out to draw bipartisan support. Stephen Douglas, more than Lincoln or any other Whig, spear-headed the drive for a multi-million-dollar bond issue to improve the woefully inadequate transportation network throughout the state. The problem came from legislators, both Whig and Democrat, representing counties that would not directly benefit from the improvements. To attract the necessary votes for approval, Lincoln proposed a payment of $200,000 to each county not immediately affected by the projects. Given the massive nature of the proposal, legislators continued to haggle over the details of the bill for much of the winter session.

Lincoln's task in pushing through a change in the location of the state capital was even more formidable. Whereas the internal improvements bill appealed to representatives of both parties and from every region of the state, the proposed move of the state capital to Springfield faced strong opposition, not just from Vandalia's supporters but also from legislators who wanted the capital moved to their own counties. Representatives from Alton, Jacksonville, and Peoria knew as well as Lincoln that having the state capital in their county created jobs and business. Not surprisingly, the debate was heated and protracted.

In the middle of this contentious legislative session, Governor Duncan once again complicated Lincoln's task by introducing another controversial national issue. The governor informed the legislators that he had received resolutions from many slave states asking Illinois's support in protesting and punishing the spread of abolitionist literature. As an example, Duncan presented Virginia's resolutions asserting that state's constitutional right to deal with slavery within its borders and asked that other states suppress and punish abolitionist pamphlets that could incite slaves to "insurrection and revolt." A second set of resolutions declared that the people of Kentucky were responsible for the institution of slavery within the state and "hold themselves responsible to no earthly tribunal, but will refer their cause to [God] alone." Mississippi's resolution stated: "We urge upon our brethren of the non-slaveholding States . . . as they value the harmony and safety of the Union," that they pass penal laws punishing those who are "plotting . . . to undermine, disturb or abolish our institutions of domestic slavery."

The early responses of northern states to the slave state resolutions had been positive. Connecticut declared that slavery was an institution controlled by the states and denounced abolitionist societies as "improper, unjustifiable, and dangerous." New York's resolutions also recognized a state's right to continue or abolish slavery within its borders and condemned abolition agitation. What should be Illinois's response to the resolutions? asked Governor Duncan.

A joint committee of the Illinois House and Senate was appointed to frame a reply. On January 12, 1837, the committee issued its report, supporting in the strongest terms the constitutional right of the slave states to maintain the institution of slavery and condemning abolitionists who were attempting to subvert that right. The committee recommended that the legislature adopt a resolution declaring that "the right of property in slaves, is [made] sacred to the slave-holding States by the Federal Constitution," of which right "they cannot be deprived . . . without their consent." It further proposed that the legislature "highly disapprove the formation of abolition societies, and of the doctrines promulgated by them." The committee also supported a resolution asserting that the federal government could not abolish slavery in the District of Columbia without the consent of its citizens.

On January 20, 1837, the resolutions with only minor amendments were adopted by a vote of 77 to 6. Lincoln was one of the six legislators voting no, but neither he nor any other member of the minority made a public statement at the time explaining the reasons for their opposition to the resolutions.

Six weeks later, Lincoln and Dan Stone, another member of the Sangamon County delegation who had voted against the resolutions, issued a written protest. Their belated objection was a cautious, lawyerly response to the adopted resolutions. In place of the declaration that slavery was a sacred right guaranteed by the Constitution, Lincoln and Stone wrote: "The Congress of the United States has no power, under the constitution, to interfere with the institution of slavery in the different states." And where the resolutions had asserted that the legislators "highly disapprove" of abolitionist societies, Lincoln and Stone stated that "the institution of slavery was founded on both injustice and bad policy; but that the promulgation of abolitionist doctrines tends rather to increase than to abate its evils." Their statement added that Congress could abolish slavery in the District of Columbia, but only if the people of the District requested it.

Lincoln waited until his more pressing legislative priorities had been approved—bills to move the state capital to Springfield and to finance internal improvements—before he and Stone issued their protest against the resolutions on slavery and abolitionist societies. Both Lincoln's timing and his measured response undoubtedly were dictated by his overriding concern that legislators sympathetic to the slave states might react by voting against the Springfield and internal improvements bills.

Lincoln's protest against slavery was noteworthy primarily because it stood in opposition to the sentiment expressed by the overwhelming majority in the Illinois legislature. But if his delayed protest was dictated by pragmatic considerations, his position was also based on principle. He believed that the Constitution guaranteed the southern states the right to maintain slavery within their borders. At the same time, he condemned the institution of slavery as an immoral blight on the national character.

Lincoln's position was not so unusual for a moderate to take, especially in the free states. Even in the slave states there were moderates, like Roger B. Taney of Maryland, who denounced the institution of slavery. Recall that Taney at the Gruber trial had expressed his belief that slavery was evil. But Taney, like Lincoln, maintained that the Constitution guaranteed the southern states the right to preserve it. By the mid-1830s, the abolitionist societies had grown increasingly vocal and powerful, and both Lincoln and Taney feared their deleterious effect on the tranquility of the Union.

Elijah P. Lovejoy was a fearless young Presbyterian preacher who had moved from Massachusetts to St. Louis in 1833 and, at the age of thirty-two, began the publication of a fiery journal of discontent, the *Observer*. Lovejoy's *Observer* attacked both Catholicism and slavery, which were particularly ill-advised targets in St. Louis where Catholics and pro-slavery sympathizers composed a majority of the population. In 1836, incensed citizens forced Lovejoy to leave the city.

Lovejoy relocated across the Mississippi River in the southwest Illinois town of Alton, where his printing press was mysteriously thrown into the river one night. The law-abiding residents of Alton were appalled by the act of vandalism and tried to make amends to Lovejoy by buying him another press. After the preacher resumed printing his anti-slavery diatribes, a mob again threw his press into the Mississippi. Abolitionists in Ohio, hearing of the recurrent vandalism, sent money to Lovejoy for a third press. He resumed publication of the *Observer* until his press, for a third time, was thrown into the river.

Abolitionists throughout the state of Illinois were now aroused and organized a local chapter in Alton. When Ohio abolitionists bought Lovejoy a fourth printing press, sixty armed abolitionists from the Alton area vowed to protect it. After the press was delivered to a stone warehouse on November 7, 1837, a hostile mob gathered and demanded that it be handed over. When the demand was rejected, shots were fired. One man in the crowd was killed. The roof of the warehouse was set on fire, extinguished, and set afire a second time. Twice Lovejoy, armed with a rifle, came out of the building and fired on the crowd. When he appeared a third time, he was spotted in the doorway and shot dead.

The murder occurred in the midst of widespread violence throughout the country. In St. Louis only a year earlier, a light-skinned mulatto named McIntosh, while resisting arrest, stabbed a law enforcement officer and murdered a prominent citizen—all within view of a large crowd. McIntosh was then seized by a mob, dragged through the streets of St. Louis, chained to a tree, and burned to death. And in Vicksburg, Mississippi, shortly after the McIntosh killing, three professional gamblers were hanged from trees.

It was not surprising, therefore, that Abraham Lincoln chose the subject of violence for his address to the Young Men's Lyceum in Springfield on January 27, 1838, only eleven weeks after Elijah Lovejoy had been murdered. There was an imminent threat to the United States, Lincoln began, but it was not from abroad. "All the armies of Europe, Asia and Africa combined, with all the treasure of the earth (our own excepted) in their military chest; with a Buonaparte for a commander, could not by force, take a drink from the Ohio, or make a track on the Blue Ridge, in a trial of a thousand years." The nation was being torn apart, instead, from within, by "wild and furious passions" of lawless mobs. The devastation stretched from New England to Louisiana.

Lincoln illustrated his point by citing the recent hangings of the three gamblers in Mississippi, which, he noted, were followed by the serial lynching of negroes "suspected of conspiring to raise an insurrection," white men "supposed to be leagued with the negroes," and, finally, sympathetic strangers from neighboring states. "[D]ead men were seen literally dangling from the boughs of trees upon every road side, and in numbers almost sufficient, to rival the native Spanish moss of the country, as a drapery of the forest."

Lincoln also condemned the burning death of the mulatto McIntosh in St. Louis. Even though McIntosh deserved to be severely punished for his murder of a prominent citizen of the city, the punishment should have been administered under the laws of the state, not imposed by the vigilante justice of the mob. Later in his speech, Lincoln summed up the critical danger posed to the nation by "this mobocratic spirit." If lawless bands can "burn churches, ravage and rob provision stores, throw printing presses into rivers, shoot editors, and hang and burn obnoxious persons at pleasure, and with impunity," he warned, "this Government cannot last." The mob violence closest to Lincoln's home, the murder of Elijah Lovejoy in Alton, Illinois, rated only that passing reference to printing presses thrown into rivers and editors shot, which he folded into a long sentence condemning general lawlessness in the nation.

Why did Lincoln speak so sparingly of the rank violence in his own state? He may have chosen to make his point subtly, aware that the young men in his Springfield audience were too familiar with reports of the Lovejoy murder to need specifics. Or he may have wanted to signal his disapproval of an abolitionist crusader like Lovejoy without condoning his murder. Whatever the motive, his gingerly treatment of the Lovejoy murder avoided the risk of alienating members of his audience or readers of the *Sangamo Journal*, who may have been more overtly hostile to the abolitionist movement. And he could still dwell on his overarching theme that the rule of law should be "the political religion of the nation."

In 1837, after two justices of the Illinois Supreme Court had licensed Lincoln to practice law in the state, he said good-bye to his New Salem friends and moved to Springfield, where he joined in partnership with his fellow Whig, John Todd Stuart. Though Lincoln was conscientious in drafting the wills and deeds that were staples of Stuart & Lincoln's Springfield law practice, he reserved his most passionate energy for the advancement of the Whig Party. When Stuart ran for a seat in the U.S. House of Representatives in 1838 against the Democrats' Stephen A. Douglas, Lincoln threw himself into the campaign, soliciting votes throughout the congressional district. "If we do our duty we shall succeed in the congressional election," Lincoln wrote Jesse Fell, a Whig newspaper editor in Bloomington, "but if we relax an *iota*, we shall be beaten."

After Stuart won the election by a plurality of only 36 votes, Lincoln anticipated an electoral challenge from Douglas. Rather than waiting for Douglas to contest Stuart's victory, Lincoln and five other Stuart supporters made a preemptive strike, sending a letter to Whig newspaper editors requesting that they investigate reports of voting irregularities that favored Douglas. The protest came in the form of a series of questions, including two that suggested minors, non-residents, and "unnaturalized foreigners" had illegally cast votes for Douglas.

Stuart maintained his narrow victory margin over Douglas. Lincoln nonetheless remained vigilant, writing Stuart that even if "we had heard Douglass* say that he had abandoned the contest, it would not be verry

---

* Early in his career Douglas spelled his name with two s's.

authentic." Beyond his skepticism about Douglas's integrity, Lincoln had already marked Douglas as his chief rival for future political office.

He was soon given the opportunity to meet Douglas in a series of public debates. The idea came from Douglas himself, who was the state Democratic Party chairman, after the Illinois Democratic Party had passed a series of resolutions at the party's state convention in support of the reelection of President Martin Van Buren. Douglas proposed that he and other Illinois Democratic leaders debate Lincoln and his Whig colleagues on the merits of the Van Buren administration's economic policies.

Lincoln prepared carefully for his major speech on December 26, 1839, aware that the state Whig organization intended to publish his attacks on Van Buren's policies as a campaign pamphlet. The most egregious error of the Democratic administration, Lincoln argued in his speech, was its destruction of the Bank of the United States in favor of a sub-Treasury system of federal depositories that were independent of both state banks and private business. In destroying the Bank of the United States, Lincoln contended, the Democrats had undercut the strength and stability of the national economy.

He rejected the argument of former President Jackson and his Attorney General, Roger Taney, that the National Bank was unconstitutional: "On examination, it will be found that the absurd rule, which prescribes that before we can constitutionally adopt a National Bank as a fiscal agent, we must show an indispensable necessity for it, will exclude every sort of fiscal agent that the mind of man can conceive." Lincoln's argument closely tracked Chief Justice John Marshall's in *McCulloch v. Maryland*—that the "necessary and proper" clause of the Constitution was broad enough to authorize a choice of legislative means to achieve legitimate constitutional goals, including the creation of the Bank of the United States.

Before he had finished, Lincoln took several swipes at Douglas's defense of the Van Buren administration's spending policies. He dismissed Douglas's claims as "wholly untrue" and contrary to the public record which he, Abraham Lincoln, had examined in detail. Despite his partisan thrusts at Douglas, Lincoln's speech was considered effective, even by the Democratic Illinois *State Register,* which reported that it was "in the main, temperate, and argumentative."

Only three years earlier, President-elect Martin Van Buren, as the chosen successor to the popular Andrew Jackson, had appeared positioned to keep the Democrats in control of the executive branch of the federal government well into the 1840s. He was a seasoned and sophisticated politician, having served as U.S. Senator from New York, Jackson's Secretary of State, and U.S. Minister to Great Britain. But no sooner had Chief Justice Taney administered the oath of office to Van Buren in March 1837 than the nation's economy was devastated by a financial panic that left bankruptcies, foreclosures, and bank closings in its wake. The Whigs blamed the debacle on Democratic economic policies, in general, and President Van Buren, in particular.

As the 1840 presidential election approached, Whigs knew that Van Buren was vulnerable, but were faced with a dilemma. Should they nominate the unquestioned leader of the party, Henry Clay, whose familiar voice proclaiming Whig principles was perhaps too strident? In the end, the Whigs chose to pass over Clay in favor of sixty-seven-year-old General William Henry Harrison, a military hero of the War of 1812, who appeared sufficiently non-controversial to challenge successfully the hapless Van Buren. "I am the most unfortunate man in the history of parties," lamented Clay, "always run by my friends when sure to be defeated, and now betrayed for a nomination when I, or anyone, would be sure of election."

Though he remained loyal to Clay, Lincoln accepted Harrison's nomination in the interest of party unity and the Whigs' calculation that Harrison had a better chance to defeat Van Buren than Clay. During the 1840 presidential campaign, Lincoln made speeches on Harrison's behalf using the same economic arguments against the Van Buren administration that he had given in his debates with Douglas. He also laid out a plan for Harrison's victory in central Illinois that provided detailed instructions to Whig county, precinct, and section electoral captains. The duty of every section captain, Lincoln wrote, was "[t]o see each man of his Section face to face, and procure his pledge . . . that he will record his vote as early on the [election] day as possible." Further, he instructed, the captain was "to add to his section the name of every person in his vicinity who did not vote with us in August, but who will vote with us in the fall, and take the same pledge of him, as from the others."

A confident Lincoln predicted that Harrison would carry the state, writing his law partner, Stuart, "The chance to do so, appears to me 25 per cent better than it did for you to beat Douglass." When state Democrats publicly objected to the Whigs' organizing tactics, Lincoln and four Whig colleagues defended themselves in a spirited rebuttal published in the *Sangamo Journal*. They pledged, moreover, that they would join the army led by their presidential candidate and "will, meet, conquer and disperse Gen. Harrison's and the country's enemies, and place him in the chair, now disgraced by their effeminate and luxury-loving chief."

Lincoln's highly partisan, sometimes demagogic support of Harrison was further demonstrated in a speech he made in Tremont, Illinois. The *Sangamo Journal* hailed the speaker's acute analysis of the Democrats' destructive war against the Bank of the United States and "his exposure of President Van Buren's vote in the New York Convention in allowing Free Negroes the right of suffrage, and his Janus-faced policy in relation to the war [on the bank]."

With Harrison saying little of substance during the campaign, his Whig surrogates, including Lincoln, lambasted Van Buren, portraying the president as an incompetent overseer of the nation's economic ruin. The Democrats retaliated by characterizing Harrison as a senile old man, who aspired to nothing more than to sit on the front porch of his log cabin wearing a coonskin cap and drinking hard cider. The Democrats' attacks backfired. The Whigs took wounded umbrage at the attacks on a national military hero and defended Harrison, who, unlike the cosmopolitan Van Buren, understood the ordinary man and would represent him well in Washington. They did not dwell on the fact that Harrison, an old Federalist, was a very rich man who owned 2,000 acres of fertile Ohio farmland.

In November, Harrison defeated Van Buren easily, though he did not carry Illinois, as Lincoln had predicted. Lincoln was nonetheless extremely pleased by his candidate's victory. At long last, a fellow Whig would occupy the White House.

From the moment he met Mary Todd, Abraham Lincoln was enchanted with her delicate beauty and exuberant personality. He wanted to dance with her "in the worst way," he told her at a party given by Mary's older sister, Elizabeth Edwards, and her husband, Ninian, at their elegant Springfield mansion in 1839. The Edwards regularly entertained everyone who mattered in Springfield, including the rough-hewed Lincoln, whose ambition and amiability counted for more than his crude manners.

Though Mary Todd, like Lincoln, was born in Kentucky, her background could not have been more different from his. She was the daughter of Robert Todd, a prosperous Lexington merchant and banker who provided Mary and her sisters with education in the finest private schools as well as all of the luxuries his considerable fortune could afford. Despite being waited on by the family's slaves, Mary did not fit the demure image of the aristocratic southern belle. She was feisty and independent-minded, qualities that Lincoln found extremely appealing. Like Lincoln, she delighted in quoting Robert Burns's poems and, best of all, she shared his commitment to Whig principles and devotion to Henry Clay, a Lexington friend and neighbor of the Todds.

The couple were married in the fall of 1842 and moved into a single room on the second floor of the Globe Hotel in Springfield. By the following spring, Mary was pregnant and Abraham was faced with an uncertain professional and financial future. Earlier, he had decided not to run for a fifth term in the state legislature. His decision did not mean he had abandoned a career in politics, but only that he had set his ambitious sights higher, to succeed his law partner, John Todd Stuart, in the U.S.

House of Representatives. In 1843, Lincoln announced his intentions. But two other leading Whigs, John Hardin and Edward Baker, with the same goal and greater party support, temporarily frustrated his plans.

Although he was forced to postpone his campaign for Congress, Lincoln remained active in Whig politics. As the party geared up for another presidential election in 1844, Lincoln once again supported the candidacy of Henry Clay. Clay's opportunity to seek the presidency for a fourth time was made possible by the freakishly abbreviated term of the Whigs' first president, William Henry Harrison. Despite the bitterly cold day of his inauguration in March 1840, Harrison did not wear an overcoat and insisted on tipping his hat repeatedly to the admiring crowds. He caught a cold that turned into pneumonia, and died one month later.

Harrison was succeeded by Vice President John Tyler, a conscientious but indecisive Virginian who was no match for the hard-driving Clay. In his leadership role in the Senate, Clay introduced a blizzard of bills calculated, in large part, to overshadow the president. The most notable was Clay's proposal for a Third Bank of the United States, which passed both houses of Congress. Tyler, after much hesitation and over the objections of most of his cabinet (who were Clay loyalists), vetoed the legislation. The president was pilloried by Clay supporters in Congress and the press as a traitor to Whig principles. When the party met in Baltimore to nominate their presidential candidate in 1844, Henry Clay was the unanimous choice.

Lincoln, as a leading member of the Clay Club of Illinois, invited his hero to visit Illinois for the first time. He and other members of the club's executive committee promised Clay "a reception as shall be worthy of the man on whom are now turned the fondest hopes of a great and suffering nation." Lincoln made speeches during the presidential campaign throughout the state of Illinois and in Indiana as well, extolling the virtues of the Whig candidate's American System. Frequently, he focused on Clay's support for a protective tariff, which he assured his listeners would benefit the economy throughout the nation.

Clay again failed to win the presidency, this time losing to Democrat

James K. Polk of Tennessee. Polk owed his thin margin of victory primarily to his support for the annexation of Texas. Clay had opposed annexation on the grounds that it would bring war with Mexico and probably extend, rather than restrict, slavery. But Clay's anti-slavery stand was too tepid for northern abolitionists, who voted for a third candidate, James Birney of the Liberty Party. Birney siphoned off just enough votes from Clay to ensure Polk's victory.

Lincoln blamed Clay's loss on the rigid, and in his view, self-defeating demands of northern abolitionists. "If the Whig abolitionists of New York had voted with us last fall, Mr. Clay would now be president, whig principles in the ascendent, and Texas not annexed," Lincoln wrote two outspoken abolitionist brothers, Williamson and Madison Durley of Hennepin, Illinois. Later in this same letter, Lincoln outlined his views on slavery and how best to deal with the institution that, increasingly, was dividing the nation: "I hold it a paramount duty to us in the free states, due to the Union of states, and perhaps to liberty itself (paradox though it may seem) to let the slavery of the other states alone; while, on the other hand, I hold it to be equally clear, that we should never knowingly lend ourselves directly or indirectly, to prevent that slavery from dying a natural death—to find new places for it to live in, when it can no longer exist in the old."

By the early forties, Lincoln and Stuart had agreed to dissolve their partnership. Soon afterward, Stephen Logan, a former circuit judge and one of the state's ablest lawyers, asked Lincoln to become his partner (though Logan insisted on a larger share of the firm's income). Before long, the firm of Logan & Lincoln had attracted more law business than it could handle. With the economy depressed and the state bankrupt, the two men represented a host of failing corporations and individual debtors. But their general practice covered the full range of legal controversies, from the defense of horse thieves and murderers to the drafting of wills and settlement of large property disputes.

Lincoln was a superb advocate before judge or jury, using the same homespun charm and quick wit that engaged virtually everyone he met outside the courtroom. He talked to juries rather than lectured them, and he was careful to shield them from intimidating technical terms. He reduced his case to plain facts, relevant precedents, and simple reason. And with his talent for argument and shining reputation for integrity, he rarely lost.

Lincoln did not mix law and politics. He represented anyone, regardless of cause, who requested his services. In 1841, he defended a black woman named Nance against the claim of a slaveholder that she belonged to him. Lincoln demonstrated that Nance had lived in Illinois for several years, declared herself free, and had purchased goods on her own account. He supported his factual argument with references to both state and federal law that protected a person of any color from being sold in a free state.

But six years later, he just as assiduously represented a slaveowner, Robert Matson, in his legal claim to recover his runaway slaves. When Lincoln entered the case, the complicated and sensational legal controversy involving Matson and his runaway slaves had already been widely reported in Coles County and the adjacent rural Illinois counties near the state's border with Kentucky. The story had begun in 1843 when Matson, a young, unmarried farmer from Bourbon County, Kentucky, purchased a large farm in the northeast corner of Coles County. To cultivate his new land, Matson brought slaves from his Kentucky farm across the border. Once his crops were harvested and stored for the winter, he sent the slaves back to his property in Kentucky. Every spring Matson renewed the process, selecting a fresh group of his Kentucky slaves to cross the border to help with the work on his Illinois farm.

In his annual ritual of importing slaves from Kentucky into the free state of Illinois, Matson consciously acted in such a way as to maintain his ownership of his slave property. Under what were then known as the "Black Laws" of Illinois—statutes designed to discourage the settlement of fugitive slaves in the state—a slaveholder retained ownership of his slaves if they entered Illinois only temporarily, as Matson intended. To clarify his intentions, Matson made a formal declaration before one of his farmhands every year that the slaves then working his Illinois farm were there temporarily, and that he planned for their return to his Kentucky property after the harvest was completed.

Matson's well-laid plan began to run into trouble in the fall of 1847 after Mary Corbin, his housekeeper (who also was his mistress), engaged in a violent argument with the wife of one of Matson's black farmhands, Anthony Bryant. Like most of Matson's workers, Bryant had been transported from Kentucky to Illinois to help with the work on his master's Illinois farm. But unlike the other slaves, Bryant had remained there permanently to serve as overseer on Matson's Illinois farm. He therefore became a free man under Illinois law.

Matson had not intended to free Bryant's wife, Jane, who had come with their four children from Kentucky to join her husband on the Illinois farm. After Jane felt the sharp lash of Mary Corbin's temper during their heated disagreement, the enraged Corbin declared that she would demand that Matson immediately send Jane and her children back to Kentucky to be sold at a slave auction for work on plantations in the Deep South. When Anthony Bryant was told of Corbin's threat to his family, he sought the assistance of two well-known abolitionists in the nearby village of Oakland, Gideon Ashmore and Dr. Hiram Rutherford. At their instruction, Bryant brought his wife and children to Ashmore's inn for protection.

Once Matson had located the slaves, he tried for several days to persuade them to return. When they refused, he swore out an affidavit, as required by Illinois law, claiming that the slaves belonged to him. Upon Matson's request, a justice of the peace issued an order to produce Jane and her four children. When they appeared before the judge, they were promptly turned over to the county sheriff and locked up as runaway slaves. Dr. Rutherford hired an attorney, Orlando Ficklin of Charleston, to represent the five incarcerated blacks, but the same justice of the peace denied that he had jurisdiction of the case. Since Bryant's wife and children could not produce "certificates of freedom," they were bound over to the sheriff to be advertised and sold for jail fees under provisions of the state's "Black Laws."

Rutherford and Ashmore immediately sued out a writ of habeas corpus on behalf of the five slaves, demanding that their bondage be justified in court. Meanwhile, Matson sued Rutherford and Ashmore for $2,500 in damages for taking his slaves from him. After the habeas corpus proceedings were joined with Matson's damage suit, Lincoln entered the legal picture, representing Matson in his suit against Rutherford and Ashmore.

Lincoln's role in the Matson controversy has never been firmly settled in the minds of historians and his biographers. Since Lincoln represented the slaveholder Matson, many of his biographers have strained to provide a satisfactory explanation that befits the author of the Emancipation Proclamation. Some have suggested that Lincoln did not seek out the legal business but was reluctantly pressed into service by Matson after the slaveholder had sought him out. But the more plausible explanation, based on the factual record, is that Lincoln was traveling outside his judicial district searching for additional legal business, not an uncommon practice among lawyers of that period. It may well have been Lincoln's intention to be hired in the Matson legal dispute, though not necessarily by the slaveholder. Whatever his motive, records show that he also was engaged as counsel in two other legal controversies in Coles County during that same fall 1847 judicial term.

On October 16, 1847, when Lincoln appeared in a crowded Charleston courtroom on behalf of Matson, he focused on a single issue: Had his client brought the slaves from Kentucky to settle them permanently in the free state of Illinois? If that were the case, he immediately conceded before the three-judge panel, then they were entitled to go free, and Matson had no legal claim to collect damages from Ashmore and Dr. Rutherford. That Lincoln made such a concession at the outset presented proof positive in some of his biographers' view that he had given away the case. But those acquainted with Lincoln's courtroom strategy recognized that it was his frequent practice to concede a hypothetical set of facts—only to argue that they did not exist. And that was precisely what he did in the Matson case.

Bolstered by testimony of one of Matson's field hands, Lincoln argued that the slaveholder had consistently declared his intentions to keep his slaves in Illinois temporarily, and that there was no evidence to contradict Matson's intentions. That made them *in transitu* under Illinois law and, therefore, they remained Matson's property. Under his rendering of the facts and relevant law, Lincoln argued that Matson was entitled to the return of his slaves as well as damages from the abolitionists Ashmore and Rutherford.

By some accounts, Lincoln only represented the slaveholder half-heartedly and performed far below his vaunted forensic skills. The problem with that interpretation is that it suggests that Lincoln, an officer of the court, in effect attempted to throw the case, which hardly speaks well of his integrity or professional reputation. The record suggests, on the contrary, that he argued Matson's case with considerable skill, even if it put Lincoln, who was known to be opposed to slavery, in the awkward position of vigorously defending a slaveholder's right to his human property.

Lincoln had seized upon the strongest argument available to him: that the slaves in dispute had been placed on Matson's Illinois farm with the slaveholder's knowledge and clear understanding that they would be returning, as slaves, to Kentucky after the harvest. His argument was described by an attorney on the other side, Orlando Ficklin, as one of "trenchant blows and cold logic and subtle knitting together and presenting of facts favorable to his side of the case." According to Ficklin, Lincoln laid out the facts "plausibly, ingeniously and forcibly." Despite Lincoln's best efforts, he lost the case. The judicial panel apparently concluded that the annual migration of Matson's slaves from Kentucky to Illinois did not comport with the intent of the state law to discourage runaway slaves.

Lincoln had dutifully supported the congressional candidacies of John Hardin and Edward Baker, each of whom served a single term in the House of Representatives. In 1846, it was Lincoln's turn and he, like Hardin and Baker before him, was nominated by the Whigs to serve the eighth congressional district of Illinois. His Democratic opponent was Peter Cartwright, an evangelical Methodist minister whose sermons proved more effective than his political speeches. Trailing Lincoln, a desperate Cartwright attacked his opponent as an infidel. Lincoln rejected the charge that he was "an open scoffer at Christianity," though he admitted that he was not a member of any church. He assured voters that he had never denied the truth of the Scriptures and had "never spoken with intentional disrespect of religion in general." Lincoln won the election handily and prepared to take his place in the 30th Congress as the only Whig representative from Illinois.

Early in December 1847, just days before the beginning of his congressional term, Lincoln moved himself and his family—Mary and their two young sons, Robert and Edward—into Mrs. Ann Spriggs's boardinghouse, located just east of the unfinished Capitol Building, on land now occupied by the Library of Congress. The Lincolns lived in a single upstairs bedroom and took their meals in a dining room with other boarders, including a fervent abolitionist, Whig congressman Joshua Giddings of Ohio, as well as Mississippi's pro-slavery representative, Patrick Tompkins. Lincoln used his superb storytelling skills to divert dinner conversation from slavery and other controversial topics. When a contentious discussion threatened the conviviality of the meal, Lincoln laid down his knife and fork, placed his elbows on the table, with his face resting between his hands, and said, "That reminds me . . ." Tension among the boarders instantly dissipated, and all at the table prepared to laugh at another Lincoln anecdote.

Once he entered the House chamber, Lincoln was totally focused on the serious political business at hand. He rarely missed a day of the congressional session and paid close attention to his committee duties. Lincoln's confidence in his own abilities increased as he tested his drafting and oratorical skills against those of his new colleagues. His quiet but assured self-confidence is conveyed in the earliest photograph taken, shortly before he began serving his congressional term. Formally posed in a dark suit, satin vest and ascot, he stares purposely at the viewer.

On the House floor, Lincoln aggressively attacked President Polk's role in starting the war with Mexico, which, as Clay had predicted, followed the United States's annexation of Texas. By the time Lincoln initiated his assault on the president, the United States had virtually won the war. Lincoln contended, however, that Mexico had not given the United States provocation for the war. To make his point, he presented an elaborate set of resolutions, aimed at the president much like a fusillade of leading questions directed at a hostile witness in a courtroom. Lincoln was convinced that the facts he had studied demonstrated that the United States troops had actually engaged the Mexican soldiers on territory that was indisputably Mexico's. There was no legitimate provocation for the war, Lincoln concluded.

He waited in vain for a response from the Polk administration. His accusations were ignored. Worse still, his charges were not even taken seriously by his fellow Whigs in the House, whom he hoped would agree with him that this could be a winning political issue in the 1848 presidential campaign.

Bold though he was in attacking the president's role in initiating the Mexican War, Lincoln was surprisingly quiescent during his first year in the House on the controversial subject of slavery, even though the issue was a source of impassioned debate. That debate focused on the merits of the Wilmot Proviso, named for its sponsor, Representative David Wilmot of Pennsylvania, which would have prohibited the extension of slavery into any territory acquired in the Mexican War. Lincoln had long opposed the spread of slavery and voted in favor of the Wilmot Proviso. But throughout the long debate, he did not make a single speech in support of the legislation.

Despite his meager influence in the House, Lincoln played a principal role in the Whigs' selection of a presidential candidate to challenge the Democratic nominee, Senator Lewis Cass of Michigan. General Zachary Taylor became Lincoln's choice, and eventually that of the Whig Party. Taylor, like General William Henry Harrison, was a war hero. And like Harrison, he seemed to have no political convictions. But Lincoln knew that Taylor could effectively blunt the Democrats' claim to the victory in the Mexican War, since Taylor had been a military leader in that victory. As to his lack of a platform, Lincoln provided a ready rationalization for Taylor's deficiencies: the general would be a passive, essentially figurehead, president who would allow Congress to make important policy decisions.

That Taylor prevailed in the 1848 presidential election was gratifying to Lincoln but did not compensate for his lackluster congressional term. In a final effort to produce important legislation, Lincoln proposed a referendum for the District of Columbia in which voters could abolish slavery. He included in his proposal provisions to attract support from moderate southerners. If the referendum succeeded, the proposal provided that slaveowners who agreed to free their slaves would be compensated in "full cash value." To further appeal to representatives from the South, Lincoln's bill required municipal officials in the District of Columbia to enforce the Fugitive Slave Law.

In the end, Lincoln's proposal satisfied almost no one. Moderate southerners feared that a successful referendum in the district would be the first critical step toward the abolition of slavery throughout the United States. Abolitionists in the North rejected the idea that slaveowners should be compensated for freeing their slaves. They were, moreover, repulsed by the proposed enforcement of the Fugitive Slave Law. The abolitionist leader, Wendell Phillips, began to refer to Lincoln as "that slave hound from Illinois"—an absurd charge, but ominous signal that efforts at compromise on the slavery issue by moderates like Lincoln would ultimately be in vain.

Chapter Three

"THE MONSTROUS INJUSTICE OF SLAVERY"

A demoralized Abraham Lincoln returned with his family to Springfield in the spring of 1849. He felt that he had accomplished nothing of significance during his congressional term and was resigned to devoting all of his professional energies to reestablishing his law practice. His public life appeared to be finished.

But during the next congressional term, while Lincoln was quietly resettling into his life as lawyer and family man in Springfield, the first in a chain of momentous events that would lead to Lincoln's presidency and exalted place in American history occurred. In December 1849, the 31st Congress faced the problem of how to deal with the spoils of the Mexican War, which had added a half billion acres of land to the United States in the California, New Mexico, and Utah Territories. One question dominated the legislative session: Would those territories be slave or free?

President Zachary Taylor—"Old Rough and Ready," as he had been known to his troops—put his military mind to work on the issue and had come up with a typically blunt-edged solution. Though Taylor was a former Louisiana planter and slaveowner, his thinking was national, not sectional, in scope. The voters in the territories should petition for statehood immediately, the president decided, and that would eliminate fights between pro- and anti-slavery forces over control of the territorial governments. Taylor had sent his agents to the territories to accelerate the process, confident that voters would exclude slavery. And that would be the end of the problem. "Old Zack is a good old soul," observed the *New York Tribune's* Horace Greeley, "but don't know himself from a side of sole leather in the way of statesmanship."

Southern legislators were outraged by Taylor's "executive tyranny" and threatened secession if slavery were excluded from the territories. Senator Jefferson Davis of Mississippi warned that the people of his state knew how to defend their institutions, even by civil war, "and will march up to the issue and meet it face to face." With equal bellicosity, William H. Seward, the freshman senator from New York, rejected Taylor's solution of leaving the slavery question to the territorial voters. The nation was governed by God's law, Seward believed, and He intended all territories to be free.

With radicals threatening irrevocably to split Congress and the nation, congressional moderates from both sections of the country turned to Henry Clay. The Kentuckian eagerly seized the opportunity to lead Congress toward a compromise on the issue of race, as he had done thirty years earlier. Now seventy-three years old and in failing health, Clay was no longer the lean, dashing figure of his political prime, but he still possessed the uncanny talent of identifying the fine line of accommodation between warring factions. In January 1850, he presented a set of resolutions to the Senate that he promised would cauterize all of the "bleeding wounds" exposed by the slavery issue.

Clay proposed that California be admitted to the Union as a free state, but that territorial governments be set up in the other lands of the Mexican cession area with no immediate decision made on the issue of slavery. The slave state of Texas would accept a reduced western boundary, ceding more land to the New Mexico Territory, but the United States, in exchange, would assume Texas's $10 million debt. The slave trade, though not slavery itself, would be abolished in the District of Columbia. And as a final enticement to the slave states, Clay proposed that Congress pass a new, tough fugitive slave law.

Early in February 1849, Clay defended his resolutions in two impassioned speeches on the Senate floor. Thousands came from Alexandria, Baltimore, and Philadelphia to sit in an overheated Senate chamber to hear Clay's plea for compromise. Clay spoke, he said, not as a Kentuckian or as an anti-slavery man, but as an American. For those, like Clay himself, who opposed the spread of slavery, his proposal allowed nature to take its course in the disputed territories. Clay was convinced that the land was not suited to the slave economy and inevitably would be free. He assured the South that their institutions were safer in the Union than outside. Secession, he warned, would lead to war—"furious . . . bloody . . . implacable."

For the last time, Clay was joined in debate by South Carolina's John C. Calhoun and Massachusetts's Daniel Webster, the two other legendary orators of the Senate who constituted "the triumvirate." Calhoun was dying of tuberculosis and had to be helped to his seat. Draped in a black cloak, he sat impassively as a fellow slave state senator read his speech, which amounted to a southern ultimatum. For the Union to survive, Calhoun demanded that the South be granted equal rights to the territories and that the North cooperate in returning fugitive slaves and cease agitating against the institution of slavery. And, finally, to ensure the South's parity with the more populous northern states, Calhoun proposed a constitutional amendment that would give the South a veto over onerous legislation. If the North was unwilling to meet his demands, Calhoun said that the two sections should part in peace. "If you are unwilling we should part in peace tell us so," he added, "and we shall know what to do, when you reduce the question to submission or resistance."

Three days after Calhoun had issued his defiant ultimatum, the third member of the triumvirate, Webster, joined the debate. Like Clay, the sixty-eight-year-old Webster was ailing. But "the Godlike Daniel," with his brooding countenance and sonorous voice, could still hold his Senate audience in thrall. Dressed in his ceremonial suit of revolutionary blue and buff, Webster gave eloquent support to Clay's compromise. To demonstrate that his allegiance was to the Union, not to his state or section of the country, Webster condemned the violent language of the abolitionists as well as the proliferating personal liberty laws in the North that prevented the recovery of fugitive slaves.

His conciliatory words toward the South shocked New England's anti-slavery intellectuals. "Why did all manly gifts in Webster fail?" asked the abolitionist Ralph Waldo Emerson. "He wrote on Nature's grandest brow, *For Sale*."

Clay fought tenaciously for his resolutions on the Senate floor and in committee. The final legislative product, the Compromise of 1850, incorporated the major provisions of his resolutions. But the success was due to more than Clay and Webster's advocacy. While the legislative battle raged, both Calhoun and President Taylor died, depriving opponents of compromise of two powerful dissenting voices. Taylor's successor, Vice President Millard Fillmore, immediately announced his support for the compromise.

Clay also needed the deft legislative skills of the young senator from Illinois, Stephen A. Douglas, known as "the little Giant." He had been elected to the Senate in 1843 at the age of thirty and was already considered a future presidential candidate. Douglas left the oratory to Clay and Webster, but maneuvered adroitly behind closed doors, splitting the resolutions into separate bills, then working and reworking the language of compromise until he had collected the necessary votes for passage.

Relieved Americans celebrated the Compromise of 1850 with cannon salutes, parades, and banquets. Ecstatic crowds gathered at Webster's and Douglas's residences to applaud. And Henry Clay was cheered by northern crowds wherever he traveled, from Baltimore to Philadelphia to New York. The legislation, all hoped, would serve as the enduring document that preserved the Union.

Two years later, after Henry Clay died, Lincoln delivered his eulogy in Springfield's Hall of Representatives. In recounting the many accomplishments in Clay's public life, Lincoln spoke proudly of Clay's pivotal role in passing the Missouri Compromise and the Compromise of 1850. Lincoln devoted the final passages to Clay's position on slavery, which reflected his own beliefs. Clay had been a slaveowner, Lincoln acknowledged, but he believed in the gradual emancipation of slaves and worked through the American Colonization Society to realize that goal. And Clay, like Lincoln himself, opposed radicals on both sides of the slavery issue. At the same time, Clay staunchly defended his belief in the human bond between the black slave and free white man. "He ever was, on principle and in feeling, opposed to slavery," Lincoln said. "He did not perceive, that on a question of human right, the negroes were to be excepted from the human race."

The Compromise of 1850, which Lincoln considered to have "settled forever" the issue of slavery in the territories, held the country together less than four years. The fissure was, at first, so subtle that even the man who would be blamed for it, Senator Douglas of Illinois, was totally unaware of the devastating potential of his action. In January 1854, Douglas, as chairman of the Senate's Committee on Territories, introduced a bill to provide a government for the vast northern portion of the Louisiana Territory, which included the present states of Kansas and Nebraska. Under the terms of the Missouri Compromise of 1820, the territory should have been designated "free soil," since it was above that legislation's boundary for slavery. But southerners had defeated earlier bills based on those terms, and Douglas feared a similar fate for his latest bill. To break the impasse, he proposed that voters in the territory decide whether it would be slave or free. In defending his proposal for popular sovereignty, the Illinois senator pointed approvingly to the Compromise of 1850 in which Congress provided that voters would decide the slavery issue in the New Mexico and Utah Territories.

As soon as Douglas introduced his bill, senators from the slave states seized the opportunity to eliminate the source of long-standing southern bitterness, the Missouri Compromise. Since Douglas's proposal effectively repealed the earlier legislation, they argued, explicit language should be written into the bill overturning the 1820 law. Douglas knew that he needed southern votes for his bill to pass, and so he reluctantly agreed to the amendment. At the same time, he assented to splitting the region into two territories: Kansas (where the South had high hopes that voters would approve slavery) and Nebraska. Caving in to southern pressure, Douglas predicted that his bill "will raise a hell of a storm."

The congressional tempest that Douglas anticipated reached seismic proportions. Antislavery senators led by Salmon P. Chase of Ohio and Charles Sumner of Massachusetts assailed the legislation as "a gross violation of a sacred pledge." The challenge to the Missouri Compromise uprooted party allegiances. Northern Democrats joined northern Whigs in opposing the legislation. Southerners, whether Democrat or Whig, overwhelmingly supported it. Having made his deal with the southerners, Douglas ferociously defended his bill in both the House and Senate. And he persuaded the Democratic president, Franklin Pierce, to put his administration's prestige behind the bill. After bitter floor debate, the Kansas-Nebraska Act was passed by Congress on May 30, 1854.

Douglas's political fortunes in the North plummeted. He was compared to Judas Iscariot; indignant women in Ohio, to make the point more vivid, presented him with thirty pieces of silver. He could travel to his Chicago home, Douglas sardonically observed, guided by the flames of his own burning effigies. When he arrived in Chicago, he was greeted by scathing criticism from the *Chicago Tribune* and other major newspapers in the city.

Lincoln did not, at first, join the chorus berating Douglas. For five years, he had stuck closely to the career path that he had charted for himself upon leaving Congress. His law practice was busy and lucrative, thanks particularly to railroad clients, like the Illinois Central Railroad, that were rapidly expanding their Illinois operations. Lincoln's political activity was limited, and his enthusiasm subdued. He had campaigned for the losing Whig presidential candidate, General Winfield Scott, in 1852, but his speeches lacked the fierce conviction of his earlier efforts.

There is no record of Lincoln's opposition to Douglas's bill during the five months of acrimonious congressional debate over the legislation. And for almost three months after the passage of the Kansas-Nebraska Act, Lincoln made no comment on the statute either in his private correspondence or public statements. His silence may be explained, in part, by his deep involvement at the time in a lawsuit on behalf of the Illinois

Central in which he defended the exemption of the railroad's property from local taxation. The case proved to be one of the most complicated and profitable of his entire career. He may also have been exercising his lawyer's caution before plunging headlong into a controversy that had attracted an embarrassingly fractured group of opponents to the legislation. Moderate Whigs, like Lincoln, found themselves uncomfortably close to radical abolitionists as well as members of the emerging nativist Know-Nothing Party, which was feeding on hatred of Catholics and immigrants of any religion.

Lincoln first condemned "the great wrong and injustice" of the Kansas-Nebraska Act at a meeting of the Scott County Whigs on August 26, 1854. Although the meeting had been called to appoint delegates to the state party convention, the Whigs' *Illinois Journal* raced past its report of the business transacted at the meeting to hail Lincoln's "ingenious" and "logical" dissection of the legislation. Emboldened by the positive response to his first attack on the Kansas-Nebraska Act, Lincoln repeated his criticism in speeches that he delivered over the next two months, making his arguments with greater clarity and rising moral indignation.

By September, Senator Douglas had recovered from the initial shock of the widespread criticism to the legislation that he had so skillfully pushed through Congress. With indefatigable energy, he barnstormed throughout the state of Illinois defending the Kansas-Nebraska Act. The legislation, he argued, honored the nation's historic commitment to the right of self-government. Douglas contended that the Compromise of 1850, for which he had worked tirelessly, superseded the Missouri Compromise of 1820 and properly returned the law governing U.S. territories to the fundamental principle of popular sovereignty. Like Henry Clay and other proponents of the 1850 compromise, Douglas now asserted that both the soil and climate of the Kansas and Nebraska Territories guaranteed that they would eventually enter the Union as free states. Opposition to the legislation came primarily from abolitionists and members of the Know-Nothing Party, he claimed, each representing a hateful, extreme constituency. Douglas urged all patriotic Americans,

North and South, who believed in fairness to all and a just and lasting peace for the nation, to reject such destructive radicalism.

As good as Douglas's arguments were, Lincoln was eager to refute them, face to face. To prepare himself for a showdown, he spent scores of hours in the state library at Springfield studying the congressional debates on the legislation, the proliferating pamphlets on the law, and relevant data including census reports on the territories. But Douglas, who was combative when he had to be, saw no need to share the public stage with Lincoln and declined to meet him in debate.

Undaunted, Lincoln prepared to challenge Douglas on the opening day of the Illinois State Fair in Springfield, October 3, after he learned that the senator was scheduled to defend the Kansas-Nebraska Act at an open-air rally. When a rainstorm forced Douglas to move to the hall of the Illinois House of Representatives for his speech, Lincoln paced back and forth in the lobby, listening intently to the senator's arguments. After Douglas had completed his harangue, Lincoln stood in the middle of the stairway and shouted to the startled men and women exiting the hall that the next day either he or Democratic congressman Lyman Trumbull, who also opposed the legislation, would answer Douglas's arguments. Lincoln invited Douglas to attend and offered him time for a rebuttal.

The next afternoon, Lincoln appeared before a large crowd on the platform that Douglas had vacated the previous day. He was dressed informally in shirtsleeves and stood a few steps away from the podium. Douglas took a chair directly in front of Lincoln, hoping to inhibit or unnerve his unwelcome adversary. But as Lincoln delivered his long, carefully calibrated attack on the Kansas-Nebraska Act over the next three hours, Douglas, not Lincoln, became agitated, interrupting the speaker with taunts and objections.

Lincoln made his major points through a combination of narrative history, logic, and legal analysis, sprinkling his arguments with the humor and practical examples for which he was so well known in the courtroom. He also took advantage of Douglas's challenges, counterpunching with cool effectiveness.

Lincoln began with the premise that the framers had tolerated slavery where it existed but clearly intended that it not spread to other parts of U.S. territories. Lincoln's exhibit A was the Northwest Ordinance, passed in 1787, which prohibited slavery north and west of the Ohio River. Were not the people who settled in those territories (later to become the states of Ohio, Indiana, Illinois, Michigan, and Wisconsin) capable of managing their own affairs? he asked. Why then did Jefferson and other "founders of liberty and republicanism on this continent" deny them what Senator Douglas had called the fundamental right of self-government? Lincoln answered that the framers valued human freedom even above self-government. Citizens of Illinois "never knew the depth of our misfortunes imposed by the ordinance of '87," he observed dryly; "we never knew how miserable we were!"

The Missouri Compromise of 1820 was an agreement reached openly between two contentious sections of the country, Lincoln conceded. But to assume that the Compromise of 1850 repealed the earlier legislation, as Douglas had argued, defied logic and common sense. To illustrate his point, Lincoln asked his audience to imagine that a man advised him to build an addition to his house. If he declined to do so, did that mean that the man could burn down Lincoln's house? Certainly not. Agreements to build the house (the Missouri Compromise) and an extension (the Compromise of 1850) were separate, and their terms independent of each other.

Making what he admitted to be a legal argument, Lincoln ticked off every provision of the 1850 legislation to show there was not a single reference to the repeal of the Missouri Compromise. No reasonable mind could conclude that the Congress that passed the 1850 legislation intended to repeal the earlier law. Lincoln noted that Douglas had attempted to bolster his argument by claiming that the Illinois legislature had instructed him to repeal the Missouri Compromise in the Kansas-Nebraska Act. He informed the audience that he had looked in vain in the records of the state legislature for such formal instruction to Douglas.

Douglas interrupted to insist that there was such a resolution. Calmly, Lincoln requested that Douglas read the entire state legislative record before he again interrupt him. True, one house of the state legislature had instructed Douglas, but the other had not. If it was all the same to Douglas, Lincoln admonished, would the senator refrain from another interruption until he had distinguished between a resolution that had passed in both houses and one that had not.

Lincoln read from an 1849 Douglas speech in which the senator had declared that the Missouri Compromise was "sacred." The audience responded to Lincoln's reading with exuberant applause, which, a reporter observed, "Judge Douglas didn't enjoy." * When Douglas shouted his displeasure, Lincoln stared directly at his antagonist. Since Douglas had so recently declared the Missouri Compromise "sacred," he said, it "illy" became him to apply unseemly names and epithets to Lincoln and other American citizens who still revered the legislative compact. Lincoln added to Douglas's discomfort by reminding him that his original Kansas-Nebraska bill introduced in the Senate in 1853 had recognized Congress's right to exclude slavery from the territory.

Lincoln rejected Douglas's contention that popular sovereignty in the Kansas and Nebraska Territories would not encourage slavery, again using an earthy metaphor to emphasize his point. Suppose I have a fence that protects my field from nearby cattle and hogs, Lincoln hypothesized. "If I go and tear down the fence, will it be supposed that I do not by that act encourage them to enter? Even the hogs would know better—much more men, who are a higher order of the animal world!" Lincoln predicted that violence would follow if the fence that had figuratively been torn down by the Kansas-Nebraska Act was not rebuilt.

The senator claimed that the repeal of the Missouri Compromise was "just and right in itself," Lincoln reminded his audience, laying the premise for his most fervent argument against slavery. No court decision or federal law, including the Compromise of 1850, had ever supported Douglas's contention. But surely Douglas was wrong at a more fundamental moral level, if he meant that the settlers of the Kansas and Nebraska Territories had a *natural* right to introduce slavery. Lincoln then

---

* Douglas had earlier served as a state circuit court judge.

reeled off a series of questions for which he left no doubt of the affirmative answer: "Is not slavery universally granted to be, in the abstract, a gross outrage to the law of nature?" "Have not all civilized nations, our own among them, made the Slave trade [a] capital [offense] and classed it with piracy and murder?" "Is it not held to be the great wrong of the world?"

The Democratic *Illinois Register* attempted to dismiss Lincoln's powerful address with a mock eulogy for his "lifeless remains" that, the newspaper claimed, had been buried by Douglas's superior arguments. But Douglas knew better and admitted privately that Lincoln was "the most difficult and dangerous opponent that I have ever met." Hoarse and exhausted from his constant public defense of the Kansas-Nebraska Act, Douglas wanted no more challenges from Lincoln.

But Lincoln pursued the senator relentlessly, challenging him to another debate two weeks later in Peoria. Douglas weighed the political risks of avoiding his increasingly aggressive and effective adversary. He decided to accept Lincoln's challenge, but on his terms.

Douglas spoke for three hours on the afternoon of October 16, long enough, he calculated, to leave Lincoln with a restless and hungry audience. But Lincoln smoothly confounded Douglas's strategy. Go home and have your supper, he told the crowd, and return refreshed at seven o'clock for his speech. To entice the Democrats in the audience, Lincoln promised to give Douglas a full hour to respond. "I felt confident you would stay for the fun of hearing him skin me," Lincoln said.

In his Peoria speech, Lincoln reiterated many of the arguments he had made in Springfield, laying out the sad history of slavery in the United States with a noticeably conciliatory tone toward the southern states. He did not challenge the constitutional right of the southern states to maintain slavery; that was the hard bargain made by the framers. He acknowledged that the slave states were not responsible for the origin of slavery, and conceded that it was an institution, once established, that was difficult to eliminate. Like his southern neighbors, Lincoln admitted that he had no easy solution for eliminating slavery. He wished, like many moderates in the South, that American slaves could be transported to Liberia to govern themselves. But that dream of colonization was not immediately realistic. He also agreed with southerners that the black man was inferior to the white man politically and socially. And he supported a fugitive slave law, so long as it protected the free black from being forced into slavery. He conceded, finally, that he valued the preservation of the Union above his profound opposition to the spread of slavery and would therefore reluctantly accept the terms of the Kansas-Nebraska Act rather than have the nation torn violently asunder.

All that said, Lincoln contended that there was no moral justification for permitting slavery to spread in the free territories of the United States. With rising passion, he rejected the argument that territorial voters should be free to perpetuate slavery. "I hate it because of the monstrous injustice of slavery itself," he said. "I hate it because it deprives our republican example of its just influence in the world—enables the enemies of free institutions, with plausibility, to taunt us as hypocrites—causes the real friends of freedom to doubt our sincerity, and especially because it forces so many really good men amongst ourselves into an open war with the very fundamental principles of civil liberty."

Attacking Douglas's self-government argument at its core, Lincoln declared that the senator's position was based on the principle that a black male was not a man. But if he was a man, as Lincoln believed, was it not a total destruction of self-government to say that he too shall not govern himself? "When the white man governs himself that is self-government," he said, "but when he governs himself and also governs *another* man, that is *more* than self-government—that is despotism."

The fundamental flaw in Douglas's argument, Lincoln argued, was that it was built on a false premise. "Judge Douglas frequently with bitter irony and sarcasm paraphrases our argument by saying 'The white people of Nebraska are good enough to govern themselves, *but they are not good enough to govern a few miserable negroes*!!.' Well I doubt not that the people of Nebraska are and will continue to be as good as the average of people elsewhere. What I do say is that no man is good enough to govern another man, *without that other's consent*. I say this is the leading principle—the sheet anchor of American republicanism."

Later in his three-hour speech, Lincoln blamed Douglas personally for the moral bankruptcy of the Kansas-Nebraska Act. "It shows that the Judge has no very vivid impression that the negro is a human; and consequently has no idea that there can be any moral question in legislation about him. In his view, the question of whether a new country shall be slave or free is a matter of as utter indifference, as it is whether his neighbor shall plant his farm with tobacco or stock it with horned cattle." Lincoln then declared that he joined the great mass of mankind, which took a totally different view: "They consider slavery a great moral wrong; and their feeling against it, is not evanescent, but eternal. It lies at the very foundation of their sense of justice; and it cannot be trifled with."

In his speeches condemning slavery, Lincoln rose to extraordinary heights of moral fervor. At the same time, as an ambitious politician, he began to maneuver for a seat in the U.S. Senate after voters in the fall elections in northern states repudiated Douglas and the Kansas-Nebraska Act. Without guile or subtlety, Lincoln asked for the support of influential Whigs around the state as well as members of the Illinois legislature, where the election of the state's next U.S. senator was scheduled for January 1855.

"You used to express a good deal of partiality for me, and if you are still so, now is the time," Lincoln wrote Charles Hoyt, a prominent Aurora merchant and leading Whig. "Some friends here are really for me for the U.S. Senate, and I should be very grateful if you could make a mark for me among your members." Besides asking his support, Lincoln requested that Hoyt provide him with "the names, post-offices, and 'political position' " of his friends in the state legislature. To Thomas Henderson, a Whig legislator, Lincoln wrote: "It has come round that a whig may, by possibility, be elected to the U.S. Senate, and I want the chance of being the man. You are a member of the legislature and have a vote to give. Think it over, and see whether you can do better than to go for me." Lincoln worked so tirelessly to win the Senate seat, observed his law partner, William Herndon, that "he slept, like Napoleon, with one eye open."

Lincoln knew that he needed virtually every anti-Nebraska vote in the state legislature to prevail. His broad solicitation efforts included entreaties to anti-Nebraska Democrats as well as Whigs. He was careful not to reject overtures from the abolitionists who had formed a new Republican Party in the state and named him to the party's executive committee. And he did not openly condemn members of the Know-Nothing Party, though he had no sympathy for their nativist views.

Meanwhile, the Whigs nominated Lincoln to be Sangamon County's representative in the state legislature. Though he did not campaign, he received the most votes of any candidate in the state. His victory, however, complicated his Senate ambitions. A state constitutional provision prohibited legislators from electing one of their own to higher office, which could give representatives unenthusiastic about Lincoln's candidacy a formal reason to reject him. Lincoln also worried that in a close Senate vote he could unwittingly tip the election to a Douglas-backed Democrat, since protocol forbade a representative from voting for himself. To keep his candidacy for the Senate viable, Lincoln announced that he was giving up his recently won legislative seat.

Once he had cleared the way for a run for the Senate, he campaigned tenaciously, keeping detailed notes of the likely votes of every member of the legislature. His efforts appeared to pay off. On the first ballot, Lincoln led all candidates, followed by the incumbent Democrat James Shields and Congressman Lyman Trumbull. But he was still a handful of votes short of election. Unfortunately for Lincoln, those crucial votes were held by anti-Nebraska Democrats who, though finding nothing objectionable about Lincoln, vowed that they would only support a member of their party. In the end, the legislature picked the Democrat, Trumbull, who had opposed the Kansas-Nebraska Act as vigorously as Lincoln.

Though the defeat was a painful blow to Lincoln's ambition, he did not show it publicly. The night after Trumbull's election, Lincoln attended a gala reception at the Ninian Edwardses, which had originally been planned to celebrate *his* victory. Elizabeth Edwards told Lincoln that she knew how disappointed he must have been. Without a visible trace of regret, Lincoln responded: "Not too disappointed to congratulate my friend Trumbull." He then walked toward the man who had defeated him, his right hand extended in congratulation.

As Lincoln predicted, the Kansas-Nebraska Act led to discord and eventually violence. Douglas's pledge of popular sovereignty for the Kansas Territory promoted a fierce competition between pro- and anti-slavery forces to win the vote. Abolitionist groups, like the New England Emigrant Aid Company, poured money and armed anti-slavery men into Kansas. Pro-slavery men from adjacent Missouri, brandishing bowie knifes and six-shooters, countered by fraudulently claiming Kansas residency and daring abolitionists to challenge them.

In 1855, pro-slavery forces prevailed in the tainted election of a territorial legislature and immediately made it a felony to challenge the right to hold slaves in Kansas. The territorial governor questioned the legitimacy of the legislature, but was soon removed from office by President Pierce and replaced with a more compliant administrator. The free-state forces, however, were not idle. Convinced that the Pierce administration would not allow a fair election to take place, they chose delegates at a convention of their own, which adopted a constitution excluding slavery, all without prior congressional approval. President Pierce denounced their action as "revolutionary" and vowed to support the pro-slavery government. The threat of civil war within the territory was palpable.

Lincoln learned the sordid details of the Kansas chaos from his friend Mark Delahay, who edited the free-state paper at Leavenworth. His hope for an uneasy peace between North and South turned to despair. "Our political problem now is, 'Can we, as a nation, continue together permanently—forever—half slave, and half free?'" he wrote Judge George Robertson of Lexington, Kentucky. "The problem is too mighty for me. May God, in his mercy, superintend the solution."

Even as the nation cracked along the fault line of slavery, Chief Justice Taney, former slaveowner and proud son of the South, was revered by political leaders in the North as well as the South. Anti-slavery senator William Seward of New York, for example, wrote Taney in 1851 of "the high regard which, in common with the whole American people, I entertain for you as the head of the Judicial Department."

Under Taney's leadership, the Supreme Court of the United States appeared to be a lonely beacon of reason in an increasingly divided nation. "Who doubts the integrity or the learning of the distinguished Chief Justice?" asked Samuel Phelps, a Whig congressman from Vermont, who announced his willingness to submit the constitutional question of slavery to the Court. "If we cannot trust the power there, where, in Heaven's name, shall we repose it?" Reverdy Johnson, a prominent Democratic from Maryland, agreed with Phelps that the slavery issue should be settled once and for all by the Court. "The members of the Supreme Court are not politicians," Johnson said. "They are born in a different atmosphere, and address themselves to different hearers."

A bill to give the Court the final authority to resolve the issue had been introduced in Congress in 1848 but, after protracted debate, was defeated. In opposing the measure, Congressman John Crozier, a Tennessee Democrat, spoke prophetically of the disaster that awaited the Taney Court less than a decade later after its *Dred Scott* decision. "If the decision should be against the North, the North would not abide by it," he said. "They would insist that the decision had been made by a Court, a majority of whose members were from the South and slaveholders; that their decision was either corrupt or their judgment had been warped by prejudice and interest."

In the early 1850s, while members of Congress wrangled over the slavery issue just a floor above the Court in the nation's Capitol, Chief Justice Taney continued his unobtrusive leadership of his judicial colleagues. Forty-two-year-old Benjamin Curtis, a Harvard graduate, leader of the Massachusetts bar, and prominent Whig (appointed to the Court by President Fillmore in 1851), recalled his first impressions of the thin and enfeebled seventy-four-year-old Chief Justice. Taney seemed to be on the verge of physical collapse, as he had for virtually his entire adult life. But in judicial conference he instantly revived. There, Curtis observed, Taney demonstrated an extraordinary ability to recite the facts of complicated cases, relevant precedents, and legal principles in fastidious detail and with great clarity. His thorough exposition of the cases was done without bias or desire to impress other members of the Court. And though colleagues like Curtis were aware of Taney's temper, it was at all times kept in check. The Chief Justice never lost sight of his primary responsibility: to serve as mediator between the increasingly irreconcilable views of his brethren.

Taney's able leadership was all the more impressive since, by the early 1850s, the passionate disagreements over slavery that dominated the national political debate had infiltrated the inner sanctum of the Supreme Court. Fortunately, the strong opinions of the justices were, for the most part, hidden from the public view. Associate Justice Peter Daniel of Virginia, who had been appointed by President Van Buren in 1841, was an avid proponent of states' rights in general, and the South's slave-driven agrarian economy in particular. Convinced that Congress had acted unconstitutionally in passing the Missouri Compromise, Daniel summarily rejected the authority of a Congress dominated by the northern states to keep slavery out of any of the territories. He hated the abolitionists and chafed at their attitude of moral superiority toward the South. "It is the unmitigable outrage," he wrote former President Van Buren, "which I venture to say, there is no true Southron from the schoolboy to the octogenarian, who is not prepared for any extremity in order to repel."

Associate Justice John McLean was at the opposite end of the political spectrum from Daniel. Almost from the beginning of his long tenure on the Court, McLean had electioneered for the presidency, flaunting his anti-slavery credentials wherever he thought it could do him the most political good. With an eye to the slavery issue, he had openly opposed the annexation of Texas and the war with Mexico. And later, when the nation became irreparably split over the issue of the spread of slavery, McLean publicly expressed his opinion that Congress had the authority to prohibit slavery in the territories.

Chief Justice Taney needed all of his considerable skills as a mediator to bring the Court together in 1851 when the justices, neither for the first time nor the last, were pressed to define the federal government's role in excluding slavery from states and territories. The case originated in Kentucky, where a slaveowner, Dr. Christopher Graham, had encouraged three of his slaves to develop their musical skills by traveling to other states for performances. They had been allowed to travel to the free states of Indiana and Ohio to perform and return to Kentucky. Later, when the slaves fled to Ohio to seek their freedom, Dr. Graham filed a lawsuit in Kentucky against a man named Strader who had assisted in the slaves' escape. Strader argued that his action in helping to relocate the slaves in Ohio was protected by the Northwest Ordinance of 1787 and the laws of Ohio, which prohibited slavery. Dr. Graham won his case in the Kentucky courts, and Strader appealed to the U.S. Supreme Court.

In *Strader v. Graham*, the justices were faced with a decision charged with explosive political repercussions. If the Court decided that the antislavery provisions of the Northwest Ordinance were binding in the case, then abolitionists might well assume that the ruling could be extended to other territories. Even if the justices did not focus on Strader's Northwest Ordinance argument, they were left with the issue of which state law, Ohio's or Kentucky's, should guide them. Did the slave musicians become legally free when they entered the free state of Ohio to perform?

In writing for a unanimous Court, Chief Justice Taney surgically removed from his opinion any consideration of the Northwest Ordinance or the laws of Ohio. The Northwest Ordinance was superseded by the Constitution, Taney wrote, and therefore the appropriate legal authority for the status of the slaves resided in the individual states. The musicians remained slaves, the Chief Justice continued, since they had voluntarily returned to Kentucky after their Ohio performance and were, as a result, still governed by the slave laws of Kentucky.

Taney's opinion was consistent with his entire record as Chief Justice and, before that, as President Jackson's Attorney General. He had never wavered in his conviction that the framers had guaranteed the southern states the right to maintain the institution of slavery. Significantly, the Chief Justice's opinion was crafted narrowly enough to attract the votes of both Justices Daniel and McLean (though McLean complained in a concurrence of Taney's dismissive treatment of the Northwest Ordinance). The Court had once again, under Taney's prudent leadership, avoided the combustible constitutional question of the federal government's authority to exclude slavery in a state or territory.

Abolitionists soon lost patience with the Court's cautious approach to the slavery issue. Their impatience turned to outrage when northerners on the Court, acting in their individual capacities as circuit court judges, unfailingly enforced the Fugitive Slave Law. That group of justices included Massachusetts's Benjamin Curtis as well as Samuel Nelson of New York and Robert Grier of Pennsylvania. Even the fervent anti-slavery Justice McLean enforced the law.

Justice Grier presided over several controversial fugitive slave law proceedings and especially felt the pressures of the abolitionists. He was an anti-slavery man and sympathized with those who insisted on strict proof of slave ownership to protect free blacks from kidnappers. But abolitionists who flouted the law were another matter. Grier called them "unhappy agitators who infest other portions of the Union, and, with mad zeal, are plotting its ruin."

Throughout this tempestuous period, the Chief Justice scrupulously avoided any public expression that might be wrongly interpreted in the charged political atmosphere. When New York's Senator Seward asked permission to inscribe a speech that he had given on French spoliation claims which, he believed, reflected Taney's views, the Chief Justice politely declined the gesture. Taney wrote Seward that he was "very unwilling to have" his "name in any way connected with a measure pending before the Legislative or Executive Departments of the Government," less his so doing "might be construed into interference."

Taney held strong political opinions, but he kept those opinions to himself and his closest friends and family members. He had watched with disgust and anxiety the rise of the Know-Nothing Party, with its virulent anti-Catholicism. And he deplored the increasing power of the abolitionists who, he feared, were driving a wedge between the North and South. Like his colleague, Justice Daniel, Taney bristled at the condescending attitude of northern politicians toward the South and their assumption that they were morally superior to southerners. And he was steadfast in his belief that the framers had made a binding constitutional pact between North and South that entitled the states to determine for themselves whether slavery would live or die. Short of a constitutional amendment, he was convinced that the federal government had no authority to alter that guarantee in the existing states or those that might be carved out of U.S. territories.

Outside his judicial tasks, Taney's life in Washington was bleak. He lived alone in a small rented apartment near the Capitol. The modest accommodations reflected, in part, the Chief Justice's desire for privacy as well as his aversion to ostentation. The sparse quarters were also a necessity because of Taney's paltry government salary of $5,000 a year. He only occasionally ventured out for dinner and then usually in response to an invitation from the president or other high government official. Meanwhile, Mrs. Taney and three unmarried daughters remained in the family house in Baltimore.

For Taney, a devoted family man throughout his adult life, summer vacations were especially important. They meant an extended reunion with his beloved wife and children and respite from the rigors of the Court, which had always sapped his limited physical energy. Beginning in 1849, the Taneys had vacationed at the Virginia resort of Old Point Comfort, near Norfolk. The Chief Justice loved the cool ocean breeze and swimming with his wife and daughters in the Atlantic surf. With an ample supply of cigars for the vacation, Taney also undertook two ambitious writing projects. First, he completed a 158-page manuscript describing his version of the war that he and President Andrew Jackson had fought against the Bank of the United States. And in 1854, in response to what he considered the superficial, though favorable, treatment of his life in Van Santvoord's *Lives of the Chief Justices of the United States*, he began writing his autobiography.

In the spring of 1855, Taney eagerly anticipated the family's annual vacation at Old Point Comfort. Both he and his wife, Anne, had been in poor health during the long winter and looked forward to the rest. Taney knew that they would be joined at the resort by their daughter, Sophia, and her baby, who had been abandoned by Sophia's husband the previous year. Taney was determined that as many members of his family as possible congregate in Old Point Comfort. As a result, he brusquely discouraged his unmarried youngest daughter, Alice, from joining her sister, Anne, and her husband, J. Mason Campbell, for a vacation in Newport, Rhode Island. Taney reproached Campbell, who had extended the invitation to Alice. "I have not the slightest confidence in [the] superior health of Newport over Old Point," he wrote his son-in-law, "and look upon it as nothing more than that unfortunate feeling of inferiority in the South, which believes every thing in the North to be superior to what we have."

Dutifully, the twenty-eight-year-old Alice joined her parents at the Virginia resort. The Taneys were somewhat concerned by news that a yellow fever epidemic had spread from New Orleans to the Virginia port cities of Norfolk and Portsmouth. But even as reports of fatalities in those two cities reached Old Point Comfort that summer, Taney assured himself and his family that the disease was caused by filth, and that the bracing sea air and clean conditions at their resort would prevent yellow fever from reaching them.

Taney had made a fatal miscalculation. In late September, Anne Key Taney, the Chief Justice's wife of forty-nine years, suffered paralysis and, a few days later, a severe stroke. She died on September 29; an autopsy found evidence of yellow fever in her body. A few hours later, on the morning of the following day, Alice Taney died of the same disease.

Taney was devastated. He was seventy-eight years old and in fragile health, and no one, including Taney himself, was certain that he possessed the physical and emotional stamina to live through the family tragedy. He found solace in his religion and began to attend mass regularly. "[I]t has pleased God to support me in the trial, and to enable me to resign myself in humble submission to his will," he wrote his colleague, Justice Curtis, in response to a touching condolence letter. "And I am again endeavoring to fulfil the duties which may yet remain to me in this world."

In December 1855, the Taneys sold the family house in Baltimore. With the help of two of his daughters, Ellen and Sophia, Taney moved into rented rooms in a group of houses known as Blogden's Row on Indiana Avenue. The next month, the distraught Chief Justice prepared for one of the most momentous terms in the history of the U.S. Supreme Court. In February, the justices would hear oral arguments in the case of *Dred Scott v. Sandford.*

Chapter Four

DRED SCOTT

By two standard measures of power—wealth and population—the North in the mid-1850s threatened to overwhelm the South. At the same time, slavery appeared to be a vanishing institution, at least in the expanding United States. The raw numbers were revealing. In 1855, the national population exceeded 23 million, yet only slightly more than 350,000 were slaveowners.

Those intimidating facts caused southern politicians to insist on parity between the two sections that had existed when the Constitution was ratified. The South's congressional representatives had pushed successfully for the repeal of the Missouri Compromise, which had skewed the sectional balance in favor of the North. The concept of popular sovereignty in the territories, sealed by the Kansas-Nebraska Act, promised (at least in theory) that the South's institution of slavery would survive. But that controversial legislation, rather than providing an uneasy peace between North and South, broke down political alliances and ushered in a frightening period of agitation. In this fearful atmosphere, there was virtually no room for compromise. The issue of slavery, it seemed, defied political solution.

It did not help that the nation was led by President Franklin Pierce of New Hampshire, an inept chief executive whose undisguised sympathy for the southern cause had alienated his political base in the northern states. Congress was hopelessly divided by section; the rhetoric on both sides grew harsher and more personally abusive. Hostility between congressmen from North and South became so acute that apprehensive representatives attended sessions armed with knives and pistols.

Could the Supreme Court of the United States impose order and reason in this increasingly desperate situation? Certainly the Taney Court, even in those tumultuous days, enjoyed a prestige that members of the popularly elected branches of the federal government could not emulate. The Chief Justice, in particular, appeared to be insulated from partisan attack. Senator Seward of New York proposed to amend a bill providing for a bust of the late Chief Justice John Rutledge by bestowing a similar honor on Taney, in spite of the custom of providing such sculptural tributes only after the death of the person portrayed. Seward wanted to honor Taney while he was still living. From the South, Senator George Badger of North Carolina, in supporting a bill to raise the justices' salaries, showered the Chief Justice with worshipful praise. "He is a noble specimen for what the judicial character should be," said Badger. "Every Senator knows that he has discharged all the duties of his high office with an integrity unimpeached, with unsurpassed learning, and with a decorum and a courtesy which has never, in a single instance, been swerved from its propriety." Even the outspoken opponent of slavery Senator Salmon P. Chase of Ohio readily concurred in Badger's encomium to Taney.

While anti-slavery men like Seward and Chase were prepared to honor Taney for his good judicial works, permitting the Chief Justice and his brethren to settle the issue of slavery for the nation was a different matter. The stakes were too high to leave the decision to a Court with a five-member southern majority. "For one, I may say, with every respect for those judicial dignitaries, that I would rather trust a dog with my dinner," groused the New York Tribune's Horace Greeley.

For abolitionists, the issue of slavery could not be confined to written law; it was a principle of morality that transcended man-made legal doctrine, even that of the Constitution. At the other extreme, southerners like Senator Robert Toombs of Georgia were equally opposed to a judicial solution to the problem. Toombs was convinced that the Court, if asked, would find the Missouri Compromise constitutional, since "there has been no assumption of political power by this Government which it [the Court] has not vindicated and found somewhere."

There was a third political group, however, which was convinced that the Taney Court held out the last best hope for a peaceful resolution to the slavery issue and the preservation of the Union. Composed of moderates from both North and South, they pointed to the proven integrity of the justices on the slavery issue in every decision of the previous decade and a half. Although southerners represented a majority on the Court during those years, the decisions from *Prigg v. Pennsylvania* in 1842 to *Strader v. Graham* in 1851 had appeared to put to rest the notion that the justices' voted their sectional prejudices.

Dred Scott, like so many other plaintiffs who have made constitutional history, lived an unremarkable life until his legal cause was brought before the U.S. Supreme Court. Though the details of Scott's early life remain sketchy, we know that he was an illiterate African-American slave owned by a Virginia planter, Peter Blow. In 1830, Blow moved to St. Louis with his wife, seven children, and six slaves (including Scott) and became the proprietor of a boardinghouse, which lost money. Two years later, Blow died and, to help pay off his debts, Dred Scott was sold to Dr. John Emerson, an Army surgeon then working at the Jefferson Barracks outside St. Louis. From 1833 to 1836, Dr. Emerson was stationed at Fort Armstrong in Rock Island, Illinois, where Scott worked for him. In 1836, Emerson, accompanied by Scott, was transferred to Fort Snelling, located in the northern part of the Louisiana Territory (near the present city of St. Paul, Minnesota). At Fort Snelling, Emerson purchased a female slave, Harriet Robinson, who became Dred Scott's wife. Emerson returned with the couple to Missouri in 1838. During the return journey, a child, Eliza, was born to the Scotts; a second daughter, Lizzie, was later born in St. Louis. In 1843 Emerson died, leaving the Scotts as part of his estate.

Dred Scott attempted to purchase freedom for himself and his family from Emerson's widow, Irene, in 1846. After his offer was rejected, Scott initiated a lawsuit against Mrs. Emerson to win his freedom. Whether the idea for the legal action came from Scott himself or from members of the Blow family, Scott's original owners, is not clear. We do know, however, that Scott persisted in his legal challenge over the course of eleven years of litigation and that the Blow family, particularly Peter Blow's son, Taylor, gave their wholehearted support to his cause.

Scott's legal claim was straightforward. When Dr. Emerson had taken Scott with him in 1833 to reside at Fort Armstrong in the state of Illinois, which prohibited slavery, the master had emancipated his slave. And later, when the Army surgeon moved with Scott to Fort Snelling, which was designated free territory under the terms of the Missouri Compromise, Emerson had again changed Scott's legal status from slave to that of a free black. A consistent line of Missouri Supreme Court decisions supported Scott's claim. In those decisions, the state's highest court had ruled that once a slave had left Missouri to reside in a free state or territory, he became free. Scott lost the first trial on a technicality, but won his case in a second trial on precisely those grounds.

Irene Emerson proved to be as tenacious as Scott in pursuing her legal interests and appealed the trial court's decision. Fortunately for Mrs. Emerson, when the lawsuit of *Scott, a Man of Color v. Emerson* reached the Missouri Supreme Court in 1852, the passions unleashed by the growing slavery controversy had effected a radical change in the court's attitude toward the state's slave laws. The earlier rulings, written in the spirit of compromise of the 1840s, had recognized the freedom of former slaves who had resided in states that prohibited slavery. As attitudes hardened in the early 1850s, the respect extended by Missouri to the laws of free states (under the doctrine of comity) disappeared, replaced by a militant defense of slavery.

In reversing Dred Scott's trial court victory, the majority opinion of the Missouri Supreme Court reflected the emerging angry judicial spirit in Missouri and the other slave states. Judge William Scott's opinion for the court rejected the notion that Missouri was obligated to recognize the laws of the free state of Illinois. He was similarly dismissive of the argument that under federal law (the Missouri Compromise) Dred Scott had earned his freedom by residing in a section of the Louisiana Territory that prohibited slavery. The Missouri courts, he wrote, owed allegiance exclusively to the state's laws pertaining to slavery. And under Missouri law, Dred Scott remained a slave and the property of Mrs. Emerson.

Recognizing that earlier decisions of his court had come to the opposite conclusion, Judge Scott suggested that those decisions had been made in a period of relative tranquility between North and South. A new vigilance in the slave states was now necessary, Scott observed, because both individuals and states "have been possessed with a dark and fell spirit in relation to slavery, whose gratification is sought in the pursuit of measures, whose inevitable consequences must be the overthrow and destruction of our government." Under these ominous circumstances, Scott declared, "it does not behoove the State of Missouri to show the least countenance to any measure which might gratify this spirit."

The Missouri Supreme Court decision forced Dred Scott's lawyer, Roswell Field, to make a difficult choice between two legal strategies. He could appeal directly to the U.S. Supreme Court. But the Taney Court's opinion in *Strader v. Graham*, decided only one year earlier, was not an encouraging precedent. Chief Justice Taney's opinion for the Court in *Strader* had declared that the status of the slave musicians who had traveled to the free state of Ohio was determined by the laws of the slave state of Kentucky, as that state's supreme court had ruled. True, the facts in the Scott case were different. The musicians in *Strader* had only traveled for a brief period in Ohio before returning to Kentucky. In contrast, Dred Scott had resided for several years in the free state of Illinois and later in the free Louisiana Territory before returning voluntarily to the slave state of Missouri. Despite the more favorable facts in Scott's case, the Missouri Supreme Court's decision, like that of the Kentucky Supreme Court in *Strader*, posed a serious obstacle to a successful appeal to the Taney Court. With the full and open support of the Chief Justice, the Court had consistently ruled that the issue of slavery was a matter of prevailing state law.

Rather than appealing directly to the Taney Court, Field devised an alternative strategy that was both ingenious and fraught with peril. He

initiated a new lawsuit in the U.S. Circuit Court in St. Louis. For purposes of his federal suit on behalf of Dred Scott, Field assumed that his
client was a free man by virtue of his residence in a free state and territory
and therefore a citizen of Missouri. As a free black, Scott was entitled to
sue the defendant, John Sanford, who was Mrs. Emerson's brother and
administrator of her late husband's estate. Since Sanford was a citizen of
New York and Scott a citizen of Missouri, according to Field's reasoning,
federal diversity jurisdiction entitled him to bring suit in the circuit
court. If successful on the jurisdictional issue, Field hoped that a jury in
federal court would decide the case on the merits and conclude, contrary
to the Missouri Supreme Court's ruling, that Scott's residence in Illinois
and the northern Louisiana Territory had emancipated him. In the lawsuit of *Scott v. Sanford*, which appeared in 1853 on the docket of the federal circuit court in St. Louis, Dred Scott sued for his freedom by
charging that John Sanford was guilty of trespass in holding a former
slave against his will.

Sanford's attorney, Hugh Garland, immediately challenged the pre-
sumption that Dred Scott was a citizen of Missouri who could bring a
lawsuit in the federal court. He filed a plea of abatement, a procedural
motion that denied Scott's claim of Missouri citizenship. Dred Scott was
not a citizen of the state of Missouri, the defense contended, "because he
is a negro of African descent; his ancestors were of pure African blood
and were brought into this country and sold as negro slaves."

Scott's attorney responded with his own motion (a demurrer), alert-
ing the judge that the legal issue had been joined. Field well knew that
the defendant's procedural motion, if granted, would not only result in
Scott's suit being thrown out of court, but also cut off other African
Americans, even those with the unchallenged status of free blacks, from
federal courts throughout the nation.

In 1854, Field and Garland argued the crucial jurisdictional issue before U.S. Circuit Court Judge Robert Wells. The judge ruled in Field's
favor, concluding that Scott, as a resident of Missouri who could sue in
that state's courts, was entitled to bring his suit in the federal circuit
court. The fact that a prospective federal litigant was black, Wells de-

cided, was not a conclusive bar to citizenship. Having ruled in favor of Dred Scott on the procedural issue, Wells ordered that a trial on the merits go forward before a jury. At the trial, however, Wells instructed the jury to rule for the defendant, Sanford. Since Scott had voluntarily returned to Missouri after residing in Illinois and the northern Louisiana Territory, Judge Wells told the jury, he must be considered a slave under Missouri law. Sanford could not therefore be guilty of trespass, since he had the legal right to restrain Scott. Obeying the judge's instruction, the jury returned a verdict for the defendant.

The verdict discouraged many of Dred Scott's supporters. As a consequence, a written plea for money to appeal to the U.S. Supreme Court, signed with Scott's mark, soon appeared in a widely distributed twelve-page pamphlet. The pamphlet began with a first-person introduction, presumed to be written by Scott, and followed with the circuit court record in the case. The introduction noted that Judge Wells had read in court from both the Illinois Constitution and the Missouri Compromise. "The judge said that according to these laws While I was in Illinois and Wisconsin I was a free man—just as good as my master—and that I had as much right to make a slave of a white man as a white man to make a slave of me." But later, the narrative continued, "the judge said that as soon as my master got me back this side of the line of Missouri, my right to be free was gone; and that I and my wife and children became nothing but so many pieces of property." Scott's appeal to the Supreme Court had been granted, but "I have no money to pay anybody at Washington to speak for me. My fellow-men, can any of you help me in my day of trial?"

At about the time that the pamphlet was distributed, Scott's Missouri attorney, Roswell Field, wrote to a Washington lawyer, Montgomery Blair, asking him to argue Scott's appeal in the Supreme Court. Blair was a member of a prominent Maryland family (his journalist father, Francis, had been an adviser to President Andrew Jackson), whose original sympathy for the South's cause had gradually been supplanted by a growing opposition to slavery. Montgomery Blair had practiced law in St. Louis before moving in 1853 to Washington, where he quickly became a respected member of the bar.

Field told Blair that the main issue raised by Dred Scott's lawsuit—whether a slave who had been taken by his master to reside in a free state or territory was emancipated—was of pressing national importance and needed to be settled. Field also emphasized an equally important issue: whether an African American could bring suit in a federal court. It was imperative, Field said, that Judge Wells's ruling in favor of Scott on the second issue be vigorously defended in the Supreme Court.

Blair agreed to argue the case without fee, but asked that others sympathetic to Scott's cause pay the court costs. He filed an eleven-page brief with the Taney Court as the attorney of record for the plaintiff in *Dred Scott v. Sandford,** which was set for oral argument before the Supreme Court in February 1856. Defending John Sanford were two of the most prominent lawyers in the country, Reverdy Johnson, the former U.S. Attorney General and senator from Maryland, and U.S. Senator Henry Geyer of Missouri. Johnson and Geyer's participation, even more than Blair's, suggested that the political implications of Dred Scott's lawsuit were well known throughout the country. Among members of the Court, however, only Justice McLean took written notice of the case (in a letter to an Ohio newspaper editor) before it was argued. And despite the obvious potential of the lawsuit to create historic news, it received little press coverage when the justices first heard oral arguments in the case, except for the abolitionist *New York Tribune*.

Neither Montgomery Blair's brief nor his oral argument impressed the *Tribune*'s Washington correspondent, James E. Harvey, who had expected a better performance from the lawyer on the "right" side of the case. Johnson and Geyer's arguments for Sanford, according to the *Tribune*, were not much better. What the *Tribune* did not tell its readers was that its Washington correspondent was a confidant of Justice McLean and would later be able to report the gist of the justices' private deliberations in the case.

When the justices met in chambers after the argument, it was immediately evident that they could not agree on either the jurisdictional

---

* The court reporter misspelled Sanford's name.

issue (whether Scott could sue in federal court) or the merits of the case. All nine justices were well aware that a majority's answer to the jurisdictional question could dictate the outcome of the lawsuit. If the Court reversed Judge Wells's ruling that Scott could sue in federal court, the justices need not decide the case on the merits. If, however, a majority of the justices accepted Judge Wells's ruling that Scott could sue, then the Court would be faced with a decision on Scott's legal status: slave or free black? Lurking in the background was the incendiary issue of the constitutionality of the Missouri Compromise. The justices could decide that question if they chose to make a definitive ruling on Scott's status while in the northern Louisiana Territory.

In their initial deliberations, the justices' positions on the jurisdictional issue cut across sectional lines. Three southerners—Chief Justice Taney (Maryland) and Associate Justices Peter Daniel (Virginia) and James Wayne (Georgia)—and one anti-slavery northerner, Justice Benjamin Curtis of Massachusetts, wanted to reopen the issue of whether Scott could sue in federal court. But two southerners, Justices John Catron (Tennessee) and John Campbell (Alabama), and two northerners, Justices Robert Grier (Pennsylvania) and John McLean (Ohio), took the position that the jurisdictional issue need not be raised again, and that the Court should proceed to the merits of the case. At first, Justice Samuel Nelson of New York leaned toward the Taney view that the Court should decide the jurisdictional issue, but he hesitated to cast the decisive vote.

The justices' discussions extended over more than two months, beginning in late February, primarily because the Court took a full month's recess in March. Early in April, Justice Curtis wrote to his uncle that the Court majority had decided that it was unnecessary to rule on the constitutionality of the Missouri Compromise, and would presumably confine their opinion to the jurisdictional issue or a narrow ruling on the merits of Dred Scott's case.

Meanwhile, the *Tribune's* Harvey reported that a majority favored reopening the jurisdictional issue but that those in the minority, most notably the correspondent's source, Justice McLean, would write a stinging dissent going to the merits of the case and concluding that Dred Scott was a free man. Harvey also took special notice of the pro-slavery bias of the southern justices, describing Alabama's John Campbell as an ardent acolyte of the late John C. Calhoun who viewed the Constitution as a legal bastion for slavery. And with chagrin, Harvey noted that the infirm Chief Justice was increasingly showing his sectional prejudice in favor of the southern cause.

Finally, on May 12, 1856, the Court made its first official announcement in the Dred Scott case. At Justice Nelson's request (and with no dissent), the Court scheduled reargument at its December term. The attorneys for both sides were specifically asked to answer two questions: Was the jurisdictional issue properly before the Court? If so, had Judge Wells ruled correctly that a free black had the right as a citizen to bring a lawsuit in a federal court?

Whether by design or not, the Supreme Court's delay had taken the Dred Scott case and the justices themselves out of the impending presidential campaign. By that action, the Court deprived its most politically ambitious member, Justice John McLean, of a platform to launch his candidacy for the nomination of the anti-slavery Republican Party.

By the end of 1855, Abraham Lincoln anticipated the demise of the Whig Party. The party's moderate political and economic policies had been rejected by abolitionists and Know-Nothings in the North. And its opposition to the spread of slavery had no appeal below the Mason-Dixon line. Lincoln continued to keep his distance from the abolitionists but began to consider other political options.

Though he was still nominally a Whig, he attended a meeting in February 1856 called by a group of Illinois newspaper editors to form a fusion party. He was greeted enthusiastically and endorsed the editors' cautious anti-Nebraska platform: restoration of the Missouri Compromise, opposition to the spread of slavery, non-interference with slavery in states where it already existed, a pledge of religious tolerance, and a vow to defend the constitutionality of the Fugitive Slave Law. Before adjourning, the men called for a state fusion convention to be held in Bloomington on May 29, and they named Lincoln as a delegate.

Only a week before Lincoln and the other delegates met in Bloomington, violence broke out in Kansas, making the peaceful settlement of the slavery issue more urgent and elusive than ever. A pro-slavery posse of eight hundred men, many of them Missourians, marched into Lawrence, Kansas, to arrest free-state leaders. The posse degenerated into a mob, dumping the presses of two anti-slavery papers into the Kaw River and looting a hotel and many private homes. Three days later, John Brown, a fearsome abolitionist, impassively supervised the murder of five pro-slavery settlers who were hacked to death with sabers in the town of Pottawatomie.

Two thousand miles away, Charles Sumner, the tall, imperious abolitionist senator from Massachusetts, rose on the Senate floor to deplore "the crime against Kansas," which he defined as "the rape of a virgin territory, compelling it to the hateful embrace of slavery." Sumner's Senate colleagues had become accustomed to his florid rhetoric. But that May day Sumner's anti-slavery invective turned personal. He struck most cruelly at the respected senior senator from South Carolina, Andrew Butler, who, by southern standards of the day, was a moderate. Butler had committed the unpardonable sin, in Sumner's eyes, of defending the pro-slavery government in Kansas. "The Senator from South Carolina has read many books of chivalry, and believes himself a chivalrous knight, with sentiments of honor and courage," Sumner intoned. "Of course he has chosen a mistress to whom he has made his vows and who, although ugly to others, is always lovely to him; although polluted in the sight of the world, is chaste in his sight—I mean the harlot, Slavery."

Two days later, Butler's nephew, Representative Preston Brooks of South Carolina, exacted violent revenge for Sumner's insult. Brandishing a gutta-percha cane, Brooks entered the Senate chamber after adjournment and approached Sumner, who was still at his desk. Brooks announced stiffly that he had come to punish a slanderer and proceeded to pummel Sumner with blow after vicious blow. Sumner attempted to rise and wrenched the bolted desk from the floor. Still, Brooks continued his assault. When his cane broke, he used the butt to finish his bloody assignment. None of Sumner's colleagues rushed to his rescue. Finally, the semiconscious victim was taken away on a stretcher.

In the North, Brooks's attack was viewed as an atrocity, and Sumner became a martyr in service of the abolitionist cause. The assault confirmed, in Ralph Waldo Emerson's mind, that the southern male was a despicably low-grade animal. But in the South, Brooks was hailed as a hero who had defended the honor of an entire section of the country. He received presents of canes and promises of more if he needed them in his congressional work. Brooks resigned his seat to allow his constituents to register their opinion. He was reelected almost unanimously.

While reports of "Bloody Kansas" and the Brooks attack circulated wildly throughout the country, Lincoln and 269 other delegates at the Bloomington convention formally organized the Illinois Republican Party. Lincoln was called to the platform to make the last major speech, which, by all accounts, was one of the greatest that he ever delivered. Lincoln's law partner, Herndon, took notes on the early portions of the speech, but put down his pen after fifteen minutes so that he could be swept up "in the inspiration of the hour." A resolute Lincoln affirmed the new party's anti-slavery platform. At the same time, he rejected the growing threats of secession from southern politicians. "The Union must be preserved in the purity of its principles as well as in the integrity of its territorial parts," he asserted. Echoing the earlier plea of Daniel Webster, Lincoln proclaimed that the nation and its bedrock value of freedom must be preserved at all costs: "It must be 'Liberty and Union, now and forever, one and inseparable.'"

Lincoln remained in Illinois to attend to his law practice while delegates to the Republican National Convention met in Philadelphia in June to nominate their first candidate for president. Justice John McLean was considered a leading contender, though he had not publicly announced his candidacy. McLean's colleague, Justice Benjamin Curtis, privately admitted that McLean would make a good president, but thought it unwise for McLean or any other justice to run for the office.

McLean did not share Curtis's concerns. Only a day after the justices had called for reargument in the Dred Scott case, McLean wrote Senator Lewis Cass of Michigan reiterating his position that Congress had the authority to prohibit slavery in the territories (even though the constitutionality of the Missouri Compromise could be decided by McLean and the eight other Justices in *Dred Scott v. Sandford*). Shortly before the Republican Convention, he wrote a letter to a member of the New Jersey delegation, which was published, expressing his support for the immediate admission of Kansas under the constitution enacted by the anti-slavery legislature. In another letter, the justice broadly laid out his views on the leading issues of the day. He favored reinstatement of the Missouri Compromise, opposed the introduction of slavery into free territory, and supported the constitutional rights of the existing slave states to maintain the institution of slavery.

McLean was Lincoln's first choice for the Republicans' presidential nomination. Besides supporting McLean's moderate anti-slavery positions, Lincoln thought that the justice was the candidate most likely to attract conservatives from the old Whig Party, a constituency he considered essential to a Republican victory. On the first ballot at the Philadelphia convention, McLean made a strong showing. But in the end, the Republicans passed over the seventy-one-year-old justice in favor of John C. Frémont. Celebrated for his explorations of the Rocky Mountains, Frémont projected a youthful and vigorous image for the new political party.

Lincoln was honored by the delegates when he received the second greatest number of votes for the Republicans' vice-presidential nomination (losing to former New Jersey senator William Dayton). Told that the Republicans had placed his name in nomination for the vice presidency, Lincoln modestly denied his growing national prominence. "I reckon that ain't me," he said. "[T]here's another great man in Massachusetts named Lincoln, and I reckon it's him."

When the Democrats met in Cincinnati to select their candidate for the presidency, they rejected both the incumbent, Franklin Pierce, and the firebrand senator from Illinois, Stephen A. Douglas, in favor of the venerable Pennsylvanian, James Buchanan. In Buchanan's long public career, almost no high national office, save the presidency, seemed to have escaped him. He had served ten years in the House of Representatives and almost eleven years in the Senate. He had been President Polk's Secretary of State and the nation's minister to both Russia and England. In that last assignment, Buchanan had been fortunate to be out of the country when the Kansas-Nebraska Act was passed, so he was not obligated to take a public stand on the legislation. In fact, Buchanan owed much of his political longevity to his skillful avoidance of taking controversial positions. In more than two decades as a legislator, he had not had his name attached to an important bill or taken a prominent role in any major debate. On the issue of slavery, Buchanan's conservative views appealed to the party's southern wing. If the federal government was not more sensitive to the South's pro-slavery position, Buchanan believed, the Union would not survive. And he was intent on preserving the Union.

Chief Justice Taney avidly read reports of the presidential race in the Baltimore and Washington papers at his vacation retreat in Fauquier White Sulphur Springs, Virginia. For the first time in half a century, Taney was spending his vacation without his beloved late wife, Anne. That, in part, may explain his despondent view of the presidential campaign. Taney also appeared to be swept up in the rising indignation of the South toward the North, a development that Justice McLean may have leaked to the *Tribune's* James Harvey during the Court's early deliberations in the Dred Scott case.

Taney's sense of foreboding over the political future of the nation was fully vented in a letter to his son-in-law, J. Mason Campbell. He told Campbell that he supported the Democrat, Buchanan, but was not sanguine about his chances of success. Taney feared that a victory by the Republican, Frémont, or the nominee of the American Party (the old Know-Nothings), former President Millard Fillmore, would guarantee that the rights of the South would be further trampled. It would be better, he wrote, for the South to secede from the Union rather than to suffer more northern humiliation. Under a Frémont or Fillmore administration, Taney was convinced that the Union would be divided into two unequal parts: the powerful North and the weak South.

In Taney's view, there was no realistic hope that the South could cleanly break away, since he believed there were enough influential southern politicians who craved power under a northern-based administration to fight off secession. "The South is doomed to sink to a state of inferiority," he concluded bitterly, "and the power of the North will be exercised to gratify their cupidity and their evil passions, without the slightest regard to the principles of the Constitution." He thought it likely that "bold and brave men in the South" might take up arms if either Frémont or Fillmore were elected, but he did not think they would be successful. "I grieve over this condition of things, but it is my deliberate opinion that the South is doomed, and that nothing but a firm united action, nearly unanimous in every state can check Northern insult and Northern aggression. But it seems this cannot be."

Lincoln did not share Taney's apocalyptic view of the nation's future. Though he had originally been a McLean man, Lincoln quickly joined ranks with Frémont's supporters. After their convention, the Republicans spread out across the northern states, chanting the party's campaign slogan—"Free soil, free speech and Frémont"—in parades and at mass meetings. And they made "Bleeding Kansas" and "Bleeding Sumner" twin symbols of the tyranny of slavery.

During the campaign Lincoln delivered more than fifty speeches on behalf of Frémont, but he carefully avoided inflammatory rhetoric. He did not mention the violence in Kansas or Sumner's beating. Nor did he challenge the South's right to maintain the institution of slavery, but only its threat to secede from the Union. Invariably, Lincoln dwelled on a single theme: a Republican administration would not allow the spread of slavery into the territories. In delivering his message, Lincoln made an open appeal to old-line Whigs and Fillmore supporters. His greatest fear was that the anti-slavery vote in Illinois would be split between Frémont and Fillmore, resulting in a victory for Buchanan. "With the Fremont and Fillmore men united, here in Illinois, we have Mr. Buchanan in the hollow of our hand," Lincoln wrote. "[B]ut with us divided . . . he has us."

Just as Lincoln feared, Fillmore siphoned off votes from Frémont, and Buchanan carried Illinois. The split between the Republican and American Party candidates among anti-slavery voters was replicated in other crucial northern states, allowing James Buchanan to win the presidency. The final tally was 174 electoral votes for Buchanan, 114 for Frémont, and 8 for Fillmore. With the shift of only a few thousand votes in two northern states, Pennsylvania and Indiana, Frémont would have been elected president. The narrowness of Buchanan's victory was underscored by the popular vote: Frémont and Fillmore's combined total exceeded Buchanan's by 400,000.

Lincoln wasted no time in using those numbers to exhort his fellow Republicans to make a greater effort in the next presidential contest. Speaking at a Republican banquet in Chicago a month after Buchanan's election, Lincoln pointed to the popular vote and the devastating result of the division between Frémont and Fillmore supporters. "Can we not come together?" he pleaded. In the future, Lincoln told his fellow Republicans, they must not let differences among voters in the North frustrate their party's determination to rededicate the nation to its first principle—that "all men are created equal."

President-elect Buchanan viewed his election victory as a mandate to preserve the fragile status quo between the hostile sections of the Union. "The great object of my administration will be if possible to destroy the dangerous slavery agitation," he wrote his fellow Pennsylvanian, Justice Robert Grier, "and thus to restore peace to our distracted country." For Buchanan, the first priority would be to rein in the abolitionists, whom he considered to be the greatest obstacle to the nation's stability.

In his last annual message to Congress, President Pierce made a similar judgment on the meaning of Buchanan's victory. The voters had rightly rejected the demands of the anti-slavery North, said Pierce, who blamed that section alone for a "long series of acts of indirect aggression." He denounced the Missouri Compromise and said that its repeal (by the Kansas-Nebraska Act) had eliminated from the statute books "an objectionable enactment, unconstitutional in effect and injurious in terms to a large portion of the States." Pierce then made a stunningly inaccurate statement, claiming that the Supreme Court had declared the Missouri Compromise unconstitutional, and had so ruled "in every form under which the question could arise." Pierce may have been influenced by an earlier advisory opinion from his Attorney General, Caleb Cushing, who concluded that the statute was unconstitutional. But the president should not have confused an advisory opinion from his Attorney General with a decision of the Supreme Court, which had made no such declaration.

Pierce's surprising announcement of the unconstitutionality of the Missouri Compromise, while factually incorrect, may have revealed a larger political truth. The leadership of the northern wing of the Democratic Party, most notably President Pierce and President-elect Buchanan, had concluded that the only way to achieve peace in the republic was to accommodate the restless, pro-slavery South. And to accomplish that delicate diplomatic task, President Pierce (and later President-elect Buchanan) attempted to eliminate a major obstacle— the claim of anti-slavery leaders in the North, including Lincoln, that Congress could prohibit slavery in the territories through statutes like the Missouri Compromise.

Only two weeks after Pierce had delivered his message to Congress, the Taney Court convened to hear the second set of arguments in *Dred Scott v. Sandford*. There is no written record indicating that Buchanan's election or Pierce's interpretation of its meaning affected the lawyers in the case or the justices. It was clear nonetheless that the constitutionality of the Missouri Compromise emerged as a central focus of the Dred Scott case. The press, which covered the furious debate in Congress on the issue following the president's speech, began to discuss the Court's likely judgment on the statute. More significant, all four attorneys who reargued the case in December 1856 addressed the subject. The intense attention on the issue made it less likely that the justices would refrain from ruling on the constitutionality of the statute, a decision that Justice Curtis had earlier predicted the Court would avoid.

Dred Scott was again represented by Montgomery Blair, who was joined at the reargument by Justice Curtis's brother, George Curtis, brought into the case specifically to defend congressional power in the territories. Blair and Curtis contended that the framers gave Congress broad authority over U.S. territories to dispose of public lands and to make rules governing temporary governments, including the prohibition of slavery. Defense attorneys Henry Geyer and Reverdy Johnson countered that the constitutional power of Congress to make rules for the territories referred only to the disposition of land, and did not authorize the establishment of territorial governments that prohibited slavery.

The lawyers devoted considerably less time to the jurisdictional issues that the Court had asked them to address in their rearguments. Blair argued that the defendant, Sanford, had waived his right to challenge Scott's claim of citizenship and right to sue in federal court, since he had agreed to Judge Wells's decision to proceed on the merits. If the Supreme Court rejected that argument, Blair provided a mass of evidence that demonstrated African Americans had exercised rights of citizenship in many states and that Missouri, in particular, had in some instances made references to them as citizens. On the merits, Blair reiterated his earlier argument that Dr. Emerson had emancipated Scott when he resided in the free state of Illinois and later in the northern Louisiana Territory, which prohibited slavery.

Senator Geyer, for Sanford, argued that "[t]rue blacks are not citizens," even if they had been freed by their masters or had traveled to free states or territories. Citizenship was limited either to native whites or those who had been naturalized. Going to the merits of the case, Geyer returned to his earlier arguments that Dr. Emerson's travels to Illinois and the northern Louisiana Territory did not free Scott and, in any event, Scott's status was ultimately determined by the decision of the Missouri Supreme Court, which ruled that the petitioner remained the property of his master. Geyer's co-counsel, Reverdy Johnson, followed with an emotional defense of the institution of slavery. "Slavery promises to exist through all time, so far as human vision can discover," Johnson told the justices, and it could well turn out that "the extension of Slavery on the continent is the only thing which will preserve the constitutional freedom we now enjoy."

By the end of the rearguments on December 18, 1856, the press acknowledged that the Dred Scott case would have far-reaching consequences for the future of the nation. Rumors about the final judgment of the Court abounded in the corridors of Congress as well as in the country's newspapers. Representative Alexander Stephens of Georgia buoyantly reported that he had heard that the Court would rule against Scott and declare the Missouri Compromise unconstitutional. The *New York Tribune*'s Washington correspondent, James Harvey, had apparently heard similar rumors. Harvey prepared his readers for the dreaded result: "Judicial tyranny is hard enough to resist under any circumstances, for it comes in the guise of impartiality and with the prestige of fairness. If the Court is to take a political bias, and to give a political decision, then let us, by all means, have it distinctly and now. The public mind is in a condition to receive it with the contempt it merits."

Alarmed by the power of a Court dominated by justices from the southern states, Representative Benjamin Stanton of Ohio proposed a realignment of the judicial circuits that would more accurately reflect the greater population in the North and West and give those sections of the country fairer representation on the Court. Unless there was such a realignment, Stanton said, the Court's decision "can have no moral power and cannot command the confidence of the people." He insisted on Congress's sovereign power in the territories, including its right to prohibit slavery, and resurrected Calhoun's claim of a state's right to nullify an unconstitutional law, such as the Kansas-Nebraska Act.

For almost two months after the rearguments in the Dred Scott case, while speculation swirled around the Supreme Court's impending decision, the justices did not hold a single formal conference. The delay was caused by the personal tragedy of Justice Peter Daniel. On January 3,

Daniel's wife was burned to death in their home when the sleeve of her blouse accidentally caught fire from a nearby candle. Justice Curtis reported that Daniel was inconsolably stricken by the tragedy and could not meet with his colleagues for at least a month. The energy of two other justices, Wayne and Taney, had been sapped by ill health. "Our aged Chief Justice," wrote Curtis, "who grows more feeble in body, but retains his alacrity and force of mind wonderfully, is not able to write much."

When the justices did finally meet on February 15, 1857, it was apparent that they held diverse and deeply felt opinions on the array of complex legal issues raised in the case. The five southern justices were prepared to strike down the Missouri Compromise as unconstitutional. But they were reluctant to deliver such a momentous decision, which would undoubtedly be interpreted in the North as a raw power play by five southerners on behalf of their section of the country.

Initially, the justices decided on a more prudent course of action. The majority opinion was assigned to the Court's most cautious jurist, Justice Samuel Nelson of New York, who was expected to write a narrow opinion affirming the decision of the Missouri Supreme Court that Dred Scott remained a slave under state law. Nelson's opinion would avoid definitive judgments on the constitutionality of the Missouri Compromise and the right of an African American to sue in federal court. It was a tidy, if extremely limited, solution that would take the Court out of the political maelstrom.

But hardly had Justice Nelson begun to write his opinion than the compromise reached by the Court majority unraveled. Justices Curtis and McLean, according to an account by Justice Grier, vowed to write dissenting opinions justifying, at length, Congress's authority to prohibit slavery in the territories.* Their challenge, in turn, brought a defiant reaction from the five justices from the southern states who had already

---

* Curtis and McLean's reported vow to write expansive dissents was highly unusual at this time in the Court's history. The normal procedure for dissenting justices was simply to record their objections or silently acquiesce.

concluded that the Missouri Compromise was unconstitutional. They promised a vigorous rebuttal to Curtis and McLean's dissents that would constitute the Court majority's decision on the issue.

Within days of the justices' original decision to assign the Court opinion to Justice Nelson, Justice James Wayne made a motion (supported by a majority of the justices) to reassign the opinion to Chief Justice Taney. It was understood that Taney's opinion would decide all of the critical issues before the Court, including the constitutionality of the Missouri Compromise and the issue of whether an African American could sue in federal court. Wayne made his motion, according to Justice Curtis, because he "became convinced that it was practicable for the Court to quiet all agitation on the question of slavery in the Territories by affirming that Congress had no constitutional power to prohibit its introduction."

Constitutional historians have long debated the credibility of the various accounts explaining the switch of the Court's opinion in *Dred Scott* from Nelson to Taney. The recollections of two justices, Catron and Grier, support the view that Curtis and McLean's pledge to write spirited defenses of the constitutionality of the Missouri Compromise caused the five southern justices to abandon their earlier position to accept a narrow Court opinion. They advocated, instead, a broader decision that would declare the statute unconstitutional. But neither Curtis nor McLean ever corroborated that version of the events leading to the assignment of the opinion to Taney. And this has left scholars to wonder why the dissenters, Curtis and McLean, both outspoken anti-slavery justices, would knowingly provoke the southern-dominated Court to declare the Missouri Compromise unconstitutional when narrower grounds for the decision were not only available but agreed upon by the majority.

An alternative to the Curtis-McLean provocation theory holds that the justices, from the outset, felt intense pressure to settle the issue of Congress's authority to prohibit slavery in the territories—once and for all time. President Pierce had given his opinion on the issue, as had members of Congress and the press. Even before they had formally met to discuss the case, many of the justices, too, were reported to hold strong views on the subject and intended to express those views in individual concurring and dissenting opinions. Taney and Daniel were said to be prepared to write extensive opinions, presumably defending the southern position that the Missouri Compromise was unconstitutional, while Curtis and McLean were poised to respond in dissent.

Under those circumstances, Justice Nelson's proposed narrow Court opinion, even if it survived, was destined to be sabotaged by more passionate advocates on both sides of the issue. It was better, reasoned Justice Wayne, that the Court give full and frank voice to the constitutional controversy, and that the nation be advised, officially, that Congress could not prohibit slavery in the territories. "With the best of intentions, with entirely patriotic motives, and believing thoroughly that such was the law on this constitutional question," Justice Curtis wrote, "he [Wayne] regarded it as eminently expedient that it should be so determined by the Court."

President-elect Buchanan, working behind the scenes, exerted further pressure on the justices to support his position that the Missouri Compromise was unconstitutional, preferably before his inauguration on March 4. In his inaugural address, Buchanan hoped to announce that all three branches of the federal government—the president, the Democratically controlled Congress, and the Supreme Court—were united in their view that Congress could not prohibit slavery in the territories. Early in February, Buchanan wrote confidentially to an old Democratic political ally, Justice Catron, to inquire if the Court was going to rule on the statute before the inauguration.

Catron replied shortly after the Court opinion had been assigned to Nelson, informing Buchanan that the justices would not decide the issue. But a few days later, after the reassignment of the opinion to the Chief Justice, Catron again wrote Buchanan to report that the Court would indeed decide the issue, though he did not indicate what the decision would be. He also told Buchanan that the President-elect's friend Justice Grier had taken no position on the issue and urged Buchanan to "drop Grier a line, saying how necessary it is, and how good the opportunity is, to settle the agitation by an affirmative decision of the Supreme

Court, the one way or the other." Catron added that Grier "has no doubt about the question on the main contest, but has been persuaded to take the smooth handle for the sake of repose."

As Catron had advised, Buchanan wrote Grier beseeching him to take a stand on the issue of the statute's constitutionality. Grier, who was not aware that the president-elect was also corresponding with Justice Catron, shared Buchanan's letter to him with Taney and Wayne. In a letter to the president-elect, Grier then told Buchanan exactly what he wanted to hear: The Pennsylvania justice had decided to join his five southern colleagues in a Court opinion declaring the Missouri Compromise unconstitutional. That made six justices in agreement with Buchanan's position, and gave the Court's decision the semblance of a national, rather than sectional, cast. But Buchanan was also told by Grier that he could not use the tantalizing inside information in his inaugural address, because the Chief Justice's opinion for the Court would not be announced before March 6, two days after Buchanan was scheduled to take the oath of office.

March 4 was a bright, sunlit day in the capital. The president-elect, attentive to the symbolic details of his inaugural ceremony, wore a homespun suit woven by a Lancaster, Pennsylvania, tailor that displayed thirty-one stars (representing the states) stitched into the lining. Buchanan's effort to demonstrate national unity was inadvertently destroyed moments before the start of the official ceremony when he was observed briefly conversing with Chief Justice Taney. Anti-slavery critics of Buchanan and the Court later accused the Chief Justice of violating the proprieties of his office by informing Buchanan of the Court's *Dred Scott* decision. That Taney, a stickler for Court protocol, would pass on such confidential information before thousands of onlookers seems highly improbable. Besides, Buchanan, as a result of Justice Grier's letter, already knew what the Court had decided.

In his inaugural address, Buchanan made only a single reference to the Dred Scott case. The judicial question of whether Congress could prohibit slavery in the territories was before the Taney Court "and will, it is understood, be speedily and finally settled," he said. "To their decision, in common with all good citizens, I shall cheerfully summit."

• • •

The Chief Justice spent the entire day of March 5 putting the finishing touches on his *Dred Scott* opinion. The next morning, eleven days before his eightieth birthday, Taney entered the Court's basement courtroom with the eight associate justices to announce the decision. For two hours the Chief Justice read his opinion in a low, almost inaudible voice.

As his colleagues had expected, Taney's opinion* answered all three of the controversial questions before the Court: Was Scott a citizen of Missouri entitled to sue in federal court? Was the Missouri Compromise constitutional? Was Scott still the slave property of John Sanford? When Taney later made written revisions in response to the criticisms of the dissenters, Curtis and McLean, his opinion covered fifty-five pages in *Howard's Reports*, the official record of Supreme Court decisions. His discussion was devoted primarily to the first two issues—twenty-four pages on Scott's claimed right to sue in federal court and twenty-one pages on the constitutionality of the Missouri Compromise. He spent the final page of his opinion on the issue of whether Scott remained a slave.

It was the duty of the Supreme Court, Taney began, to supervise the lower federal courts and to review all legal errors, including whether Dred Scott was a citizen who had properly brought his suit before U.S. Circuit Court Judge Wells. Once the Chief Justice had introduced the issue of Scott's citizenship, it seemed as if the deep reservoir of southern resentment over the slavery issue suddenly poured out. He declared that Dred Scott was not a citizen entitled to sue in federal court, and he made the point over and over again with bold, conclusive statements supported by conspicuously threadbare documentation.

Taney asserted that Dred Scott and every other American black, whether free or not, was forever destined to remain in a degraded status in civilized society and could never rise to the level of national citizen. This proposition was evident, wrote Taney, by even a cursory review of European history and was "too plain to be mistaken." For more than a

---

* Taney insisted that he spoke for the Court, but he did not have a majority for his opinion on one major issue: whether the Court had jurisdiction to decide Scott's citizenship.

century before the Declaration of Independence and U.S. Constitution were written, blacks had "been regarded as beings of an inferior order, and altogether unfit to associate with the white race, either in social or political relations; and so far inferior, that they had no rights which the white man was bound to respect." The framers of both the Declaration and the Constitution subscribed to this view, he contended.

Taney did not offer a single source of proof for his sweeping generalization. He lumped all of those who signed the Declaration and the Constitution together, the slaveholders of the South with the opponents of slavery in the North. He dismissed the idea that the Declaration of Independence's proclamation that "all men are created equal" should be taken literally. Blacks were permanently excluded, according to Taney, because they were considered a degraded class.

That the Declaration was a statement of ideals did not appear to occur to Taney. Yet there was significant historical evidence to underscore the idealistic purpose of the Declaration. The slaveholder Thomas Jefferson, for example, had castigated George III for exporting the institution of slavery to the colonies, an action, wrote Jefferson in his first draft of the Declaration, that made the British monarch responsible for waging "cruel war against human nature itself."

As proof of the intentions of the framers of the Constitution, Taney pointed to provisions protecting the slave trade for twenty years and requiring the return of fugitive slaves. But placing those provisions in broader historical context could just as easily have served as a rebuttal to Taney's argument. While it was true that the framers protected the slave trade for twenty years, Congress in 1808 immediately forbade it, a tangible indication that slavery was increasingly disfavored in the young republic. The fugitive slave provision, moreover, dealt only with the rights of slaveowners over their human property and said nothing about the status of free blacks. Taney insisted that blacks were neither citizens nor persons under the Constitution, but he ignored a third constitutional clause, which provided that slaves be counted as three-fifths of the free population for purposes of representation and taxation. That provision implicitly recognized that even slaves, not to mention free blacks, were considered persons by the framers for certain purposes, and not merely property.

The Chief Justice attempted to bolster his argument by citing miscegenation statutes from Maryland and Massachusetts that existed at the time the Constitution was ratified. Taney purposely selected statutes from one slave and one anti-slavery state to demonstrate what he considered the pervasive recognition of the black's inferior status. But the statutes did not prove Taney's point, since they penalized whites as well as blacks. He also referred to Connecticut statutes that forbade blacks to travel freely and excluded them from schools in the state. The problem with Taney's argument was that the statutes he cited did not fully reflect the status of blacks in the original thirteen states. Even in Maryland, free blacks were allowed a degree of freedom closed to slaves. And in Massachusetts, free blacks enjoyed the same right to vote as whites. Like free blacks in other states, they could also hold property, marry, and sue in their state's courts, the same rights available to white *citizens*.

What, then, were the attributes of a citizen of the United States at the time that the U.S. Constitution was ratified? Despite a long and often confusing discussion of state and federal citizenship, Taney never defined the essential requirements for national citizenship. In fact, five of the thirteen states that constituted the original Union gave free blacks the vote, a sure indication, Justice Curtis wrote in his dissent, that they were considered citizens. The free blacks whom Taney insisted could never be citizens of the United States may well have voted to ratify the Constitution!

At the time of Dred Scott's suit against John Sanford, the laws of many states, including Missouri, permitted free blacks to own property and to sue in the state courts, legal rights generally associated with citizenship. Judge Wells had ruled in Scott's favor on the citizenship issue on the basis of the petitioner's residence in Missouri and his right to sue in the state courts. But Taney argued that nothing that happened in the United States after the Constitution was ratified could make the slightest difference in the Court's interpretation of citizenship for the purpose of suing in federal courts. The original understanding of the framers was all that mattered. And those men, Taney insisted, never intended blacks to share in the rights of U.S. citizenship with whites.

Under Taney's interpretation of the Constitution, the general phrases of the document could not derive meaning by virtue of the unforeseen needs and experiences of future generations of Americans. That narrow constitutional perspective was significantly at odds with the opinion over twenty-five years earlier of Chief Justice John Marshall, who proclaimed that "it is a constitution we are expounding." By that, Marshall meant that the document was not to be read with codelike precision, but to be interpreted broadly as a governing blueprint for the ages. For Taney, the constitutional status of blacks in American society, a status that he struggled to define in his *Dred Scott* opinion, was forever frozen in 1789.

Having emphatically dismissed Scott's citizenship claim, Taney next declared that the Missouri Compromise was unconstitutional. He accomplished this daring judicial feat by adopting a severely constricted interpretation of Congress's constitutional authority under Article I to make all "needful rules and regulations respecting the territory and other property belonging to the United States." The Chief Justice acknowledged that the first Congress had enacted a statute enforcing all provisions of the Northwest Ordinance of 1787, including the prohibition of slavery in that vast territory north of the Ohio River. But he maintained that the framers limited the prohibition to the Northwest Territory, and that no future Congress could act, as the first Congress had done, to exclude slavery in any other territory acquired by the United States.

Congress could acquire future territory for the United States, Taney wrote, but could not forbid slavery. That decision could only be made by the voters in the territories when they applied for statehood. Congress's constitutional role, Taney argued, was confined to serving as a "trustee" for the people of the United States, preserving the final decision on slavery for the territorial voters. He concluded that the Congress that passed the Missouri Compromise had exceeded its constitutional authority, not only under the "rules and regulations" provision, but also by depriving slaveowners of their property without due process of law. In making these confident assertions, Taney did not offer a single reference to constitutional history or judicial precedent to support his position.

More than a quarter century earlier, Chief Justice Marshall had drawn broad perimeters within which Congress could exercise its constitutional authority. In giving wide scope to Congress to regulate commerce and to pass "necessary and proper" legislation, for example, Marshall acknowledged that Congress must have the flexibility to act in ways that the framers may not have contemplated. He also wrote an opinion which recognized Congress's extensive authority to govern U.S. territories, an opinion that Taney's labored reading rendered meaningless. In 1857, a generation after Marshall had delivered his authoritative opinions, Taney turned the constitutional clock backward, insisting on a single, historically fixed meaning to the territory clause.

On the fifty-fifth and final page of Taney's opinion, the Chief Justice came to his third major conclusion: Dred Scott remained a slave under Missouri law. This had been the conclusion of the Missouri Supreme Court in 1852 and the federal circuit court in 1854. Taney himself had made the same point six years earlier in the Court's *Strader* decision in which he wrote that the status of a slave was determined by state law. That had been the holding of Justice Nelson's original *Dred Scott* opinion written for the Court majority in mid-February. Had Nelson officially spoken for the Court, or had Taney crafted his later opinion along similar lines, the Chief Justice's reputation for judicial probity would have been preserved.

Instead, Taney's convoluted *Dred Scott* opinion became an easy target for ridicule and attack. It was savaged by scholars for its strained reasoning and meager documentation. And it was viewed by the majority of Americans, primarily in the North, as a partisan and unconscionable defense of slavery. The opinion was all the more shocking because Taney, over the two decades that he had served as Chief Justice, converted legions of skeptics into true believers in his fairness, pragmatism, and judgment. But in his *Dred Scott* opinion, where careful scholarship and political wisdom were desperately needed, he failed miserably.

Why, it must be asked, did Taney squander his judicial reputation with this one, extremely vulnerable opinion?

Taney's opinion can justifiably be criticized on many counts, but not the one often made—that it was the impulsive tirade of a southern zealot. On the issue of black citizenship, Taney had come to the same conclusion twenty-five years before he delivered his *Dred Scott* opinion. In 1832, as President Jackson's Attorney General, Taney had written an elaborate and outspoken advisory opinion which concluded that the Constitution condemned African Americans to an inferior status in the United States. No African American, whether slave or free, was entitled to the same constitutional rights as a white. This was the considered legal opinion of Attorney General Taney in 1832 as well as Chief Justice Taney in 1857.

Although Taney's constitutional opinion on the status of American blacks had not changed in twenty-five years, his political views on slavery had been dramatically transformed. As a respected lawyer in Maryland in the early 1820s, Taney had freed his slaves, advocated colonization for free blacks, and, generally, taken the relatively enlightened positions of a southern moderate. Ten years later, when Taney served in Andrew Jackson's cabinet, slavery was still largely a muted issue in national political debate; Taney's advisory opinion to the president on slavery was not published.

By the mid-1850s, the debate over slavery had become a public obsession that split the nation. Taney, like virtually every other moderate southerner of his generation, felt pressure to defend the culture and independence of the South, including the institution of slavery. And his fealty to the South, like that of most other southern moderates, was combined with a fear and hatred of northern abolitionists whose extreme views, he believed, threatened both the South and the Union. In 1856, Taney seriously considered what would, for him, have been unthinkable a decade earlier: the South's secession from the Union. That drastic political act, Taney wrote his son-in-law, was preferable to further capitulation to the northern aggressor.

Taney's despair caused him to conflate his constitutional and political views in his far-reaching *Dred Scott* opinion. He thought that he was performing a great service for his country by eliminating the divisive issues of African-American citizenship and the Missouri Compromise from the national debate. Like President Buchanan, he hoped that the Court's decision would silence abolitionist agitation and preserve the Union.

As transparently partisan as Taney's opinion was, the supporting concurrences of his fellow southerners on the Court were worse. Two of the justices, Campbell of Alabama and Catron of Tennessee, had actually offered earlier private opinions that the Missouri Compromise was constitutional. In 1857, however, both wrote stridently, and unpersuasively, that the statute was unconstitutional. Their colleague, Justice Daniel of Virginia, made the ludicrous claim that "the property of the master in his slave" stood above every other property right protected in the Constitution.

The long-anticipated dissent by Justice McLean was lengthy (thirty-six pages), discursive, and full of moral indignation. But it was not an impressive legal document. Only Justice Benjamin Curtis, among all of the justices, wrote a judicial opinion that discussed all of the relevant constitutional issues with admirable detachment and scholarly thoroughness.

Curtis's dissent ran to sixty-seven pages and, with McLean's, took five hours to read in court the day after Taney had read his opinion. Early in his dissent, Curtis refuted the Chief Justice's sparsely documented conclusion that African Americans could never be citizens or persons under the Constitution who were entitled to sue in federal court. Curtis's discussion focused on specific statutes in several states under the Articles of Confederation and the Constitution that explicitly gave free blacks rights commonly associated with citizenship. Among the five states that had extended voting rights to free blacks, Curtis noted, was the slave state of North Carolina, which had by statute described free blacks as citizens. Curtis took special exception to Taney's example of the miscegenation law from his home state of Massachusetts as proof of the black's inferior status. Both before and after the Constitution was ratified, Curtis pointed out, Massachusetts had given free blacks the vote, a right that he declared incontrovertibly conferred citizenship.

Curtis questioned the propriety of deciding the Dred Scott case on the merits since, under Taney's reasoning, the Court should have disposed of it on jurisdictional grounds. If Scott and every other American black were deprived of the citizenship necessary to sue in federal court, Curtis wrote, then there was no legitimate basis for ruling on the constitutionality of the Missouri Compromise or whether Scott remained a slave. Taney's opinion on the merits of the case was extrajudicial, he concluded, and not binding constitutional law.

Curtis had decided that Scott could sue in federal court and therefore felt justified in discussing whether the Missouri Compromise was constitutional. At the time of the ratification of the U.S. Constitution, Curtis wrote, Virginia had already ceded the Northwest Territory and the framers also knew that two other states, Georgia and North Carolina, were contemplating ceding territories to the United States. It defied logic and common sense to conclude, as Taney did, that the framers intended to limit Congress's broad authority under the territory clause to the Northwest Territory. And if the framers anticipated that Congress would acquire and make regulations for future territories, that constitutional authority, reasonably interpreted, must include the conditions set out in the Missouri Compromise. Curtis rejected Taney's claim that the Missouri Compromise unconstitutionally deprived a slaveowner of his slave property as a flawed exercise in both history and law. He traced due process rights back to the Magna Carta and concluded that no such protection of human property prevented Congress from prohibiting slavery in U.S. territories.

On the merits of Dred Scott's claim of freedom, Curtis noted that Scott had married his wife, Harriet, in an official ceremony at Fort Snelling that validated Scott's status as a free black, since slaves were not allowed to marry. He also maintained that the Missouri Supreme Court's ruling that Scott remained a slave was contrary to that state's settled law. The state court was obligated to recognize Scott's free status under the doctrine of comity, he wrote, unless the Missouri legislature had passed a law rejecting the doctrine. No such law had been passed.

Although Curtis was a committed anti-slavery man, he spoke of the institution of slavery as a judge, not a moralist or politician. Slavery, he wrote, was contrary to natural law. He supported his statement with a survey of both international and American law to show that slavery only existed under explicit provisions of municipal statutes. In contrast to Curtis's observation on the limited legal status of slavery, Justice McLean declared in his dissent that slavery "has its origin in power and is against right."

Curtis's calibrated dismemberment of Taney's opinion rankled the Chief Justice. Taney's irritation deepened after Curtis sent a copy of his dissent to a Boston newspaper for publication. The public reaction to the Supreme Court's *Dred Scott* decision in the North had been vitriolic in the extreme.* Curtis's published dissent was seized upon by the Court's critics to further discredit the decision. Already stunned by the rage with which his opinion was greeted in the North, Taney was further piqued by what he considered Curtis's politically motivated decision to give his dissent to an anti-slavery newspaper before all of the opinions of the justices in the case had been officially published.

Taney's bitterness erupted in an exchange of letters with Curtis after the Massachusetts justice had requested of the Court clerk to see a copy of the Chief Justice's opinion. Curtis had heard that Taney made extensive revisions of his opinion after his courtroom reading and wanted the opportunity to respond in his dissent to the Chief Justice's changes. Unknown to Curtis, Taney, in consultation with Justices Wayne and Daniel (who were the only other members of the Court still in Washington), had decided that no one would be allowed to see his opinion before publication. That decision puzzled Curtis, since it was common practice for the justices to review any revisions made by their colleagues before the official publication of a Court decision.

Taney stood by his decision and insisted that no one, not even a judicial colleague, would be permitted to see his revised opinion before pub-

---

* The Court's judgment, editorialized the *New York Tribune*, was "wicked," "atrocious," and no better than what could be heard in any "Washington bar-room." The Chicago *Democratic-Press* expressed a "feeling of shame and loathing" for "this once illustrious tribunal."

lication. After Curtis appealed directly to Taney to see a copy of his opinion, the Chief Justice suggested that Curtis was making the request for political purposes. Curtis denied Taney's accusation and reiterated his request to see the Chief Justice's revisions as a matter of judicial courtesy. Taney replied that he had made no significant changes in his opinion and again refused, adding that he deplored Curtis's insistence on continuing the "unpleasant correspondence that you have been pleased to commence." Later, after Taney's opinion was published, Curtis noted that the Chief Justice had added eighteen pages of revisions.

Taney's graceless and inappropriate rejection of Curtis's request would have been inconceivable before the Court's *Dred Scott* decision. The Chief Justice was known for his exceptional courtesy and fairness in his dealings with his colleagues. Curtis, among others, had marveled at these qualities in his private journal. But the unexpectedly stormy reaction to his *Dred Scott* opinion skewed Taney's judgment, even in his relations with his colleague from Massachusetts.

Benjamin Curtis resigned from the Court shortly after his altercation with Taney. He gave as his official reason his desire to return to private practice in Boston. And it was true that Curtis, one of the leading lawyers in the country before his appointment to the Supreme Court, had complained of the penurious Court wages compared to his previous income as a practicing attorney. But Curtis's resignation had more to do with his disillusionment with the Court than his desire for a larger income. He believed that the justices in the *Dred Scott* majority had abandoned their traditional constitutional role in the interests of political expediency. Taney's furious reaction to his request to see the Chief Justice's opinion was a further indication to Curtis that he could make a greater contribution to his profession as a private attorney in Boston than as a dissenting justice on the Taney Court.

If Taney was disturbed by Curtis's resignation, he did not record his feelings in his correspondence. On a subject that obviously did concern him, his *Dred Scott* opinion, Taney defended himself passionately. In response to a letter from a sympathetic Congregational minister in Massachusetts, Taney expounded on his view of the "unfortunate" African race that he had consigned to a degraded status under the Constitution. "Every intelligent person," Taney wrote, "whose life has been passed in a slaveholding state and who has carefully observed the character and capacity of the African race, will see that a general and sudden emancipation would be absolute ruin to the negroes, as well as to the white population."

Taney told the minister that he had freed his slaves and they "have shown by their conduct that they were worthy of freedom; and knew how to use it." But, in general, he considered emancipation in Maryland to have been a failure. Most freed slaves appeared to have suffered extreme privation that could have been prevented had they remained in bondage, he wrote. Most slaveowners treated their slaves humanely and relieved them of the anxieties of caring for themselves. He admitted that slaveholders could abuse their human property, but he did not think that occurred very often. The greatest threat to the slave's best interests was not the slaveowner, but the "discontent and ill feeling" produced by outside agitators.

Taney requested that the minister not make his letter public since, as Chief Justice, he "ought not to appear as a volunteer in any political discussion." But that did not mean that Taney was reluctant to defend every sentence in his *Dred Scott* opinion. He compared the torrent of criticism of his opinion to that he experienced when, as Andrew Jackson's Secretary of the Treasury, he had removed federal deposits from the Bank of the United States. In a letter to former President Franklin Pierce, Taney wrote that "the war is waged upon me in the same spirit and by many of the same men who distinguished themselves on that occasion by the unscrupulous means to which they resorted." Taney did not name the men who had again waged war on him, and it would probably have been impossible for him to do so. His major antagonists in the Bank War— Nicholas Biddle, Henry Clay, and Daniel Webster—had long since died. But there was no doubt that Taney's defiant spirit, so vibrant when he fought beside Jackson against the bank, had returned.

"At my time of life when the end must be near," he wrote Pierce, "I should have rejoiced to find that the irritating strifes of this world were over, and that I was about to depart in peace with all men; and all men in peace with me. Yet perhaps it is best as it is. The mind is less apt to feel the torpor of age, when it is thus forced into action by public duties. And I have an abiding confidence that this act of my judicial life will stand the test of time and the sober judgment of the country."

Chapter Five

"THE BETTER ANGELS OF OUR NATURE"

Lincoln had pledged to accept the Taney Court's decision in the Dred Scott case in a campaign speech that he delivered in the summer of 1856 at Galena, Illinois, for Republican presidential candidate John Frémont. While conceding that his party would do all in its political power to prohibit the spread of slavery in U.S. territories, Lincoln denied the Democrats' charge that Republicans were "disunionists." The U.S. Supreme Court was the tribunal to decide whether Congress had the constitutional authority to exclude slavery from the territories, he told the crowd. He vowed that Republicans "will submit to its decisions; and if you [Democrats] do also, there will be an end to the matter." Lincoln's promise was more a challenge to Frémont's pro-slavery opponents to respect the law than a vote of confidence in the Taney Court. His pledge nonetheless reflected his abiding faith in the rule of law and, implicitly, in the integrity of the justices who served on the Supreme Court.

Lincoln made no public comment for months after Chief Justice Taney announced the Court's *Dred Scott* decision in March 1857. "Having devoted the most of last year to politics," he wrote Charles Gilfillan, a prominent Republican in St. Paul, Minnesota, in May 1857, "it is a *necessity* with me to devote this, to my private affairs." He was, by then, one of Illinois's most successful corporate lawyers. One of his clients, the floundering Illinois Central Railroad, still owed him almost $5,000 in legal fees, which he finally collected after he secured a court order against the railroad's Illinois property.

Later in the year, Lincoln was hired by a coalition of railroad clients and bridge owners to defend their interests in the first railroad draw-bridge to span the Mississippi River between Illinois and Iowa. The owner of the steamboat *Effie Afton* had sued for damages after the vessel had crashed into a pier of the bridge and burst into flames. Lincoln made a field trip to the scene of the accident to study measurements of the river's currents (mild on the day of the collision) and the construction of the bridge; he also interviewed the bridgemaster and the bridge's engineer. When he appeared in the federal circuit court in Chicago, where Justice John McLean of the U.S. Supreme Court presided, he contended that transportation over the railroad bridge was as important to the nation's future as river navigation under it. And then, taking full advantage of his research, he argued to a jury that the bridge presented no hazard to navigation, and that the pilot of the steamboat had been negligent in hitting the bridge. The jurors split 6–3 in favor of Lincoln's clients, and the jury was discharged.

Despite Lincoln's rising income, he and Mary continued to live in the same modest cottage at Eighth and Jackson Streets in Springfield that had been their home for the previous thirteen years. But with three growing sons, Robert, Tad, and Willie, the Lincolns were cramped for space. Lincoln did not protest when Mary arranged for an extensive renovation, almost doubling the size of the house and transforming it into a handsome two-story Greek Revival structure. The Lincolns were invited to parties almost every night of the week and, for the first time, Mary could reciprocate with gracious entertainment of her own. More than three hundred guests attended a party in their newly decorated home.

Although Lincoln enjoyed the parties and his unprecedented prosperity, he never lost sight of his overriding goal to achieve high public office. He planned to challenge Stephen A. Douglas for his Senate seat in the 1858 election. When Douglas delivered a major address in the state legislative chamber early in June 1857, Lincoln sat attentively in the audience. Douglas had been asked by the federal grand jury in Springfield to discuss three pressing national issues: the Mormon rebellion in the Utah Territory; the continuing conflict between pro- and anti-slavery forces in Kansas; and the Taney Court's *Dred Scott* decision. It was an ideal forum for Douglas to display his command of the controversial subjects; he was already looking beyond his Senate reelection campaign to the presidential race of 1860, when he hoped to unite the southern and northern wings of the Democratic Party behind his candidacy.

Appearing before an overflow crowd, Douglas looked fitter than he had in years. Observers credited his good health to his recent marriage to the beautiful Adele Cutts, who was nearly twenty years younger than her husband, a widower with two children. Douglas's figure was trimmer, his complexion clear, and his clothes neat and clean, a sure sign of his bride's influence on the habitually hard-drinking senator.

Douglas spoke with his usual confidence and fluency, dramatically making his points without a written text (though he would later write out his speech for publication). He disposed of the first two topics expeditiously. Congress should rescind Utah's territorial status, and President Buchanan should immediately send U.S. troops to quell the Mormon rebellion. On the issue of slavery in Kansas, Douglas loftily said that popular sovereignty would decide the conflict; if the free-staters in the territory, who comprised the majority, did not vote, they would deserve to suffer the political consequence.

Douglas saved his most passionate oration for the third topic, the *Dred Scott* decision. He applauded the "honest and conscientious" judges on the Taney Court and accused the critics of their decision of striking "a deadly blow at our whole republican system of government." Labeling Republican detractors "enemies of the Constitution," he suggested that their outraged reaction was tantamount to revolution. Chief Justice Taney had spoken for all law-abiding Americans, said Douglas, who, like the senator himself, believed that the framers of the Declaration of Independence and the Constitution had created the American government for the white race alone. He agreed with Taney that whatever privileges the framers extended to the degraded African American were conferred as a matter of grace, not constitutional right. Echoing the Chief Justice's opinion, Douglas declared that "negroes were regarded as an inferior race, who, in all ages, and in every part of the globe . . . had shown themselves incapable of self government."

If the Republicans have their way, Douglas warned, they will force "the amalgamation between superior and inferior races." He claimed that the Republican leaders who had condemned the *Dred Scott* decision demanded "perfect and absolute equality of the races." The audience cheered as Douglas listed the parade of predicted racial horrors if the Republicans prevailed: the instant emancipation of all slaves; blacks voting and holding public office next to whites; and, inevitably, black men marrying white women "on an equality with white men!" Even as he spoke, Douglas ominously reported, certain Republican-controlled states were taking measures to eliminate legal distinctions between black and white. Was Illinois prepared for this insidious attack on the integrity of the white race?

Lincoln had been silent about *Dred Scott* for three and a half months, but Douglas's race-baiting defense of the decision provoked him to speak out. He only did so, however, after he had meticulously prepared a rebuttal to the man he hoped to replace in the Senate. For two weeks after Douglas's address, Lincoln spent his days in the library of the Illinois Supreme Court poring over the *Dred Scott* opinions. He also read commentaries and criticisms of the decision in the Republican press.

At just past eight-thirty on the evening of June 26, Lincoln stepped to the rostrum in the Illinois House of Representatives carrying an armload of legal volumes. Addressing an audience that was much smaller than the one that had heard Douglas two weeks earlier, Lincoln said that he was there "partly by the invitation of some of you, and partly by my own inclination." He devoted little time to the first two topics of Douglas's address, the Utah rebellion and the struggle between pro- and anti-slavery forces in Kansas. He agreed with the senator that it was necessary for the federal government to put down the Utah rebellion but wondered what happened to Douglas's commitment to popular sovereignty. Douglas's inconsistency, said Lincoln, showed that his embrace of the doctrine "was a mere deceitful pretense for the benefit of slavery." As to Kansas, Lincoln questioned Douglas's good faith in calling for elections in the territory. Douglas knew, Lincoln charged, that the vast majority of free-staters had not registered to vote because they believed that the elections had been rigged by pro-slavery forces.

Having dismissed Douglas's positions on the Utah and Kansas controversies as duplicitous, Lincoln concentrated the brunt of his attack on the senator's defense of the *Dred Scott* decision. He promised to follow Douglas's example in not discussing the merits of the decision, "believing I could no more improve on McLean and Curtis, than he could on Taney." At the outset, he challenged Douglas's assertion that criticism of the Court's decision was synonymous with violent resistance to it. "But who resists it?" Lincoln asked. "Who has, in spite of the decision, declared Dred Scott free, and resisted the authority of his master over him?"

Lincoln assured his audience that he had as much respect for the Supreme Court as Douglas, perhaps, he hinted, a good deal more. And when the justices fully settled all constitutional issues before them, he did not question the finality of the decision, either the particular holding in a case or the general policy set out by the Court for the country. To do otherwise, he admitted, might constitute "revolution." His criticism of *Dred Scott*, however, was not that of a revolutionary, but that of a lawyer and loyal American who believed that the Court's opinion was "erroneous." The Court had often overruled its own erroneous decisions, Lincoln noted, "and we shall do what we can to have it to over-rule this. We offer no *resistance* to it."

How can a reasoned challenge to a disputed Court decision make a man "an enemy of the Constitution?" Lincoln reminded his audience that President Andrew Jackson had challenged a famous Court decision, *McCulloch v. Maryland*, when he vetoed the bill to recharter the Bank of the United States. Was Jackson an enemy of the Constitution? Were others who opposed the recharter of the National Bank, including a young Democratic politician named Stephen A. Douglas? Lincoln could have added, but did not, that under Douglas's reasoning, President

Jackson's Attorney General, Roger B. Taney, should also have been added to the senator's list of revolutionaries.

The *Dred Scott* decision was based on fallacious constitutional history, charged Lincoln, who honed in on Taney's claim that African Americans were purposely excluded by the framers of the Constitution. Contrary to Taney's historical argument, said Lincoln, Justice Curtis demonstrated in his dissent "with so much particularity as to leave no doubt of its truth" that free blacks voted in five of the original states and, in proportion to their numbers, "had the same part in making the Constitution that the white people had."

Lincoln relied heavily on Curtis's dissent to challenge Taney's version of constitutional history. But once he confronted the Chief Justice's assertion that the Declaration of Independence's words "all men are created equal" were limited to white men, his arguments became his own: "I think the authors of that notable instrument intended to include all men, but they did not intend to declare all men equal in all respects. They did not mean to say all were equal in color, size, intellect, moral developments, or social capacity. They defined with tolerable distinctness, in what respects they did consider all men created equal—equal in 'certain inalienable rights, among which are life, liberty, and the pursuit of happiness.' This they said, and this [they] meant."

He appealed to Democrats as well as Republicans to reject Taney's reading of the Declaration as no more than "an interesting memorial of the dead past . . . thus shorn of its vitality, and practical value; and left without the *germ* or even the *suggestion* of the individual rights of man in it." The Declaration, he insisted, was written for all time as "a standard maxim for free society." And contrary to Taney's opinion, the framers meant "to declare the *right*, so that the *enforcement* of it might follow as fact as fast as circumstances should permit."

The *Dred Scott* decision guaranteed "the spread of the black man's bondage," Lincoln lamented, further frustrating the framers' noble aspirations. "In those days," he said, "our Declaration of Independence was held sacred by all, and thought to include all; but now, to aid in making the bondage of the negro universal and eternal, it is assailed, and sneered at, and construed, and hawked at, and torn, till, if its framers could rise from their graves, they could not at all recognize it." He accused the Taney Court of joining pro-slavery politicians in state legislatures and those in Congress, like Douglas, who "have closed the heavy iron doors upon him [the African American], and now they have him, as it were, bolted in with a lock of a hundred keys."

For most of his speech assailing the *Dred Scott* decision, Lincoln spoke of Chief Justice Taney and his defender, Senator Douglas, as if they were one person. But when he dealt with the senator's charge that Republicans favored amalgamation of the races, Lincoln focused on Douglas alone. He rejected Douglas's "counterfeit logic" that "because I do not want a black woman for a slave I must necessarily want her for a wife. I need not have her for either, I can just leave her alone. In some respects she certainly is not my equal; but in her natural right to eat the bread she earns with her own hands without asking leave of any one else, she is my equal and the equal of all others."

For the first time, Lincoln had publicly denounced a decision of the U.S. Supreme Court and, more particularly, a majority opinion of Chief Justice Taney on the issue of race. Some Illinois Republican leaders, like Gustave Koerner of Belleville, found Lincoln's response to Douglas (and Taney) overly modulated and cautious, much too close to the failed approach of conservatives in the defunct Whig Party. At the same time, the Democratic press belittled Lincoln's speech as inferior in both merit and passion to Douglas's, and eagerly anticipated the Republican challenger's thorough drubbing in the 1858 senatorial race. But Douglas himself was not so certain. He knew from earlier experience that Lincoln was a formidable adversary. And with his attack on *Dred Scott*, Lincoln had grasped an issue that resonated politically in Illinois and throughout the northern and western states.

Six months after Douglas had offered his optimistic assessment of democratic prospects in Kansas, pro-slavery forces in the territory attempted to eliminate any possibility that the free-state majority would prevail.

They convened a constitutional convention in the tiny town of Lecompton, where the delegates wrote a document imposing slavery on the population. Their purpose was to submit the constitution to Congress and request admission of Kansas into the Union as a slave state. Leaders of the Lecompton convention realized that Congress would balk unless they made some effort to poll territorial voters. They were unwilling, however, to submit the entire constitution to a referendum. Instead, voters were limited to a choice between accepting the constitution "with slavery" or "without slavery." Either way, slaveholders already settled in the territory could keep their existing slave property. In a blatantly fraudulent election, the Lecompton constitution "with slavery" passed overwhelmingly. But shortly afterward, anti-slavery settlers, who represented a sizable majority in the recently elected territorial legislature, submitted the entire Lecompton constitution to the voters, and it was decisively defeated.

In Washington, an anxious President Buchanan received reports of the growing crisis in Kansas. He wanted the dispute resolved quickly before there was further bloodshed between pro- and anti-slavery factions, which, he knew, would erode his political support. Ultimately, the president was persuaded by members of his cabinet, particularly Secretary of the Treasury Howell Cobb of Georgia, to endorse the Lecompton pro-slavery constitution and urge Congress to admit Kansas as a slave state. Buchanan and his advisers calculated that his decision would placate the southern base of his party without provoking a rebellion by northern Democrats.

The president did not anticipate the ferocious reaction of Illinois's Senator Douglas, who denounced the tainted election supporting the pro-slavery Lecompton constitution as a violation of popular sovereignty. Douglas demanded a private meeting with Buchanan and, in a tense confrontation, informed the president that he would oppose the constitution. "Mr. Douglas," Buchanan admonished, "I desire you to remember that no Democrat ever yet differed from an Administration of his own choice without being crushed." He reminded Douglas of two Democrats who had rebelled against President Jackson and were driven from the party. A defiant Douglas shot back, "Mr. President, I wish you to remember that General Jackson is dead."

Douglas staked his reputation and his political future on his fight in Congress with Buchanan over the Lecompton constitution. The galleries and lobby of the Senate chamber were packed on the day that "the little Giant" took the floor to challenge the president and the southern wing of his party on the question of popular sovereignty in Kansas. Douglas condemned the plan adopted by the Lecompton convention as a "system of trickery and jugglery to defeat the fair expression of the will of the people." So long as the voters were fairly allowed to register their preferences, said Douglas, he did not care whether the slavery clause in the Lecompton constitution was "voted down or voted up."

After he had read reports of the speech, Lincoln took special note of Douglas's stated indifference to slavery, which he carefully filed away for later use.

The Buchanan forces worked the corridors of Congress assiduously, cajoling, threatening, even bribing wavering Democrats. In the end, the Senate narrowly voted to accept the Lecompton constitution, but Douglas persuaded enough western Democrats in the House to defeat the measure. Douglas's triumph repelled his southern Democratic colleagues and guaranteed that he would not have their support in his campaign for the party's 1860 presidential nomination. The president, too, bitterly resented Douglas's victory and vowed to punish him for his disloyalty.

Lincoln warily read accounts of Douglas's battle with the president over the Lecompton constitution. The split between Douglas and Buchanan within the Democratic Party was, of course, good news for Lincoln, as were reports that Buchanan loyalists would mount organized opposition to Douglas's reelection. But those advantages were balanced against a resurgence of Douglas's popularity among Illinois Democrats who had opposed the Kansas-Nebraska Act and now rallied behind his party leadership. Equally alarming, leading abolitionists, like the *New York Tribune*'s Horace Greeley, praised Douglas's courage and principled opposition to slave interests in Congress and suggested that Republicans support his reelection.

Was it possible, an incredulous Lincoln asked, that his Republican Party might ignore him at the party's June convention and nominate his sworn Democratic enemy, Senator Douglas? "What does the New-York Tribune mean by it's constant eulogising, and admiring, and magnifying [of] Douglas?" an irate Lincoln asked Republican senator Lyman Trumbull, who had left the Democratic Party over its pro-slavery stand. "Does it, in this, speak the sentiments of the republicans at Washington? Have they concluded that the republican cause, generally, can be best promoted by sacraficing us here in Illinois?"

Lincoln need not have worried. Long-distance prodding from Greeley on behalf of Douglas only strengthened the resolve of Illinois Republicans to nominate Lincoln. "There seems to be a considerable notion pervading the brains of political wet-nurses at the East, that the barbarians of Illinois cannot take care of themselves," sniped the *Chicago Tribune*. Republican Party regulars in the state quickly swung into action, lining up county after county for Lincoln. They also devised a plan, innovative at the time, to select their candidate for the U.S. Senate at the party's state convention before the legislature voted for the nominee, as had been done in the past. By the time Republicans met in Springfield on the sultry afternoon of June 16, 1858, it was a foregone conclusion that Lincoln was their "first and only" choice for the Senate.

In accepting the nomination that evening, Lincoln delivered his "House Divided" speech, which was destined to become one of the most famous orations in American history. The opening passages set the desperate tone of the entire address. The Kansas-Nebraska Act had not resolved the slavery issue, Lincoln told the delegates, but rather had plunged the nation into crisis. The time for compromise was past; Americans must choose one side of the issue or the other. "A house divided against itself cannot stand," Lincoln declared. "I believe this government cannot endure, permanently half *slave* and half *free*." He did not expect the Union to dissolve, "but I do expect it will cease to be divided." He hoped that the opponents of slavery would succeed in pushing slavery to "ultimate extinction." If they failed, then the advocates of slavery "will push it forward, till it shall become alike lawful in *all* the States, *old* as well as *new*—*North* as well as *South*."

The second section of the address, less lyrical and much longer than the first, linked Senator Douglas, former President Pierce, President Buchanan, and Chief Justice Taney in a conspiracy to nationalize slavery. Lincoln accused Douglas of initiating the conspiratorial plot with his sponsorship of the Kansas-Nebraska Act, which repealed the Missouri Compromise's restriction on slavery in the territories. President Pierce had worked successfully with Douglas to make certain that the legislation passed. In his inaugural address, President Buchanan had not only supported the legislation but prepared the public for the final pro-slavery action of the conspiracy, Chief Justice Taney's opinion for the Court in *Dred Scott*.

"We can not absolutely *know*," Lincoln admitted, that Douglas, Pierce, Buchanan, and Taney had actually worked together in "preconcert." But he insisted that their conspiracy was real and, to make his point more vivid, introduced a metaphor familiar to every man in his audience who had helped build a farmhouse or barn: "[W]hen we see a lot of framed timbers, different portions of which we know have been gotten out at different times and places and by different workmen—Stephen, Franklin, Roger and James, for instance—and when we see these timbers joined together, and see they exactly make the frame of a house or a mill, all the tenons and mortices exactly fitting, and all the lengths and proportions of the different pieces exactly adapted to their respect places . . . in such a case, we find it impossible to not believe that Stephen and Franklin and Roger and James all understood one another from the beginning, and all worked upon a common place or draft drawn up before the first lick was struck."

Lincoln was too sophisticated a lawyer to think that his charge of conspiracy would hold up in a court of law. He nonetheless believed the conspiracy to be a political fact, if not the basis for a legal prosecution. And he presented his theory deliberately, making arguments that he defended throughout his senatorial campaign. According to Lincoln, the four conspirators had, through their coordinated actions, perpetuated the enormous moral wrong of slavery. Douglas, Pierce, and Buchanan had openly worked in political tandem to discredit the Missouri Compromise and eliminate the possibility that Congress could prohibit slavery in the territories. As to Taney, Lincoln had no knowledge that the Chief Justice had communicated with the three other men when he wrote his *Dred Scott* opinion. But he suspected that they had been told of Taney's opinion before it was announced.

It did not seem to matter to Lincoln that he could produce no tangible evidence to support his conspiracy theory. He was wrong on virtually every factual assumption connecting the four men. True, Douglas and Pierce had collaborated on pushing through the Kansas-Nebraska Act, but Buchanan was out of the country when it was passed, and Taney had nothing to do with the legislation. When he announced his theory, Lincoln knew, moreover, that two of the conspirators, Buchanan and Douglas, were openly feuding over the fate of slavery in Kansas. Having studied the *Dred Scott* decision, Lincoln also was aware that Douglas's commitment to popular sovereignty was undermined by Taney's opinion prohibiting Congress from excluding slavery in a territory and, implicitly, denying the same authority to a territorial government. Finally, Lincoln's belief that Douglas, Pierce, and Buchanan had been informed of the *Dred Scott* decision before it was publicly announced was mistaken. Based on historical records, only Buchanan had prior knowledge of the decision, and his information was received from Justice Grier, not Taney, though the Chief Justice was aware of Grier's communication with the president.

Although he had audaciously charged the Chief Justice of the United States with conspiracy, Lincoln was not done with Taney. He said that Taney's opinion in *Dred Scott* forbade Congress or a territorial government from excluding slavery, but that the Court had not yet decided whether a state might enact the same prohibition. He was certain that Taney and his colleagues would soon answer that open question. They had cleverly provided "another nice little niche, which we may, ere long, see filled with another Supreme Court decision, declaring that the Constitution of the United States does not permit a state to exclude slavery from its limits." That Court decision, Lincoln declared, was "all that slavery now lacks of being alike lawful in all the States." Unless "the present political dynasty shall be met and overthrown," he warned, "[w]e shall *lie down* pleasantly dreaming that the people of *Missouri* are on the verge of making their State *free;* and we shall *awake* to the *reality,* instead, that the *Supreme* Court has made Illinois a *slave* state."

The only way for Republicans to avoid that tragic end was to vigilantly oppose slavery. Politicians like Senator Douglas, who did not care whether slavery was extinguished or not, were the enemy. "[H]e *cares* not whether slavery be voted *down* or voted *up,*" Lincoln charged, referring to Douglas's statement in his Senate speech on the Lecompton constitution. Such indifference on the moral issue that would determine the future course of the United States was intolerable.

Lincoln had never spoken with such urgency about slavery. He had always opposed the institution but, until the passage of the Kansas-Nebraska Act four years earlier, had assumed that it would gradually disappear. By the summer of 1858, he realized that his goal of a slave-free United States was fast slipping away. In raising the specter of a nation in which slavery was pervasive, Lincoln was surely exaggerating the immediate danger. The powerful states in the North and West were not likely soon to succumb to southern pressure. But Lincoln's conspiracy theory was more than a rhetorical device to dramatize the dire state of the Union. He believed that the pro-slavery minority in the nation, assisted critically by Democratic leaders in the North, like Douglas, Pierce, and Buchanan, and a southern-dominated Supreme Court, led by Chief Justice Taney, could well prevail. It was therefore essential that he expose Douglas for his unprincipled stand on the issue that mattered most— slavery—and alert Republicans and the nation to the continuing threat posed by the Taney Court.

To Lincoln's chagrin, his "House Divided" speech was widely misinterpreted, even by those who were sympathetic to his message. Was he calling for militant action by the North against the South? asked John L. Scripps, the editor of the Chicago *Daily Democratic Press.* Lincoln replied that sectional warfare was neither his intended message nor his desire. He reminded Scripps that he had long been on record as recognizing the Constitution's protection of slavery in the southern states. At the same time, he opposed Supreme Court decisions that permitted the spread of slavery into new territories and free states. Whenever those efforts were "fairly headed off, the institution will then be in course of ultimate extinction; and by the language used I meant only this."

Senator Douglas, speaking to a huge crowd from the hotel balcony of the Tremont House in Chicago, attacked Lincoln's speech as a call to arms "of the free states against the slave states." Again pledging his allegiance to the principle of popular sovereignty, Douglas said it was wrong for Congress to impose its will on either slave or free states. "It is no answer . . . to say that slavery is an evil and hence should not be tolerated," he chided. "You must allow the people to decide for themselves where it is a good or an evil." Lincoln ought to have greater faith in the people in the states to decide what is best for them. Self-government, Douglas proclaimed, was "the great safe guard of our liberties."

At Douglas's invitation, Lincoln had sat in a balcony chair during the Tremont House address and heard the senator describe him as a "kind, amiable, and intelligent gentleman." Douglas's courtesies did nothing to soften Lincoln's attack on him the following night for distorting his "House Divided" speech. Lincoln had said "a hundred times" that the free states had no right to enter into the slave states "and interfere with the question of slavery at all." He had also said many times that the framers of the Constitution had disfavored slavery and had shown their intentions by the passage of the Northwest Ordinance, which had prohibited slavery. The framers further demonstrated that they "expected the ultimate extinction of that institution," Lincoln contended, by drafting the constitutional provision providing that the slave trade could be cut off after twenty years.

On the subject of states' rights, Lincoln assured his Chicago audience that he had no desire to interfere with the cranberry laws of Indiana, the oyster laws of Virginia, or the liquor laws of Maine. But slavery was different. He did not agree with Douglas that slavery was "as an exceedingly little thing—this matter of keeping one-sixth of the population of the whole nation in a state of oppression and tyranny unequaled in the world." Unlike the apathetic Douglas, Lincoln said that he was a member of a large majority of the American people who looked upon the institution of slavery as "a vast moral evil."

Throughout July and early August, Lincoln stalked Douglas, listening to his speeches, then immediately announcing that he would reply to the senator either later that night or the next day. In his relentless attacks on his Senate opponent, Lincoln repeated his conspiracy charge against Douglas, Pierce, Buchanan, and Taney. They had deceived Congress and the people in the territories into thinking that they could exclude slavery when the conspirators knew in advance that the Taney Court was going to prevent it. He taunted Douglas for not contradicting him and charged anew that the senator "was a party to that conspiracy and to that deception for the sole purpose of nationalizing slavery."

From late summer until mid-October 1858, Lincoln and Douglas traveled almost ten thousand miles between them, crisscrossing the state by train, riverboat, and carriage. Each gave a prodigious number of speeches. By campaign's end, Douglas had addressed prospective voters in 130 speeches and Lincoln in slightly less than half that number, though Lincoln's total did not include the scores of times he made informal remarks to small groups along dusty roads and in towns where crowds had gathered.

The two men faced off in seven debates, one in each congressional district of the state, except those encompassing Chicago and Springfield where the candidates had already made major speeches. Although Douglas was a superb debater, he had only reluctantly agreed to the formal confrontations with Lincoln. The nationally known senator did not want to enhance his opponent's stature by sharing a platform. But he preferred the debates to the risk of appearing afraid to meet Lincoln's arguments in direct verbal combat.

On the hot, hazy day of August 21, shortly after dawn, eager farmers and their families began to converge on Ottawa, a town of more than eight thousand residents in the fertile agricultural region of northern Illinois that was the site of the first debate. They came on foot and by horseback and in rickety wagons. Once they reached their destination, they were greeted by cannon blasts, marching bands, and rural fife and drum corps. Brightly sashed marshals patrolled on horseback while local entrepreneurs sold slices of watermelon and drafts of lemonade. Beggars and jugglers vied for the crowd's attention with itinerant peddlers hawking painkillers and miracle elixirs. Flags and banners festooned Lafayette Square where Lincoln and Douglas were scheduled to debate that afternoon.

About noon, Lincoln stepped down from one of the seventeen railroad cars that Republicans had chartered for the eighty-mile trip from Chicago to Ottawa. Amid shouts of "Hurrah for Lincoln," the candidate was ceremoniously escorted to the mayor's house in a carriage decorated with evergreens by "the fair young ladies of Ottawa." Shortly afterward, Douglas rode into town in an elegant carriage drawn by four spirited horses. He was welcomed, a correspondent for the *Philadelphia Press* observed, like "some mighty champion who had . . . saved a nation from ruin."

When Douglas and Lincoln appeared together on the platform specially built for the debate, the contrast between the two men was striking. The top of the dwarfish Douglas's head barely reached Lincoln's shoulders. The senator dressed with sartorial flair, wearing a wide-brimmed white felt hat, dark blue coat with shiny silver buttons, light trousers, and highly buffed shoes. Lincoln effected just the opposite image. The sleeves of his scruffy black frock coat were too short and his pants, also black, did not extend past his ankles. Douglas spoke in a deep, mellifluous baritone, Lincoln in a shrill, high-pitched tenor. Douglas's confident gait and thespian gestures (a defiant scowl here, a grandiose bow there) were calculated to intimidate, persuade, and entertain his audience, all at once. The tall, gaunt Lincoln stood awkwardly on the platform. When he crouched, slowly rising to make a dramatic point, his body seemed to unfold in disjointed parts.

By prearrangement, Douglas opened the debate and immediately put

Lincoln on the defensive with a barrage of prosecutorial questions. Was it not true, asked Douglas, that Lincoln and Senator Lyman Trumbull had devised a strategy in 1854 to create a radical abolitionist Republican party out of the ruins of the old Whig and Democratic parties? Could Mr. Lincoln please tell the audience where he stood on slavery: did he favor its forced abolition throughout the country? Should slavery be forbidden in every territory, even if the majority of voters favored it? Did Lincoln truly believe that blacks were equal to whites? "For my part," Douglas declared, "I do not regard the negro as my equal, and positively deny that he is my brother or any kin to me whatever." And his conviction, Douglas asserted, was identical to that of the founding fathers, including Washington, Madison, and Jefferson. They intended that the nation prosper under just the circumstances that Lincoln feared—half slave and half free.

Lincoln was stunned by Douglas's aggressive attack, and did not fully recover from the onslaught. His denial of Douglas's unsubstantiated charge that he and Trumbull had helped form an abolitionist party in 1854 was hesitant and lacked fiery indignation. If his name had appeared as a sponsor of an abolitionist party's platform, it had been done, he said, without his authorization. His initial response to Douglas's insinuations about his anti-slavery position was to read from his 1854 Peoria speech in which he confessed that he did not have a solution for the slavery problem. And while he did not match Douglas's negrophobic remarks, Lincoln conceded that there were "physical differences" between the races. He also declared that blacks were not equal to whites politically or socially, and opposed permitting them to vote or serve on juries. Lincoln insisted nonetheless that blacks had the same rights as whites to earn a living and pursue the American ideal of life, liberty, and happiness. He repeated his conspiracy theory, but became mired in legal jargon (he "took a default" on Douglas's silence to the charge) in defending it. When Douglas emphatically denied the accusation, Lincoln responded weakly: "I do not say that I *know* such a conspiracy to exist, but I *believe* it."

After the debate, a group of sturdy Republican supporters lifted Lincoln onto their shoulders, as if in triumph. Lincoln was embarrassed by his clumsy exit (his long limbs had dangled awkwardly over the shoulders of his bearers). More important, he was dissatisfied with his performance. The Ottawa contest had exposed Lincoln's weakness in the give-and-take of extemporaneous debate. He was at his best when he read carefully prepared speeches. But he was a fierce competitor and an indefatigable worker, and shortly after leaving Ottawa, he sat down with his closest campaign advisers in Chicago to prepare for the next debate. When he arrived in Freeport, a town north of Chicago near the Wisconsin border where the second debate was scheduled to occur, Lincoln was not only prepared to answer Douglas's Ottawa charges, but ready to confront his opponent with his own set of pointed questions.

Freeport was staunchly Republican, which may have explained the renewed vigor and confidence with which Lincoln opened the second debate. Backed by research in Springfield newspapers done by his law partner, William Herndon, and other supporters, Lincoln emphatically repudiated Douglas's charge that he and Trumbull had secretly met in Springfield to form an abolitionist party in 1854. No such meeting had ever taken place, Lincoln asserted. Douglas may have mistakenly referred to an abolitionist meeting in another county in which neither Lincoln nor Trumbull took part. It was "most extraordinary," said Lincoln, his words dripping sarcasm, that his world-famous opponent would make this reckless charge, which "the slightest investigation would have shown him to be wholly false." The crowd laughed and cheered its approval.

Lincoln answered Douglas's other questions directly and without a hint of the defensiveness that had hurt his Ottawa performance. He was opposed to the admission of new slave states and would be "exceedingly sorry" to have to pass on the question. But if the people of a prospective state did "such an extraordinary thing as to adopt a Slave Constitution, I see no alternative, if we own the country, but to admit them into the Union." His opposition to slavery in all federal territories, and his belief that Congress had the authority to forbid it, were a matter of long public record. On the issue of permitting slavery in a new territory, Lincoln said that he would have to consider it in the larger context of whether such a decision would further aggravate the slavery question in the nation.

It was now Lincoln's turn to ask the questions. If the Supreme Court should rule that the states could not exclude slavery, would Douglas support such a decision?

Douglas brushed off the inquiry as unworthy of his serious deliberation. Lincoln might just as well have asked him to approve a horse theft. Such a Supreme Court decision would be a violation of the Constitution, "an act of moral treason," Douglas declared, "that no man on the bench could ever descend to."

A second Lincoln question could not be so flippantly dismissed: Did the voters in a territory have the legal right to exclude slavery before they applied for admission to the Union? Lincoln knew that his inquiry would force Douglas to explain the contradiction between his endorsement of the *Dred Scott* decision and his commitment to popular sovereignty. Taney's opinion had appeared to eliminate the possibility that a popularly elected territorial government could exclude slavery, since the Chief Justice had ruled that Congress, which retained authority over territorial governments, could not itself prohibit slavery in the territories.

In addition to challenging Douglas's support for the *Dred Scott* decision, Lincoln's question contained a second poisonous political pill. If Douglas chose to embrace the principle of self-government by supporting the territorial voters' right to decide the fate of slavery, despite the *Dred Scott* decision, he would probably gain adherents among the voters in the free state of Illinois. But while that might help him in his senatorial election, it could frustrate his presidential aspirations. The Buchanan administration, backed by southern Democrats, assumed that the *Dred Scott* decision had given a definitive answer to Lincoln's question: no territorial government could prohibit slavery. Should Douglas declare his opposition to their interpretation, the breach between the Illinois senator and the Buchanan-southern alliance of his party would surely deepen.

In his response, Douglas reasserted his commitment to popular sovereignty, though he found a way to preserve the principle without contradicting the Taney Court's decision. The Court's pronouncements on "the abstract question" of whether slavery could exist in a territory or not, said Douglas, had no practical relevance. Regardless of the Court's decision on the issue, "the people have the lawful means to introduce it or exclude it as they please, for the reason that slavery cannot exist a day or an hour anywhere unless it is supported by local police regulations." Since only a local legislature could protect slavery, its refusal to do so would effectively exclude it. "[I]f the people are opposed to slavery," he reasoned, "they will elect representatives to that body who will by unfriendly legislation effectually prevent the introduction of it into their midst."

Contemporary accounts by Lincoln's supporters credited their candidate's question with depriving Douglas of the White House. In the Freeport debate, they maintained, Lincoln had cleverly forced Douglas to choose sides between his principle of popular sovereignty and the support of the Buchanan-southern wing of his party. But that version of history ignores the fact that Douglas had already announced his position prior to the Freeport debate, though he had spoken more cautiously on the issue before Lincoln posed his question. A more serious problem with the interpretation is that Douglas, always the practical politician, had written off his chances of reconciliation with the Buchanan administration and the southern Democrats. He knew that they would never forgive him for his opposition to the pro-slavery Lecompton constitution; his declaration at Freeport, later known as the "Freeport Doctrine," only reenforced their enmity toward him. If he was to be elected president in 1860, he would have to win in the northern and western states, not the South. Lincoln had come to the same conclusion. "He cares nothing for the South—he knows he is already dead there," Lincoln had written the previous summer.

What Lincoln hoped to accomplish with his question was more modest than his most avid supporters claimed: he wanted to make Douglas's position a part of the public record, so that he could not later equivocate on the issue. But while Lincoln succeeded in that goal, Douglas's open declaration weakened a central tenet of Lincoln's campaign—his insistence that Douglas was a conspirator in the plot to nationalize slavery. Douglas's Freeport Doctrine supporting territorial voters' right to exclude slavery locally not only further exposed his disagreement with a fellow conspirator, President Buchanan, but also showed that he was not the resolute pro-slavery advocate that Lincoln claimed.

Immediately after Douglas demonstrated his independence from the pro-slavery Democrats, however, he indulged in his now familiar race-baiting. With great flourish, he told his Freeport audience that during his last visit to their town he had seen the black leader, Frederick Douglass, lounging romantically with a white woman in the back of a horse-drawn carriage while the woman's beautiful daughter sat on the box seat of the coach and the owner of the carriage drove. "[I]f you, Black Republicans, think that a negro ought to be on a social equality with your wives and daughters, and ride in a carriage with your wife, whilst you drive the team," he said tauntingly, "you have a perfect right to do so." And those same "Black Republicans" would, he assumed, "vote for Mr. Lincoln."

Lincoln and Douglas exchanged charges and countercharges in the third debate at Jonesboro, in the extreme southern region of the state, and then at Charleston, in Coles County, where Thomas Lincoln and his family had lived (and the townspeople proudly displayed an eighty-foot painting of young Abe Lincoln riding on an oxen-driven wagon). For the fifth debate, the candidates traveled by train to Knox College in Galesburg, a Republican stronghold settled by anti-slavery Scandinavians. Before an enthusiastic crowd, Lincoln declared that "the entire records of the world, from the date of the Declaration of Independence up to within three years ago, may be searched in vain for one single affirmation, from one single man, that the negro was not included in the Declaration of Independence." A week later, at Quincy, Douglas said that there could be no appeal of the *Dred Scott* decision "this side of heaven" and accused Lincoln once again of fomenting violence instead of respect for the law.

Finally, Lincoln and Douglas boarded the riverboat *City of Louisiana* to sail down the Mississippi to their seventh debate, at Alton. By this time, Douglas's energy and effectiveness had noticeably waned; he was so hoarse his voice barely rose above a whisper. Lincoln, meanwhile, appeared more invigorated by each successive debate. Douglas once again returned to his major theme: "I care more for the great principle of self government than I do for all the negroes in Christendom." In his response, one of the most poignant of his campaign, Lincoln said that his disagreement with Douglas over slavery represented "the eternal struggle between these two principles—right and wrong—throughout the world. . . . The one is the common right of humanity and the other the divine right of kings."

Election day, November 2, was cold and rainy across Illinois. Lincoln voted early and later joined friends at the Springfield telegraph office to receive the returns. As expected, both parties secured their traditional bases of support, the Republicans in the more populous northern counties, the Democrats in the poorer, rural south. The middle region of the state, where both candidates knew that their election would be won or lost, split almost evenly between the parties. In statewide elections, votes for the National Democratic candidates, who represented the Buchanan-backed third party organized to undermine Douglas, were modest (just over 5,000). But that total enabled the Republicans to win a narrow popular majority in the races for state treasurer and superintendent of education.

Neither Lincoln nor Douglas was on the ballot, but the votes for state legislators, who would determine the Senate race, were distributed along the same lines as those for the statewide offices. But although Republican state representatives received a slight majority of all of the votes cast, they faced a daunting task in trying to wrest control from the Democrats in the legislature where the next U.S. senator would be chosen. Since the Democrats retained eight of the thirteen holdover seats in the legislature, Republicans needed to win more than half of the contested seats. Compounding the Republicans' challenge was the fact that the legislature had last been reapportioned in 1850, which favored the Democratic south over the increasingly more populous northern counties. Although Republicans won 50 percent of the popular vote, they captured only 47 seats in the legislature, while the Democrats, with 48 percent of the popular vote, won 53 percent of the seats. As a result, when the legislature met in early January 1859, Douglas won reelection to another six-year term in the U.S. Senate.

Lincoln had narrowly lost another senatorial election, his second in four years, and was deeply disappointed. Still, he took satisfaction in his extraordinary effort on behalf of a cause that he profoundly believed in. "I am glad I made the later race," he wrote an old friend, Dr. Anson Henry. "It gave me a hearing on the great and durable question of the age, which I could have had no other way; and though I now sink out of view, and shall be forgotten, I believe I have made some marks which will tell for the cause of civil liberty long after I am gone."

Lincoln was only half right in his self-appraisal. He was justly proud of his campaign against the spread of slavery, which he had conducted with moral fervor and eloquence. But he had woefully miscalculated his political future. Far from being buried in obscurity, Lincoln would, within a few months, become a national leader of the Republican Party and a candidate for the presidency.

Lincoln was not the only Republican politician in 1858 to draw nefarious links between the Taney Court and pro-slavery forces in the nation. Senator William Seward of New York, who was the early front-runner to win the Republican nomination for president in 1860, described the justices of the Taney Court as sycophantic courtiers to President Buchanan in a plot to make slavery legal throughout the nation. According to Seward, the Dred Scott case was, from the beginning, a trumped-up litigation created by slave interests to provide the Court with the opportunity to indelibly constitutionalize slavery. In secret conversations emanating from the White House, he said, Buchanan had worked hand-in-glove with the justices to effect the prearranged result that Taney announced in the *Dred Scott* decision. Seward charged that Buchanan and the Taney Court had forgotten "that judicial usurpation is more odious and intolerable than any other among the manifold practices of tyranny."

Taney was so infuriated by the attack of his former Senate admirer that he vowed to refuse to administer the oath of office to Seward, should he win the presidency. Seward's charges were, to be sure, outlandishly exaggerated. The Dred Scott case was instigated by a slave in pursuit of his freedom, not by slaveholding puppeteers. And as the prolonged and convoluted deliberations by the justices in the case attested, there was no preordained result.

But Taney's indignation, like the charges themselves, appeared overblown. After all, Buchanan had initiated communication with both Justices Catron and Grier while the Court was deciding Dred Scott's fate. Grier told Taney about his contact with Buchanan and, with the Chief Justice's knowledge, informed the president-elect of the Court's result. The communications between Buchanan and Grier did not constitute a carefully organized cabal on behalf of pro-slavery interests. But they were not innocent exchanges either, and Taney knew it.

Taney claimed that his *Dred Scott* opinion was his final word on the case, and that he would not dignify his critics with responses to their mounting attacks. But the Chief Justice was a proud and determined man and could not completely restrain himself. In September 1858, eighteen months after he had announced the Court's *Dred Scott* decision, Taney wrote a thirty-page addendum to his official opinion. His supplement plowed the furrows of his original opinion more deeply, defending in considerable detail his claim that at the time of the Declaration of Independence the black man had no rights that the white man was obligated to recognize. His additional research was undertaken, he wrote, to put to rest any remaining questions about the judicial authority for his original opinion. He also wanted to clarify any ambiguities about the scope of the decision. He noted, at the outset, that a federal circuit court in Indiana had erroneously allowed an African American whose ancestors were not slaves to bring suit; the *Dred Scott* decision made clear, he wrote, that the entire black race, whether slave or free, was forever degraded and could not, as a matter of right, sue in a federal court.

Citing common law decisions in Great Britain and treaties dating back to the late seventeenth century, Taney reiterated his claim that European nations had always considered blacks inferior under both their domestic laws and the laws of nations. He was comparably dogmatic in asserting that the framers of the Constitution viewed the "ignorant, degraded, savage" blacks imported from Africa as so many packaged commercial goods, treated no differently under the law than "bales of woolen goods or puncheons of rum." He noted, further, that the framers had no intention of undermining their existing social and political institutions by advocating the wholesale emancipation of slaves. At the end of his supplement, Taney wrote defiantly that he had read criticisms of his opinion, but all were "founded upon misrepresentations and perversions" of the points he had made for the Court. "They cannot mislead the judgment of any one who is in search of truth, and will read the opinion; and I have no desire to waste time and throw away arguments upon whose who evidently act upon the principle that the end will justify the means."

Taney's supplement was not added to the Supreme Court's official decision because the Chief Justice did not receive the necessary consent from his judicial colleagues for its inclusion. Taney therefore instructed his chosen biographer, Samuel Tyler, to publish it in his memoirs. The public was first made aware of Taney's supplement when Tyler's biography was published in 1872.

In tracing Taney's prolonged pursuit of vindication for his *Dred Scott* opinion, one might conclude that the Chief Justice thought of nothing else in the aftermath of the disastrous Court decision. But that was not possible for the man who remained Chief Justice of the United States. Only a few months after he had written his supplement, Taney was deeply engaged in two cases with far-reaching implications for the nation that were argued before the Court. Both involved an abolitionist firebrand named Sherman Booth, the Connecticut-born, Yale-educated editor of the Milwaukee *Free Democrat*.

Booth's wilful challenge to federal judicial authority began in 1854 after he had learned that a fugitive slave named Joshua Glover, who had worked for two years in a sawmill outside Racine, Wisconsin, had been arrested and taken to the Milwaukee county jail at the behest of his Missouri owner. Mounting his horse, Booth rode through the streets of the city, stopping at each corner to shout: "Freemen! To the rescue! Slave catchers are in our midst! Be at the courthouse at two o'clock."

Shortly before the crowd assembled, a county court judge issued a writ of habeas corpus for the release of Glover. But U.S. District Judge Andrew Miller, who had authorized Glover's arrest, intervened, persuading the sheriff not to serve the writ. Miller was a native of Pennsylvania, a friend of James Buchanan, and like Buchanan, he believed that the Fugitive Slave Law must be enforced. He had already scheduled a hearing in which he was expected to authorize Glover's return with his owner to Missouri under the provisions of the federal statute. Concerned about the growing assembly of a hostile abolitionist crowd in Milwaukee, Judge Miller postponed the hearing and waited in vain for federal troops to respond to the local U.S. attorney's request for help.

On the evening of March 10, Booth harangued a huge crowd that had converged on the courthouse, denouncing the Fugitive Slave Law and calling for the release of Glover. The mob demanded the prisoner. When Glover was not surrendered, they battered down the jail door and seized him. The liberated prisoner was driven down one of Milwaukee's main streets, his manacled hands raised in triumph, shouting: "Glory! Hallelujah!" He was promptly put on a schooner headed for Canada. For good measure, local authorities arrested and jailed the slaveowner and the federal deputies who had incarcerated Glover, charging them with kidnapping and assault and battery.

Judge Miller again intervened, authorizing the prisoners' release. But he could not control the raging abolitionist sentiment that was sweeping the state of Wisconsin. A month after Glover's release, abolitionists held a convention in Milwaukee (forming a league that was later considered the founding of the Wisconsin Republican Party) and proclaimed a state's right to nullify an unconstitutional federal law. They urged defiance of the Fugitive Slave Law in language reminiscent of Jefferson's Kentucky Resolutions of 1798 (opposing the Alien and Sedition Acts) and the late South Carolina senator John C. Calhoun's southern manifesto. Like Jefferson and Calhoun, they declared that the U.S. Constitution was a compact among the states and entitled an individual state to declare an unconstitutional federal law null and void. Impassioned states' rights advocacy, long the political preserve of the South, had been transported to the northern state of Wisconsin.

A federal commissioner exacerbated the volatile situation by arresting Booth for assisting in the escape of the fugitive slave, Glover. At his hearing, Booth condemned the Fugitive Slave Law and declared that, rather than seeing the writ of habeas corpus and jury trial stricken under the federal statute, he would "prefer to see every Federal officer in Wisconsin hanged to a gallows fifty cubits higher than Haman's." He applied to the Wisconsin Supreme Court for a writ of habeas corpus for his release, arguing that he was unlawfully held since the Fugitive Slave Law was unconstitutional.

With the full court in recess, Associate Justice Abram Smith, an avowed abolitionist, wrote an outspoken states' rights opinion in which he agreed with Booth. Ignoring circuit court opinions by members of the U.S. Supreme Court affirming the constitutionality of the Fugitive Slave Law, Smith asserted a state court's right to nullify the federal statute, which he pronounced unconstitutional. He also issued a warning to the federal government not to interfere with the judicial authority of state courts. Unless the federal government paid heed to his warning, Smith wrote, "I solemnly believe that there will be no peace for the state or the nation, but that agitation, acrimony and hostility will mark our progress, even if we escape a more dread calamity, which I will not even mention."

After Booth was released, federal authorities appealed to the full state supreme court to reconsider Smith's decision. When the Wisconsin Supreme Court affirmed Smith's nullification decision, abolitionists across the country rejoiced. Massachusetts senator Charles Sumner congratulated Booth's attorney and the state of Wisconsin for taking the lead in the abolitionists' cause. The *New York Tribune*, while lamenting "the virus of a National Bench" on the slavery issue, applauded "a most refreshing example of independence of this influence" in the Wisconsin Supreme Court.

While an appeal of the Wisconsin decision to the U.S. Supreme Court was pending, a resolute U.S. District Court Judge Miller demanded that a federal grand jury indict the fugitive slave's rescuers. Otherwise, said the judge, the rule of law would be replaced by brute force. Dutifully, the grand jury complied with the judge's demand, and Booth, among others, was arrested for a second time. He was then seriously ill but, when his health improved, was again indicted. With prosecutorial zeal, Judge Miller instructed the jury at Booth's trial to find him guilty. Do not commit "moral perjury" by ignoring the clear dictates of the federal statute, he counseled. The jury followed the judge's lead and convicted Booth. Miller sentenced the defendant to a month in jail and fined him $1,000 plus court costs.

Since there was no federal prison facility in Wisconsin, Booth was incarcerated in the Milwaukee county jail. For a second time, he applied for a writ of habeas corpus to the Wisconsin Supreme Court. And the state supreme court, again, issued the writ, declaring that Booth was unlawfully held and ordering his release.

Judge Miller was, by then, the subject of scathing criticism around the state; he was labeled "a disgrace," "a tyrant," and "an old Granny and a miserable Doughface." Unbowed, Miller defended his decision in a statement issued in his courtroom. But his judicial resources in the case were exhausted. The federal government's effort to quell the abolitionist revolt in the courts of Wisconsin was transferred to the Attorney General in Washington, who prepared the appeal of the state supreme court's decisions to the U.S. Supreme Court.

When the Booth cases* were argued before the Taney Court in January 1859, the justices heard only one side of the argument—that of Attorney General Jeremiah Black defending Booth's arrests and conviction under the Fugitive Slave Law, which he maintained was constitutional. Neither Booth's lawyer nor the state of Wisconsin appeared in the courtroom to contest the federal government's case. By their prior words and

---

* The first Booth case concerned the writ of habeas corpus issued from the Wisconsin Supreme Court after the defendant's initial arrest and incarceration in the Milwaukee county jail; the later case arose from the state supreme court's second writ releasing Booth after a federal jury, at Judge Miller's instruction, convicted the defendant under the provisions of the Fugitive Slave Law.

actions, the defendant and the Wisconsin Supreme Court demonstrated that they did not recognize the jurisdiction of the U.S. Supreme Court to render a final judgment on the issues before them.

Two months later, Chief Justice Taney, speaking for a unanimous Court, resoundingly affirmed federal judicial authority to interpret the nation's laws. In an opinion that was reminiscent of the most forceful nationalistic opinions of Chief Justice Marshall, Taney declared that neither Booth nor the state of Wisconsin had the power under the Constitution to defy the legitimate authority of the federal government. In every significant particular, Taney's opinion in the Booth cases was the very antithesis of his *Dred Scott* ruling. His language was restrained, his tone somber. Where his *Dred Scott* opinion was filled with tendentious arguments, the Chief Justice's *Booth* opinion was carefully reasoned and securely anchored to the text and history of the Constitution. Like his predecessor, Chief Justice Marshall, Taney offered a broad vision of the framers' intentions when they replaced the Articles of Confederation with the Constitution of the United States.

After reviewing the facts of the cases and defiant state court decisions in elaborate detail, Taney posed this basic constitutional question for resolution: Did a state supreme court possess final judicial authority in cases arising under the Constitution and the laws of the United States? "[I]f the Supreme Court of Wisconsin possessed the power it has exercised in relation to offences against the act of Congress in question," Taney wrote, "it necessarily follows that they must have the same judicial authority in relation to any other law of the United States." If that were so, he continued, every federal law—the entire criminal code of the United States, all federal revenue laws, every regulation prohibiting fraud or violence in the various departments of the federal government—would be subject to the final judicial authority of the Wisconsin Supreme Court. And if Wisconsin's highest judicial tribunal could claim that authority, so could the supreme court of every other state.

But the framers of the U.S. Constitution never contemplated or authorized such state autonomy. Wisconsin could properly administer the laws of the state, but never those of the federal government. "[T]he sphere of action appropriated to the United States is as far beyond the reach of the judicial process issued by a State judge or a State court, as if the line of division was traced by landmarks and monuments visible to the eye," Taney wrote. In the Booth cases, he continued, the state supreme court had no more authority to interfere with the enforcement of the Fugitive Slave Law in Wisconsin than it could do so if the defendant had been imprisoned under the same federal statute in Michigan or any other state of the Union. To accept Wisconsin's authority to pass final judgment on a federal statute would undermine the grand constitutional design.

In contrast to his *Dred Scott* opinion, Taney drew his major conclusions from a judicious interpretation of the Constitution. The Constitution was not formed primarily to guard the nation against dangers from abroad, but "to secure union and harmony at home." Based on the painful experience of the failed Articles of Confederation, the framers knew that the individual states must cede substantial powers to the federal government. Otherwise, the general government would not be "strong enough to execute its own laws by its own tribunals, without interruption from a state or State authorities." Denying that necessary power to the federal government, wrote Taney, would inevitably have encouraged "local passions or prejudices" and led to acts of aggression by one state against another. The framers therefore provided for "a common arbiter between them, armed with power enough to protect and guard the rights of all, by appropriate laws, to be carried into execution peacefully by its judicial tribunals."

The authority of the federal courts to superintend the nation's laws was given in "clear, precise, and comprehensive terms," Taney continued. The framers were well aware of the heavy burden that they placed on the Supreme Court of the United States. He noted that they did not leave it to Congress to create the Court by ordinary legislation, for he conceded that the states would not trust the impartiality of a tribunal created by the federal legislature. It was, rather, established by the people of the states when they ratified the Constitution. "So long, therefore, as this Constitution shall endure, this tribunal must exist with it, deciding in the peaceful forms of judicial proceeding the angry and irritating controversies between sovereignties, which in other countries have been determined by the arbitrament of force."

Since Taney had concluded that no state court had the authority to release any prisoner held by authority of the United States, it was not necessary for him to discuss the constitutionality of the Fugitive Slave Law. But in the final paragraph of his opinion, Taney nonetheless cleared up any misunderstanding on the issue that may have been caused by the Wisconsin Supreme Court's decisions. The federal statute, he wrote, was constitutional in all of its provisions. He did not elaborate on that judgment. Instead, he returned to his overarching theme: the need for the Court to retain appellate review of judicial decisions concerning all federal laws. "And if any argument was needed to show the wisdom and necessity of this appellate power," he concluded, "the cases before us sufficiently prove it, and at the same time emphatically call for their exercise."

Taney anticipated that there would be great demand for copies of the *Booth* decision, and ordered that his opinion be published in pamphlet form. But there was no significant demand, and no pamphlet was ever printed. The lack of widespread interest in his *Booth* opinion was due, in large part, to the precipitous drop in the Supreme Court's prestige. In 1859, two years after *Dred Scott*, no one, it seemed, viewed the Court's decisions impartially. Reaction to Taney's opinion divided along predictable political lines. The Wisconsin legislature passed resolutions denouncing the Court's decision as a usurpation of states' rights and a blow to the cause of human liberty.* In defending the *Booth* decision, the Democratic *National Intelligencer* condemned the Wisconsin legislature's action as exposing "the deformity of Nullification."

---

* Attorney General Jeremiah Black, concerned about the rebellious atmosphere in Wisconsin, did not immediately ask the federal district attorney in Milwaukee to seek a court order to rearrest Booth. Federal authorities finally took Booth into custody in March 1860. Still defiant after his jail term had expired, Booth refused to pay his fine and remained locked up in a Milwaukee federal building until he was liberated by a band of abolitionists in the summer of 1860, only to be recaptured a few days later. He was pardoned by President Buchanan shortly before he left office.

That Taney's exemplary *Booth* opinion, one of his finest, was reduced to such a simplistic political calculus was unfortunate. But the Chief Justice was largely to blame. The fact that his conclusion reenforced the loathing that southerners (including Taney) felt for abolitionists did not help. But the problem went deeper. Had Taney's *Dred Scott* opinion demonstrated the judicial discipline and political wisdom of *Booth*, reaction to both important opinions would have been markedly different. And the nation, as well as the Supreme Court, would have been infinitely better served.

After Douglas had narrowly defeated Lincoln to reclaim his Senate seat, the unsuccessful challenger soberly took stock of his personal finances. "I have been on expences so long without earning any thing," Lincoln wrote Norman Judd, the chairman of the state Republican central committee, "that I am absolutely without money now for even household purposes." Politics had taken him away from his lucrative law practice, and he vowed to devote himself in 1859 to earning a living for his family.

But even as Lincoln resumed his daily professional chores, his mind returned again and again to the future of the Republican Party. As the 1860 presidential election approached, he worried that Republicans would repeat their mistake of 1856 when they failed to prevent the split of the anti-slavery vote in the crucial lower northern states between their candidate, John Frémont, and the American Party's nominee, Millard Fillmore. In his private correspondence, Lincoln counseled other Republicans to reject extreme policies that could undermine the party's appeal to the broad spectrum of anti-slavery voters.

When Ohio Republicans adopted a platform that called for repeal of the Fugitive Slave Law, Lincoln warned Ohio governor Salmon P. Chase that the platform, if adopted nationally by the Republicans, would be suicidal. "I have no doubt that if that plank be even *introduced* into the next Republican National convention, it will explode it," he wrote Chase. He also opposed a constitutional amendment proposed by nativist Republicans in Massachusetts that would have prevented naturalized citizens from voting for two years. Having fought against the oppression of blacks, Lincoln wrote, he could hardly approve discrimination against *"white men,* even though born in different lands, and speaking different languages from myself." At the same time, he urged fellow Republicans to build upon the party's anti-slavery platform of 1856 to include a modest protective tariff and federally sponsored internal improvements, policies that were popular throughout the lower northern states.

Although he steadfastly worked to enlarge the Republicans' moderate base, Lincoln never forgot the party's raison d'être—its opposition to the spread of slavery in the territories. Nor did he forget or forgive his perennial nemesis, Senator Douglas, whose commitment to popular sovereignty, Lincoln believed, was an insidious invitation to perpetuate slavery in the North as well as the South. After Douglas published an article in *Harper's Magazine* in which he amended his Freeport Doctrine to allow territorial voters to "control" but not to prohibit slavery, Lincoln publicly attacked Douglas's newest version of popular sovereignty. Under Douglas's theory, he angrily concluded, one man could make a slave of another, and "neither the slave nor anybody else had a right to object."

Lincoln's denunciation of Douglas's article was made in September 1859, in one of a series of speeches that he delivered at the invitation of the state Republican Party in Ohio, where Douglas was already campaigning for Democratic candidates. Though Lincoln and Douglas did not share the same platform, their exchanges effectively resumed their now famous 1858 debates. Lincoln held Douglas primarily responsible for lowering Americans' resistance to the institution of slavery. After Douglas derisively ranked the black below the white man but above the crocodile in the natural order, Lincoln grimly commented that the senator had demoted the black to the subhuman category of brute. When Republicans soundly defeated their Democratic opponents in Ohio's state elections, Lincoln was given part of the credit for the victories.

By the fall of 1859, Lincoln was considered a leader of the Republican Party, not just in Illinois and Ohio but, increasingly, throughout the northern states. The Lincoln-Douglas debates had been widely reported and his virtual tie with the Democrats' leading statesman in the 1858

Senate race naturally elevated his political stature. After campaigning for Ohio Republicans, Lincoln accepted invitations to speak in Iowa, Indiana, Kansas, and Wisconsin. There was even talk, at first limited to a few editors of small-town Illinois newspapers, that Lincoln should be the Republican nominee for president.

Lincoln initially dismissed the idea, saying that he was not qualified for the presidency. After all, he had served only briefly in national office, as a member of the House of Representatives, and neither Lincoln nor anyone else rated the experience as a noteworthy term of public service. Compared to the leading candidates for the Republican nomination, U.S. Senator (and former Governor) William Seward of New York and Ohio governor (and former U.S. senator) Salmon Chase, his credentials were unimpressive. Besides, Lincoln preferred to serve in the Senate and was already considering another campaign against Douglas in 1864.

Slowly, however, a Lincoln presidential movement began to take shape. The first step for Lincoln's incipient candidacy, spearheaded by leaders of the Illinois Republican Party, was to make him the state's favorite son at the Republican Convention. Since Illinois was one of the critical lower northern states (carried by Buchanan in 1856), the block vote of the state's delegates for Lincoln would carry political clout beyond the numerical total. While his backers worked to build consensus for Lincoln in the Illinois delegation, Norman Judd, who was a member of the Republican National Committee, guaranteed that his nomination would be greeted tumultuously—by casting the decisive committee vote to hold the convention in Chicago rather than St. Louis.

For his part, Lincoln quietly promoted his name and moderate positions beyond Illinois's borders, pasting his Senate campaign speeches into a scrapbook in preparation for publication. At the same time, he generously complied with out-of-state requests for his political views. In December 1859, he sent a statement to be read aloud at a Jefferson Day celebration of Boston Republicans in which he declared that Republicans were the true trustees of the libertarian principles of the author of the Declaration of Independence. He accused the pro-slavery Democrats of perverting their Jeffersonian heritage by speaking only in "glittering generalities" that were confined to "superior races."

Lincoln prepared with particular care for the speech that he had been invited to deliver at Henry Ward Beecher's Plymouth Church in Brooklyn, New York, in February 1860. The invitation came from anti-Seward Republicans, including two of the city's leading editors, the *Tribune*'s Horace Greeley and the *Evening Post*'s William Cullen Bryant. When Lincoln arrived in New York City, his sponsors treated him with the elaborate courtesy usually reserved for established national leaders. He stayed at the elegant Astor House and sat for a full-length portrait in the studio of the celebrated photographer Mathew Brady.

After he was informed that he would be speaking at Manhattan's Cooper Union rather than Plymouth Church, Lincoln hastily revised his speech to appeal to a larger, secular audience. On the evening of February 27, a crowd of fifteen hundred New Yorkers turned out to hear him. He wore a new black broadcloth suit for the occasion, for which he had paid $100 to a Springfield tailor. After he mounted the speaker's platform in the hall and was introduced by Bryant, Lincoln delivered a consummate political address, which, overnight, transformed his candidacy from that of parochial favorite son to serious contender for the Republican nomination for president.

His objective was to show that his moderate Republican beliefs offered the best hope of protecting the nation's essential constitutional values. In the first section of his speech, Lincoln provided fresh proof that the majority of the founding fathers had disapproved of slavery and authorized the national legislature to prohibit it in the territories. Drawing on his research of the records of the Constitutional Convention and debates in the early Congresses, Lincoln demonstrated that at least twenty-one of the thirty-nine men who signed the Constitution voted to outlaw slavery, either in support of the Northwest Ordinance, its ratification in the first Congress, or subsequent legislation, such as the Missouri Compromise. By citing the historical record, Lincoln emphasized that he was a *conservative* who wanted to preserve, not uproot, the nation's political principles.

To the feverish talk of secession in the South, Lincoln responded with calm reassurance that the Republican Party would not interfere with the institution of slavery in states where it already existed. In every Republican document, he reminded his audience, his party had pledged to honor the constitutional rights of the southern states to protect slavery within their state borders. But Republicans would go no farther in placating the South's demands and would, he promised resolutely, resist all efforts to permit the spread of slavery. In his conclusion, he implored the crowd: "LET US HAVE FAITH THAT RIGHT MAKES MIGHT; AND IN THAT FAITH, LET US, TO THE END, DARE TO DO OUR DUTY, AS WE UNDERSTAND IT."

During his address, Lincoln was frequently interrupted by applause. At the end, he received a standing ovation, many in the audience waving their hats and handkerchiefs in support of their new hero. Four New York newspapers published Lincoln's entire speech the next day. Greeley, who had only recently counseled Republicans to support Senator Douglas, exulted: "Mr. Lincoln is one of Nature's orators." Later, the Cooper Union speech was printed and reprinted as a party pamphlet by the *Tribune* and other northern newspapers.

The speech "went off passably well," Lincoln modestly wrote Mary. Before returning to Springfield, the homesick Lincoln made a campaign swing by train through New England. He gave speeches in Connecticut and Rhode Island, and in four towns in New Hampshire, though his ostensible purpose for a visit to the Granite State was to spend time with his son, Robert, now a student at Phillips Exeter Academy. At first, Robert's wealthy prep school friends did not know what to make of his "homely" father. But after Lincoln addressed an assembly of five hundred in Exeter, they, like virtually everyone else who heard the candidate throughout his tour of the East, concluded that he was a statesman who could very well be the next president of the United States.

Did Lincoln now have serious presidential ambitions? asked Senator Lyman Trumbull in April. "The taste *is* in my mouth a little," he replied. He was in regular contact with his Illinois supporters, especially Judge David Davis, who acted as his unofficial campaign manager. Together, they devised a strategy for Lincoln's victory at the Republican Convention in Chicago in May. Their most daunting challenge was to deny the nomination on the first ballot to the front-runner, Senator Seward. They knew that the New York senator was a popular and exceedingly gifted politician, but also that he was viewed in some Republican quarters as too radical to carry the lower northern states necessary for election. If uncommitted delegates could be persuaded to withhold their votes from Seward on the first ballot, they concluded, then Lincoln's moderation would make him the ideal compromise candidate.

On May 18, the day that Republicans were scheduled to vote for their presidential nominee, Lincoln waited restlessly in his Springfield law office to hear the telegraphed results. Edward Baker, editor of the Republican *Illinois State Journal*, burst into Lincoln's office to announce that Seward had received 173 1/2 votes on the first ballot, 59 1/2 short of the total necessary for nomination; Lincoln was second, with 102 votes. Lincoln walked over to the telegraph office to receive the second ballot results. Seward still led with 184 1/2 votes, but Lincoln now trailed by only 3 1/2 votes, largely as a result of the wholesale switch to him by the Pennsylvania delegation. For the third ballot, Lincoln moved to the *Journal* office. Although Seward retained most of his voting strength, the other delegates stampeded to Lincoln, whose total after the third roll call was only 1 1/2 votes short of that needed for the nomination. When four Ohio delegates changed their votes from Governor Chase to Lincoln, the nomination was his. Outside the *Journal* office in Springfield, Lincoln accepted congratulations from a swelling crowd of well-wishers and then headed home to tell Mary.

Meanwhile, the Democrats held their convention in Charleston, South Carolina, where the intransigence of delegates from the lower southern states virtually guaranteed the demise of the party. The Alabama delegation introduced a platform that, in reality, was an ultimatum from the states of the Deep South to their fellow Democrats and the nation. It demanded a congressional code protecting slavery in the territories. The northern Democrats countered with a proposal endorsing popular sovereignty. In the interests of party unity, they urged the party to rally behind Senator Douglas. But the frenzied southern delegates were in no mood for compromise. The Alabama delegation walked out, followed by eight other southern states, leaving the Democrats without a nominee.

In June, after Republicans had nominated Lincoln, the northern Democrats met in Baltimore and made Douglas their candidate for the presidency. Meeting in another hall in the same city, southern Democrats chose Vice President John Breckinridge of Kentucky as their nominee. For all intents and purposes, the splintered Democratic Party appeared to have handed the election to the Republicans. "I hesitate to say it," Lincoln wrote Simeon Francis, the former editor of the *Illinois State Journal*, "but it really appears now, as if the success of the Republican ticket is inevitable."*

By tradition, presidential candidates did not actively campaign, but left it to their supporters to stump for them (as Lincoln had done for previous Whig and Republican presidential candidates). Lincoln therefore remained in Springfield during the fall campaign while Seward, Chase, and other prominent members of the Republican Party crisscrossed the northern states on his behalf. In the major cities in the North, the party held massive rallies and parades, often led by "Wide-Awakes," an organization of young Republicans with a penchant for nocturnal torchlight marches and flowing black capes. Fence rails were eagerly bought by Lincoln enthusiasts who wanted to show solidarity with their candidate, the Illinois "rail-splitter." Campaign songs proliferated, including "Honest Abe of the West," which was sung to the melody of "The Star Spangled Banner."

In Springfield, Lincoln was not idle. He patiently sat for photographers and portrait painters and gave scores of interviews to reporters. He also provided autobiographical information to a host of writers, though he would not embellish the facts of his life to suit eager hagiographers. The most successful of the campaign biographies was a thirty-two-page

---

* Republicans had balanced their ticket by nominating Hannibal Hamlin of Maine, a former Democrat, to run as their candidate for vice president.

pamphlet written by John L. Scripps, now an editor at the *Chicago Press and Tribune*, which eventually sold more than a million copies.

A Republican victory was assured, Lincoln believed, so long as he could prevent open warfare among the party's far-flung constituencies. Throughout the campaign, he adamantly refused to make any policy statements that would give any Republican faction, East or West, cause to take issue with him. His studied silence also prevented his opponents from further distorting his positions, though it did not stop persistent and virulent attacks from southern Democrats who called Lincoln "a blood-thirsty tyrant" and railed against his "free love, free Nigger" party.

In the early evening of November 6, Lincoln joined friends at the state Capitol to receive the returns in the general election. Early results relayed from the telegraph office showed that he had carried Illinois and Indiana, and was doing well in all of the western states. Later, after Pennsylvania was securely in Lincoln's column, he walked to Watson's Saloon, where he was welcomed as "Mr. President" and ate a prearranged supper prepared by Republican women. Instead of going home afterward, he circled back to the telegraph office to await the returns from the eastern states. Only at about 2:00 a.m., after he learned that New York had voted decisively for him, was he certain that he had won the presidency.

The final tally showed that Lincoln had received 1,866,452 votes, just under 40 percent of the nationwide total, but still nearly a half million votes more than his nearest challenger, Senator Douglas. And in the electoral college, Lincoln won 180 votes, representing a clean sweep of all of the free states except New Jersey, which gave 4 votes to Lincoln and 3 to Douglas. The southern Democrat, Breckinridge, finished a distant second in the electoral college, with 72 votes. Douglas, who had flouted custom to campaign vigorously, claimed only 12 electoral votes.

Lincoln carefully camouflaged his growing apprehension as secession threats increased in the South with news of his election. He immediately moved into an office in the state Capitol and energetically met with an inexhaustible stream of well-wishers and office-seekers every weekday morning and afternoon. Visitors were surprised to discover that the president-elect was growing a beard. Otherwise, he seemed remarkably unchanged, entertaining them with homespun anecdotes and tall tales. He also begun selecting members of his cabinet, extending the first invitation to Seward to be his Secretary of State.

While cheerfully going about his business, Lincoln refused publicly to express his views on the secessionist danger. The closest he came to giving an opinion on the issue that divided North and South was his insertion of two paragraphs in a speech delivered by Senator Trumbull in which he reiterated his view that slavery was protected in the South under the Constitution. Predictably, this familiar restatement of his position was wildly misinterpreted. The *Boston Courier* said that the statement reflected the president-elect's intention to abandon Republican principles. But the *Washington Constitution* read the same statement to mean that Lincoln had declared war on the South. "This is just as I expected, and just what would happen with any declaration I could make," Lincoln wrote Henry J. Raymond, editor of the *New York Times*.

South Carolina was the first southern state to transform its secessionist rhetoric into action. On November 10, the state's two U.S. senators resigned and most of its federal judges left office soon afterward. A month later, the state legislature scheduled a convention in Charleston in which delegates unanimously voted to secede from the Union. Bands played and cannons boomed their approval. Jubilant crowds danced in the streets of the state Capitol. THE UNION IS DISSOLVED was the banner headline in the *Charleston Mercury*. South Carolina officials lowered the American flag, replacing it with the state's Palmetto flag, and took over all federal buildings, including the post office, the customhouse, and the arsenal. The state militia trained its guns on the last bastion of federal power in the state, the small garrison at Fort Sumter in Charleston Harbor.

Six more southern states soon followed South Carolina's lead, formally declaring that they were no longer members of the United States of America. Even as the nation was breaking up, Lincoln stubbornly believed that moderate Unionists in the South would restore order and reason to the region. He wrote a confidential letter to Alexander Stephens of Georgia, who had served with him in the House of Representatives, pleading his case for the Union. "Do the people of the South really enter-tain fears that a Republican administration would, *directly* or *indirectly*, interfere with their slaves?" he asked. "I wish to assure you, as once a friend, and still, I hope, not an enemy, that there is no cause for such fears." But while giving Stephens that assurance, Lincoln also told the Georgian that he believed that slavery was wrong and should be re-stricted. "You think slavery is right and ought to be extended," he con-tinued, and that was "the only substantial difference between us," but he added that such a disagreement was not cause for the breakup of the Union.

Lame-duck President Buchanan, in one of his final acts of futility, an-nounced that the South had no constitutional right to secede, but con-ceded that the federal government could do nothing about it. Congress worked harder to head off the impending crisis. A blizzard of compromise proposals were offered, each attempting to find a way to keep the south-ern states in the Union. The most promising of them, offered by Senator John Crittenden of Kentucky, extended the Missouri Compromise de-marcation line of slavery westward to the Pacific Ocean. While the Crit-tenden proposal was in committee, congressional Republicans asked for guidance from their leader in Springfield. "Stand firm," Lincoln advised. "The tug has to come, and better now, than any time hereafter." Without Republican support, the Crittenden bill failed to pass.

On the morning of February 11, 1861, Lincoln bid farewell to his friends at Springfield's Great Western Railroad depot. Before entering his private railway car, he sadly told them that he was leaving "not know-ing when, or whether ever, I may return, with a task before me greater than that which rested upon Washington." For the next twelve days, Lincoln and his entourage—which included his private secretary John Nicolay, his political advisers Norman Judd and Judge Davis, as well as Mary and their three boys—traveled slowly through six northern states. In small Ohio towns like Milford and Xenia, and in large eastern cities, Lincoln's deprecating humor delighted the immense crowds that came out to greet him. His purpose, he said, was "that I may see you and that you may see me, and in the arrangement I have the best of the bargain."

At Westfield, New York, he planted a kiss on the cheek of eleven-year-old Grace Bedell, who had written him a letter during the presidential campaign urging him to grow a beard. Interspersed with his lighthearted banter, Lincoln repeatedly promised to preserve the Union—and that meant "every star and stripe of the glorious flag." To achieve that overriding goal, he told the New Jersey legislature in Trenton, "[i]t may be necessary to put the foot down firmly."

As Lincoln's train wound its way through Pennsylvania toward Washington, Allan Pinkerton, the head of the Pinkerton National Detective Agency, received a tip that a small band of southern sympathizers planned to assassinate the president-elect when he changed trains in Baltimore. The detective recommended that Lincoln alter his schedule so that he would pass through Baltimore incognito late at night. At first, Lincoln refused. But after Senator Seward's son, the senator himself, and General Winfield Scott all advised him that the threat was credible, he agreed to follow Pinkerton's plan. At 3:30 a.m. on February 22, Lincoln, wearing a soft felt hat and a large overcoat draped loosely over his shoulders, changed trains in Baltimore unnoticed and arrived in Washington two and a half hours later. After a correspondent for the *New York Times* incorrectly reported that Lincoln had worn a disguise that included a Scotch plaid hat and long military coat, cartoons mercilessly ridiculed him, showing a silly-looking Lincoln clad in tam and kilt. Lincoln regretted that he had taken the threat (never proven) seriously, but he could do nothing to erase the perception of his ignoble entry into the nation's capital.

Once he had settled into his suite at the Willard Hotel, he concentrated on completing his cabinet selections. In addition to Seward, Lincoln had named Edward Bates of Missouri to serve as Attorney General, and Montgomery Blair, the lawyer who had argued Dred Scott's case before the Supreme Court, to be Postmaster General. The most critical remaining appointment was that of Secretary of the Treasury. Lincoln had already discussed the post with Ohio governor Salmon Chase. But Seward strenuously objected to a Chase appointment, hoping to keep his Republican rival outside the administration. When Lincoln insisted on

Chase, Seward withdrew his acceptance to serve in the cabinet, confident that the president-elect needed him more than the Ohio governor. But Lincoln calmly sent word to Seward that, while he preferred the New Yorker, he was prepared to appoint another man in his place. Only hours before Lincoln was to take office, he tactfully asked Seward to reconsider his decision to withdraw from the cabinet, and he did.

By March 4, the day of Lincoln's inauguration, seven states had seceded from the Union and formed the Confederate States of America. With sharpshooters stationed atop every building along the inaugural route, Lincoln and Buchanan left the Willard at noon to ride together in an open carriage down Pennsylvania Avenue to the Capitol. The two men were escorted to a specially built platform at the east portico for the ceremony.

Lincoln had worked laboriously on his inaugural address, determined to be firm but conciliatory toward the South. He insisted that the southern states had no constitutional right to secede, because the Union was perpetual and could not be broken up without the consent of all the states. With the Chief Justice seated nearby, he again attacked the *Dred Scott* decision, suggesting that the Taney Court would not have the final word on the issue of slavery: "[T]he candid citizen must confess that if the policy of the government on vital questions affecting the whole people is to be irrevocably fixed by decisions of the Supreme Court the instant they are made in ordinary litigation between parties in personal actions, the people will have ceased to be their own rulers, having, to that extent, practically resigned their government into the hands of that eminent tribunal." He also vowed to protect federal government property during the crisis, but promised that the Union would not initiate hostilities against the states that had seceded. "In *your* hands, my dissatisfied fellow countrymen, and not in *mine*, is the momentous issue of civil war," he stressed.

Appealing directly to the South, he added, "We are not enemies, but friends," putting a more positive emphasis on the words that he had earlier written to Alexander Stephens (who, by this time, had agreed to serve as the provisional vice president of the Confederacy). He concluded plaintively: "We must not be enemies. Though passion may have strained, it must not break our bonds of affection. The mystic chords of memory, stretching from every battlefield, and patriot grave, to every living heart and hearthstone, all over this broad land, will yet swell the chorus of the Union, when again touched, as surely they will be, by the better angels of our nature."

And then he took the oath of office from the author of the *Dred Scott* decision, Chief Justice Roger B. Taney.

Chapter Six

"ALL THE LAWS BUT ONE"

In 1860, while Lincoln was successfully running for president, Taney remained in the nation's capital, cared for by his unmarried daughter, Ellen, in their modest residence on Indiana Avenue. The Chief Justice suffered an attack of pneumonia early in the year and later compounded his health problems by slipping on the marble pavement at the entrance of the Capitol. His extended absences from Court sessions stirred speculation that resignation from the office that he had held for twenty-four years was imminent. But the eighty-three-year-old Taney quickly quelled the rumors, saying that duty required him to continue his public service.

He eagerly read newspaper reports of the presidential campaign but refused to reveal his preference in public, even after supporters of Senator Douglas claimed, incorrectly, that Taney favored their candidate. In private, Taney supported the southern Democrat, John Breckinridge, as did most of his friends in Baltimore. He did not, however, think Breckinridge would win, largely because the southern states were split among the two Democratic candidates, Breckinridge and Douglas, and the Constitutional Union Party candidate, John Bell of Tennessee. As a result, Taney renewed his gloomy prediction of 1856 that the southern states would continue to suffer under the tyranny of the more powerful and populous northern states unless they united in common purpose, which he doubted, to secede peacefully from the Union.

There is no written record of Taney's opinion of the Republican candidate, Abraham Lincoln, but he could not have been favorably disposed toward the one presidential candidate who denounced his *Dred Scott* opinion and repeatedly charged that the Chief Justice was a conspirator in a national pro-slavery plot. After Lincoln was elected, Taney feared the worst—that the Republican's election would provoke slaves throughout the southern states to rebel against their masters. That did not happen, but Taney nonetheless remained pessimistic about the prospects of a continued peaceful Union.

In an isolated piece of good news, Taney was informed that the justices could move in December from their basement home in the Capitol to the vacated Senate chambers immediately above their old courtroom (the Senate was relocated in the new north wing of the Capitol). The Court's change of residence was long overdue, grumbled Justice Catron, who blamed the dark, dank basement quarters for the bad health of many of the justices.* Finally, the justices occupied an ornate courtroom appropriate for the highest tribunal in the nation. An elegant chandelier was suspended from the ceiling and Ionic columns of marble formed a colonnade across the eastern wall. Spectators sat on red velvet cushions and could admire busts of former Chief Justices that were arranged around the walls. For the first time, the justices had a proper robing room and a law library, which filled the space of the old courtroom.

But the commodious new surroundings did nothing to alter the pervasively melancholy atmosphere in the courtroom. At the conclusion of his argument during the December term, Maryland's Reverdy Johnson condemned the secessionist movement in the South and gravely predicted that the Court's session might be the last in which the justices interpreted a Constitution obeyed by all. Another advocate, George Paschal of Texas, announced at the conclusion of his argument that the

---

* Besides Taney, Justices Catron, Grier, and McLean had suffered through prolonged periods of sickness. A fifth Justice, Daniel, had died the previous July after a long illness.

nation was "on the brink of another revolution" and that, regrettably, his state would probably not recognize the jurisdiction of the Supreme Court by the time the justices had rendered their decision in his case.

The Justices did not need to be reminded of the perilous state of the Union. Two members of the Court, John Campbell and Samuel Nelson, took it upon themselves to serve as intermediaries between the outgoing Buchanan administration and representatives of the secessionist states. Campbell played a particularly active role in seeking a compromise to head off an irreparable split between the North and South. Though a states' rights Alabamian, Campbell had never been sympathetic to the extreme pro-slavery views of the secessionists; he had been briefly considered as a compromise candidate for the presidency at the Democrats' national convention in Charleston.

In December 1860, Campbell thought that a workable compromise between the sections was still possible, based upon a permanent settlement of the slavery issue. He favored a solution drawn roughly along the lines of the proposal introduced by Senator Crittenden of Kentucky, extending the Missouri Compromise's line westward, but was willing to consider other possibilities. After failing to arrange a meeting directly with President Buchanan, Campbell discussed his ideas with Buchanan's Secretary of State, Jeremiah Black, and later with Lincoln's appointed successor to Black, William Seward.

On the last day of the Court's term, one week after Lincoln's inauguration, Chief Justice Taney announced the unanimous Court decision in an important fugitive slave case that, under ordinary circumstances, would have captured the attention of the entire nation. But by the second week in March 1861, every major federal government decision, whether judicial, legislative, or executive, was viewed in partisan sectional terms, including Taney's Fugitive Slave Law opinion in *Kentucky v. Dennison*.

The dispute had begun after a slave girl held in Louisville, Kentucky, had been permitted to visit her mother, who lived in Virginia. The slave's owner planned to travel to Virginia and agreed to take his slave with him, stopping in Ohio before boarding a train to their ultimate destination. In Ohio, the slave was seized by abolitionists and taken into a state court, where the judge declared her free.

Kentucky's governor, Beriah Magoffin, demanded that the governor of Ohio, William Dennison, surrender Willis Lago, a "free man of color," who had been indicted by a county grand jury in Kentucky for helping the slave girl to escape in violation of the state's law. Governor Dennison, who had promised during his election campaign never to return a fugitive slave to a southern state, did not immediately respond to his fellow governor's demand. Eventually, on the advice of Ohio's attorney general, Dennison rejected the demand, arguing that the charge against Lago was not a felony under Ohio law, the common law applicable at the time the Constitution was adopted, or the laws of civilized nations. Lago therefore had not committed a serious crime that required his extradition. Governor Magoffin reacted angrily to Dennison's rebuff, reminding him that "the Constitution was the work of slaveholders; that their wisdom, moderation, and prudence gave it to us," and that "[n]on-slaveholding states were the exception, not the rule."

Kentucky took the case directly to the U.S. Supreme Court, which agreed with the petitioner that it had original jurisdiction since a state was party to the lawsuit. In his opinion for the Court, Chief Justice Taney first lectured Ohio's governor on the legal wrong that he had committed. The applicable law, he wrote, was that of the demanding state, and Kentucky's statutes made assisting the escape of a slave a felony. He also read from the Fugitive Slave Law of 1793, which said that it was the duty of the executive authority of a state to surrender fugitives from justice. But then, just as he appeared to have handed Kentucky a victory, Taney snatched it away. He drew a distinction between Congress's authorization of a state officer to perform a duty and forcing him to do so. Under the federal statute, Governor Dennison had a duty to extradite Lago, but it did not follow, wrote Taney, "that he may be coerced, or punished for his refusal."

When Taney's predecessor, John Marshall, had performed a similar sleight-of-hand exercise in his famous *Marbury v. Madison* opinion, even Marshall's arch enemies, the Jeffersonian Republicans, did not complain. Like Taney in his *Dennison* opinion, Marshall in *Marbury* had delivered a lecture—in that case to President Jefferson and his Secretary of State, James Madison, on their constitutional duty to deliver a judicial commission to William Marbury, a last-minute appointee of the lame-duck Federalist president, John Adams. But having made the case for Marbury, Chief Justice Marshall then refused to order Madison to deliver the commission, conceding that the Court lacked jurisdiction to do so. Marshall, therefore, did not risk a confrontation with the president, his Secretary of State, or the Republican-controlled Congress, since he did not force the Jefferson administration to do anything.

Taney appeared to emulate Marshall's effort in *Marbury*, first lecturing the anti-slavery Ohio governor on his illegal action but admitting, alas, that the technicalities of the law prevented the Court from enforcing it. But his opinion, unlike Marshall's in *Marbury*, was attacked by his political enemies as well as his friends. The *New York Evening Post* labeled it "judicial twaddle," a hopelessly inept effort by the author of the Court's despised *Dred Scott* opinion. The southern press was not much kinder, expressing bewilderment at the impotence of the Supreme Court to enforce the Fugitive Slave Law.

With the nation edging toward civil war, Taney's opinion in *Dennison* appeared to acknowledge the limited power of the Supreme Court to influence major events. It seemed that Taney, the pragmatic Chief Justice of the pre–*Dred Scott* Court, had returned. But just three months later, Taney attempted once again, as he had in *Dred Scott*, to wield his judicial power to affect the course of the nation's history. This time, he directly challenged the constitutional authority of the beleaguered wartime president, Abraham Lincoln.

The day after his inauguration, Lincoln received a bleak report from Major Robert Anderson, commander of the small federal garrison at Fort Sumter in Charleston Harbor. The major would need 20,000 additional soldiers to defend the fort. Without reinforcements, Anderson warned, the fort would have to be surrendered to Confederate troops in six weeks unless food was sent to his men.

Lincoln was plagued by indecision. If he did not respond to Major

Anderson's request, Fort Sumter, one of the last federal military outposts in the lower South, would be lost to the Confederacy without a shot being fired. The defeat would be a devastating symbolic blow to the authority of the federal government. But if the president forced the issue, sending men and supplies through the inevitable barrage of Confederate cannonfire, then the civil war that he hoped to avoid would surely follow.

Lincoln's cabinet was split on the issue. Secretary of State Seward recommended that the Union give up the fort, which he did not think could be successfully defended. Seward also had political reasons for taking this position; unknown to Lincoln, he had secretly assured Justice Campbell that Fort Sumter would be surrendered. Salmon Chase, Lincoln's Secretary of the Treasury, took the other side of the argument, supporting Major Anderson's request for reinforcements and provisions, so long as it could be done without starting a war. Postmaster General Montgomery Blair was even more insistent than Chase. Prompt reinforcements for Fort Sumter were necessary, he said, to "vindicate the hardy courage of the North and the determination of the people and their President to maintain the authority of the Government."

On April 6, Lincoln sent a messenger to inform the South Carolina governor, Francis Pickens, that a fleet would sail from New York with provisions for the soldiers at Fort Sumter, but that the fresh troops carried in frigates accompanying the unarmed supply ships would not attempt to reinforce the garrison unless they were fired upon. By this action, Lincoln wanted to convey the peaceful intentions of his administration. At the same time, he made clear that he would not willingly surrender the federal fort.

At 4:30 a.m. on April 12, General Pierre G. T. Beauregard, commander of the Confederate troops in Charleston, gave the Confederacy's answer to the president, ordering more than 4,000 rounds of mortar and cannon shots and shells to rain down on Fort Sumter. Gale-force winds prevented the Union's task force from reaching the fort during the bombardment. Thirty-three hours later, Major Anderson surrendered. The war had begun.

Lincoln issued a proclamation on April 15 calling for 75,000 militiamen to put down the insurrection in the seven states of the lower South, which was "too powerful to be suppressed by the ordinary course of judicial proceedings." From the Midwest to New England, exuberant recruits responded to the president's call to arms. Volunteers almost instantly filled Ohio's quota of thirteen regiments, wrote Governor Dennison, but "without seriously repressing the ardor of the people, I can hardly stop short of twenty." Two of Massachusetts's regiments were on the march forty-eight hours after Lincoln's proclamation, the state's governor reported, and two more would be headed south by the end of the week.

But the euphoric response to Lincoln's proclamation in the North was balanced, ominously, by the negative reaction from the eight states of the upper South. Both Lincoln and Confederate president Jefferson Davis were aware that these eight states could determine the outcome of the conflict. If they joined the cause of the seven states of the lower South, the Confederacy's ability to wage war would increase exponentially: its population would more than double and its manufacturing capacity triple. Within weeks of the president's proclamation, four of those states—Arkansas, North Carolina, Tennessee, and Virginia—announced their intention to join the Confederacy.

The secession of Virginia was particularly damaging to the Union. It was the most populous state in the South, and its manufacturing capacity was almost as great as that of the original seven states of the Confederacy combined. Virginia also offered the South superb military leadership. After declining to lead the Union forces, General Robert E. Lee, scion of one of Virginia's first families and a career Army man (second in his 1829 class at West Point and a hero of the Mexican War), left the U.S. Army and, in a matter of weeks, was appointed commander of Virginia's military forces.

The number of slaves and slaveowners in the four remaining states of the upper South—Delaware, Kentucky, Maryland, and Missouri—was significantly less than in any of the states that had seceded. This fact did not prevent the governors of two of the states—Kentucky and Missouri—from defiantly rejecting the president's request for troops. Governor Magoffin proclaimed, "Kentucky will furnish no troops for the wicked purpose of subduing her sister Southern states." Missouri's governor, Claiborne Jackson, denounced Lincoln's call for troops as "illegal, unconstitutional, and revolutionary in its object, inhuman and diabolical." Fortunately for the North, the gubernatorial rhetoric did not persuade the legislatures of Kentucky or Missouri to vote for secession. The third border state, Delaware, was never seriously tempted to join the Confederacy; its governor did not overtly respond to Lincoln's call for troops but quietly allowed volunteers to join the Union forces.

Maryland posed a special problem for Lincoln and the Union. The state surrounded the nation's capital on three sides (Virginia was on the fourth). The only railroad access to Washington from the North was through Baltimore, which meant that the Union troops expected to defend the District of Columbia would be transported through that city. Telegraph lines linking the federal government with the northern states also ran through the state.

But Maryland was by no means secure for the Union. It had voted for the southern Democrat, Breckinridge, in the 1860 presidential election, and its legislature was controlled by Democrats sympathetic to the South. The white population of the tobacco-rich southern region as well as that along the Chesapeake Bay's eastern shore was slave-dependent and drawn to the Confederacy. The northern and western sections of the state, where there were virtually no slaves, were loyal to the Union. Baltimore, which contained a third of the state's population, was divided between Union and southern sympathizers. The Confederate flag was proudly displayed in front of many of Baltimore's buildings and private residences. The governor of the state, Thomas Hicks, was a fainthearted Union loyalist, but Baltimore's mayor and police chief supported the Confederacy.

Aware of the rising tension in Baltimore, Governor Hicks and Baltimore's mayor, George William Brown, sent a telegram to Lincoln urging him not to send Union troops through the city. The next day, April 19, the Massachusetts 6th Regiment arrived at the railroad station in the eastern section of Baltimore and proceeded to the depot on other side of the city, where their connecting train waited to transport them to Washington to defend the nation's capital. In transit, the Union troops were attacked by a mob of southern sympathizers who hurled stones and pavement bricks and fired pistols at the young recruits. Inexperienced and frightened, the troops in the rear sections returned the mob's fire. The deadly toll, four members of the 6th Regiment and twelve civilians, were the first fatalities of the war. That night a reluctant Governor Hicks, at the urging of Mayor Brown and the Baltimore police, authorized the destruction of railroad bridges north of the city to prevent further entry into the city by Union troops.

After the bloodshed, Lincoln agreed to a temporary detour of Union troops around Baltimore. A few days later, a committee from Baltimore met with the president and ratcheted up their demands: no Union troops should be permitted to move throughout the state. Lincoln refused. "You would have me break my oath and surrender the Government without a blow," he replied sternly. "There is no Washington in that—no Jackson in that—no manhood nor honor in that." He reminded them that Union soldiers were neither birds who could fly over Maryland nor moles who could burrow underground. Military forces from the North therefore would continue to be transported through the state to defend the Union. "Go home and tell your people that if they will not attack us, we will not attack them; but if they do attack us, we will return it, and that severely."

Lincoln's brave talk was mostly bluff. In fact, there were no Union troops in a position to deliver severe blows to secessionists in Maryland or anywhere else. Only one fully equipped military unit, the shaken Massachusetts 6th, had arrived in Washington. Anticipating an imminent Confederate attack on the capital from Virginia's militia or Maryland secessionists, Winfield Scott, General of the U.S. Army, ordered sandbags and barricades to protect government buildings.

Lincoln peered anxiously through the northern windows of the White House, waiting in vain to see the distant outline of ships with reinforcements sailing down the Potomac. "Why don't they come?" the frustrated president asked. "I don't believe there is any North," he told officers and wounded men of Massachusetts 6th Regiment. "The [New York] Seventh Regiment is a myth. Rhode Island is not known in our geography any more. *You* are the only Northern realities."

Maryland remained dangerously volatile. Secessionists in northern Maryland destroyed railroad bridges between Washington and the North and cut telegraph lines. The state legislature, dominated by southern sympathizers, was scheduled to meet in Frederick on April 26. Anticipating a secessionist vote, General Scott recommended to the president that he be given the authority to arrest secessionist politicians in advance. Lincoln declined to give the order. If Maryland voted to secede, he told Scott, he would act decisively to put down the rebellion with "the bombardment of their cities—and of course the suspension of habeas corpus." Those drastic measures were not immediately necessary. The legislature did not vote to secede. Meanwhile, northern troops managed to filter into the capital in increasing numbers by a circuitous route, first ferrying down Chesapeake Bay to Annapolis, then boarding trains to Washington.

But the threat of sabotage in Maryland persisted and, as a result, Lincoln suspended the ancient writ of habeas corpus for the critical area between Philadelphia and Washington. The order allowed military commanders to arrest suspected secessionists and imprison them indefinitely without an indictment, judicial hearing, or trial. One of the men incarcerated by Union soldiers was John Merryman, a wealthy landowner, state legislator, and cavalry officer from Cockneysville, Maryland, who was accused of burning railroad bridges and destroying telegraph wires in northern Maryland after the April 19 Baltimore riot. Merryman was seized in his bedroom at 2:00 a.m. on May 25 and imprisoned at Fort McHenry in Baltimore Harbor later that morning.

At Fort McHenry, Merryman was given immediate access to his lawyers, who drafted a petition for a writ of habeas corpus demanding that the prisoner be brought before a civilian court to hear the specific charges against him. The petition was delivered to Chief Justice Taney on the same day that Merryman had been imprisoned. The next day, Taney signed the writ ordering General George Cadwalader, commander of military forces at Fort McHenry, to appear before him and deliver Merryman to the federal circuit courtroom in Baltimore at eleven o'clock on the morning of May 27.

The excited gaggle of newspaper reporters that gathered on the 27th at Baltimore's Masonic Hall, where the circuit court convened, anticipated a dramatic confrontation between Taney and Cadwalader. The wizened Chief Justice, who had made a special trip to Baltimore to hear Merryman's case, took his place on the bench at the appointed hour. But neither General Cadwalader nor Merryman showed up. Instead, Cadwalader sent his aide-de-camp, a Colonel Lee, resplendent in full military uniform complete with bright red sash and sword at his side.

The colonel first apologized to Taney for General Cadwalader's absence, which, he said, was unavoidable because of pressing military business at Fort McHenry. He then read aloud a statement from Cadwalader (who was himself a lawyer and the brother of a federal judge) in which the commander made the military case for Merryman's incarceration. The prisoner was "charged with various acts of treason, and with being publicly associated with, and holding a commission as lieutenant in a company having possession of arms belonging to the United States, and avowing his purpose of armed hostility to the Government." Cadwalader said that his action had been authorized by President Lincoln, who had suspended the writ of habeas corpus to protect the public safety. He admitted that he must execute his responsibility with "judgment and discretion," but he nevertheless was instructed that "in times of civil strife, errors, if any, should be on the side of safety of the country."

Cadwalader next offered conciliatory words but, at the same time, admonished Taney for forcing the confrontation: "He [Cadwalader] most respectfully submits for your consideration that those who should co-operate in the present trying and painful position in which our country is placed, should not, by reason of any unnecessary want of confidence in each other, increase our embarrassments." Finally, the general asked for a postponement of the proceeding until he could receive further instructions from the president—a signal that General Cadwalader expected to take his orders from Lincoln, not the Chief Justice.

Taney did not respond to Cadwalader's statement nor did he ask if the government planned to have counsel argue its constitutional position. He appeared to be marking time, impatiently, until he could bring the session to a close. Merryman's counsel formally asked Colonel Lee if he had produced the body of John Merryman, as required by the writ of habeas corpus. No, Lee replied.

The Chief Justice immediately announced his decision: "General Cadwalader was commanded to produce the body of Mr. Merryman before me this morning, that the case might be heard, and the petitioner either be remanded to custody, or set at liberty, if held on insufficient grounds, but he has acted in disobedience to the writ." He then issued a second writ addressed to General Cadwalader, directing him to appear before the Chief Justice at twelve noon the following day to show cause why he should not be held in contempt of court.

News of Taney's latest order to General Cadwalader spread quickly through the streets of Baltimore. It was anxiously reported that Maryland's native son, Chief Justice Taney, was determined to preserve the civil liberties of the state's citizens even when faced with the awesome power of the U.S. military and that of the nation's chief executive, President Lincoln. Taney himself seemed to have been swept up in the drama. The next day, walking to court leaning on the arm of his grandson, Taney Campbell, the Chief Justice remarked that he might be imprisoned in Fort McHenry by nightfall, but nothing would stop him from doing his duty.

More than two thousand people milled outside Baltimore's Masonic Hall at noon on May 28 awaiting reports on the high-stakes chess match between Taney and the U.S. military taking place in the packed courtroom. Taney asked the marshal, Washington Bonifant, if he had delivered his written order to General Cadwalader. Bonifant handed the court clerk a folded piece of paper with his written answer. The marshal reported that he had tried to serve the writ, but had been detained at the outer gate of Fort McHenry. He sent in his name but had been told that there was no answer.

Taney anticipated Cadwalader's rebuff and had prepared a written response. He had issued his order directing the general to appear in the federal courtroom, he said, because John Merryman was illegally detained in Fort McHenry. Taking direct aim at Lincoln, Taney declared that "[t]he President, under the Constitution and laws of the United States, cannot suspend the privilege of the writ of *habeas corpus*, nor authorize any military officer to do so." He also condemned General Cadwalader for failing to perform his duty. Since Merryman was not a member of the U.S. military subject to the laws of war, Cadwalader was obligated "to deliver him over immediately to the civil authority, to be dealt with according to law."

After reading his short written statement, Taney spoke emotionally on the disrespect for the law that he believed had been shown by General Cadwalader. He observed that the marshal, having been prevented from serving legal papers to the commander at Fort McHenry, could have summoned a posse to help him perform his official duty. But such action would have been futile, Taney added ruefully, since any posse would have been repelled by a superior military force. He wished that the general were before him, he continued, so that he could inflict just punishment—a hefty fine and Cadwalader's imprisonment. Under the unfortunate circumstances, he conceded that his only option was to give the reasons for his judgment in a full opinion. He would then "report them with these proceedings to the President of the United States, and call upon him to perform his constitutional duty to enforce the laws. In other words, to enforce the process of this Court."

"Sensation," wrote the court reporter, describing the reaction of the audience after Taney had completed his extemporaneous remarks. On his return to the home of his married daughter, Anne Campbell, after the court session, Taney was congratulated by scores of well-wishers. One of them was Mayor George William Brown. "Mr. Brown, I am an old man, a very old man," Taney responded, "but perhaps I was preserved for this occasion." Brown replied, "Sir, I thank God that you were." Taney told the mayor that he thought the danger of his imprisonment had passed but predicted, accurately as it turned out, that Brown himself would be incarcerated.

The Baltimore newspapers, as well as those from the secessionist states, agreed with the mayor that Taney had acted with both courage and honor. Predictably, the northern press condemned the Chief Justice as zealously as southern sympathizers praised him. The *New York Tribune* commended General Cadwalader for his "rebuke to the hoary apologist for crime." And a reporter for the *New York Times* wrote that Taney's purpose was "to bring on a collision between the judicial and military departments of the government, and if possible to throw the weight of the judiciary against the United States and in favor of the rebels." Such a traitorous design was not surprising, the *Times* reporter added, since Taney was at heart a rebel who had expressed the wish "that Virginians would wade to their waists in northern blood."

After issuing his decree to Cadwalader on the 28th, Taney began writing the judicial opinion that he had promised to send to President Lincoln for immediate action. As was his habit, he reworked the opinion over several drafts to make his points with the utmost force and clarity. When he was finished, Taney wrote at the top of the first page that the case was "Before the Chief Justice of the Supreme Court of the United States at Chambers," in an obvious effort to call attention to the authority of his high office, though, in fact, he was acting in his capacity as a circuit court judge.

At the outset of his opinion, Taney expressed bewilderment that General Cadwalader had claimed that the writ of habeas corpus could be suspended by President Lincoln. "I certainly listened to it [Cadwalader's claim] with some surprise, for I had supposed it to be one of those points of constitutional law upon which there was no difference of opinion, and that it was admitted on all hands, that the privilege of the writ could not be suspended, except by act of congress." The clause in the Constitution providing for the suspension of the writ,* he noted, was placed in the ar-

---

* Article I, section 9, provides that "The privilege of the writ of habeas corpus shall not be suspended, unless when in cases of rebellion or invasion the public safety may require it."

ticle which dealt with the authority of Congress, not the president. Congress's prerogative to suspend the writ, he continued, had been recognized by President Thomas Jefferson when he sought to bring Aaron Burr to justice in 1806 after he had accused the former vice president of heading a conspiracy against the United States. And Jefferson's view that Congress alone possessed the power to suspend the writ was reiterated by Chief Justice Marshall in an opinion dealing with the legal claims of two other citizens who had been accused of participating in the Burr conspiracy.

Taney next addressed the president's constitutional authority under Article II, and looked for any textual justification for the broad power that Lincoln had claimed. "But there is not a word in it that can furnish the slightest ground to justify the exercise of the power," he wrote. "The short term for which he is elected, and the narrow limits to which his power is confined, show the jealousy and apprehension of future danger which the framers of the Constitution felt in relation to that department of the government, and how carefully they withheld from it many of the powers belonging to the executive branch of the English government which were considered as dangerous to the liberty of the subject." Curiously, Taney expressed no concern about the even shorter term of office of members of the House of Representatives, whose role in suspending the writ he readily conceded.

The Chief Justice acknowledged that the Constitution made the president commander in chief of the U.S. Army and Navy and of the militia. But he described this authority as largely ministerial and, in any case, severely circumscribed by Congress and the states. Congress was responsible for appropriations for the armed forces, Taney noted, and the states controlled the appointment of officers of the militia. Taney then listed important civil duties beyond the authority of the president. He could not appoint ordinary officers of government or make a treaty with a foreign nation or Indian tribe, without the advice and consent of the Senate, and could not appoint even inferior officers, unless he was authorized by Congress to do so. He could not arrest anyone charged with a crime against the United States. Nor could he deprive any person of life, liberty, or property without due process of law—a judicial function,

Taney emphasized. The only power left to the president in protecting due process, he added, was to see "that the laws shall be faithfully executed."

If military officers like General Cadwalader, under instruction from Lincoln, could deprive citizens of their civil liberties "upon any pretext or under any circumstances," wrote Taney, "the people of the United States are no longer living under a government of laws, but every citizen holds life, liberty and property at the will and pleasure of the army officer in whose military district he may happen to be found." His duty, Taney concluded, "was too plain to be mistaken." He directed the clerk of the court to send a copy of his opinion, under seal, to President Lincoln. "It will then remain for that high officer, in fulfilment of his constitutional obligation to 'take care that the laws be faithfully executed,' to determine what measure he will take to cause the civil process of the United States to be respected and enforced."

The certitude with which Taney marched toward his conclusion in his *Merryman* opinion was reminiscent of some of his best opinions (*Booth,* for example) and his worst (*Dred Scott*). The Chief Justice suggested that the basic constitutional issue—whether Lincoln had the authority to suspend the writ of habeas corpus—was settled beyond debate. Lincoln had acted illegally, period. Every source that Taney consulted on the issue—constitutional text, history, Court precedent, treatise, the common law roots of the privilege in Great Britain (which he explored in considerable detail)—unerringly supported his position.

Taney's *Merryman* opinion proved that the Chief Justice, well into the ninth decade of his life, was still capable of writing a formidable piece of judicial advocacy. He began with the premise, which he deemed irrefutable, that the framers had intended to give the exclusive authority to suspend the writ of habeas corpus to Congress. His interpretation, he noted, was supported by two of his most illustrious predecessors on the Court, Chief Justice Marshall and Justice Joseph Story (in his treatise on constitutional law).

To achieve his goal of proving that Congress alone could suspend the writ, Taney systematically reduced the president's constitutional powers to Lilliputian proportions. Here Taney displayed the artistry of a partisan trial lawyer rather than the detachment of a judge. His interpretation was starkly at odds with Taney's own reading of presidential power when he had been President Jackson's Attorney General. In defending Jackson's broad constitutional powers in the Bank War, Attorney General Taney discovered deep wells of presidential authority, totally independent of both Congress and the Supreme Court. And Chief Justice Taney, in an earlier judicial opinion that raised an issue much closer to Lincoln's plight in 1861, declared that the governor of Rhode Island could use martial law to put down an armed insurrection. The power to do so, Taney wrote in words equally applicable to the president of the United States, "is essential to the existence of every government, essential to the preservation of order and free institutions, and is necessary to the State of this Union as to any other government."

No wartime U.S. president has ever accepted the impotent constitutional role that Taney assigned to Lincoln. And even in peacetime, presidents have interpreted their powers liberally. Jefferson boasted that he exercised extremely limited executive authority, but nonetheless he unilaterally sent ships to the North African coast to protect the nation's interests against marauding Barbary pirates. And it was the same Jefferson who completed negotiations for the Louisiana Purchase, doubling the size of the United States, without a vote of Congress.

Even with Taney's lopsided analysis, there was much to admire in his opinion. It was, after all, a clarion call for the president, and the military forces under his command, to respect the civil liberties of American citizens. General Cadwalader's imprisonment of John Merryman and his refusal to hand him over to the civil courts raised important constitutional questions. If Taney's opinion could have been read without reference to the furious sectional battle that was tearing the country apart, it would surely have commanded respect. But how could his opinion be read *without* reference to the dire situation facing Lincoln and the Union forces?

Taney's refusal to place the Merryman case in historical context gave his opinion a gauzy, surreal quality. Nowhere in his opinion did the Chief Justice suggest that Lincoln was dealing with a major insurrection in which eleven states had seceded from the Union and secessionists in other states, like Maryland, posed a significant and immediate threat to the nation's security. His references to the Burr conspiracy, and Jefferson and Marshall's declarations at that time that only Congress could suspend the writ of habeas corpus, were true enough. But the threat of the so-called Burr conspiracy, which involved a small, ragtag group of adventurers whose ultimate goal remains a mystery to this day, in no way rose to the level of danger to the republic that Lincoln faced in April and May of 1861.

Taney's rigid demeanor in court and his single-minded opinion directing Lincoln to obey his order left no doubt that the Chief Justice was intent on forcing a showdown with the president. Once he had written his opinion, he did all in his power to draw attention to it. Without waiting for a response from Lincoln, he made his opinion available to the public. It was published in newspapers and journals throughout the country and, with Taney's encouragement, printed as a pamphlet. After the opinion was published in early June, Taney accepted congratulations from far-flung admirers, including a letter from former President Pierce of New Hampshire.

Taney's response to Pierce reveals much about the Chief Justice's perspective on the nation in crisis. "The paroxysm of passion into which the country has suddenly been thrown appears to me to amount almost to delirium," he wrote Pierce. "I hope that it is too violent to last long, and that calmer and more sober thoughts will soon take its place: and that the North, as well as the South, will see that a peaceful separation, with free institutions in each section, is far better than the union of all the present states under a military government, and a reign of terror preceded too by a civil war with all its horrors, and which end as it may will prove ruinous to the victors as well as the vanquished. But at present I grieve to say passion and hate sweep everything before them."

Taney's letter made clear that the Chief Justice, unlike Lincoln, believed the South had a constitutional right to secede from the Union. But Taney obviously was prepared to go further. He was convinced that a peaceful separation of the southern states from the Union served the best interests of both sections of the nation. While his opinion—that the voluntary dissolution of the Union was preferable to civil war—might have been a tenable one to take before U.S. forces surrendered Fort Sumter, it should have raised serious conflict-of-interest problems for the Chief Justice of the United States in the summer of 1861.

Other prominent southerners who had served the federal government admirably were faced with the same choice as Taney. General Robert E. Lee shared Taney's judgment that slavery was morally wrong, but he nonetheless left a distinguished career in the U.S. Army to join the Confederacy to defend the more laudable aspects of southern culture and history. U.S. Supreme Court Justice John Campbell of Alabama resigned his high position in the federal government for a different reason. After failing in his negotiations with Secretary of State Seward to reach a peaceful compromise between North and South, Campbell submitted his resignation to return to Alabama in the belief that his continued useful service on the Supreme Court would be undermined by the public's lack of confidence in the objectivity of his opinions.

Chief Justice Taney chose to remain on the Court. As his conduct in the Merryman case demonstrated, he was determined to use his judicial office to challenge what he considered to be the excesses of the wartime Lincoln administration at every opportunity.

Lincoln took no immediate public notice of Taney's judicial order in the Merryman case. If the president was angered, or chastised, by the Chief Justice's lecture on civil liberties, he did not say so in any recorded conversation or letter. In June 1861, he had much else on his mind. With Congress adjourned, he had already blockaded southern ports, closed the mails to "disloyal" publications, called for thousands of new recruits for the Union army, and authorized the payment of $2 million from the U.S. Treasury to private citizens in New York to expedite the recruiting effort. None of these executive actions was expressly sanctioned by the Constitution. In an address to a special session of Congress on the Fourth of July, Lincoln defended his sweeping executive actions taken after the surrender of Fort Sumter. He reminded Congress of his inaugural pledges: to preserve the Union, protect government property, and give the secessionists no cause for initiating hostile action against the United States. He had honored each of his commitments, he said. The armed conflict triggered by the bombardment of Fort Sumter was a rebellion by traitorous individuals against the federal government, not a war between two sovereignties (as contended by the Confederate States of America). In this Fourth of July address, and for the remainder of his presidency, Lincoln spoke of a rebellion, not a civil war. If he mentioned the secessionist states as a group, he referred to the "so-called Confederate States of America." The distinction was important to him because it signaled to foreign nations to keep out of the internecine dispute. It also provided Lincoln with the constitutional rationale to take extraordinary emergency measures to put down the insurrection, including the suspension of the writ of habeas corpus.

In a pointed reference to Taney's *Merryman* opinion, Lincoln said that "the attention of the country has been called to the proposition that one who is sworn to 'take care that the laws be faithfully executed,' should not himself violate them." The president insisted that the Constitution gave him the authority to suspend the writ of habeas corpus, though he emphasized that he had exercised the power "very sparingly." Where Chief Justice Taney concluded that the power was indisputably Congress's because it was placed in Article I, which dealt with legislative authority, Lincoln stressed that the text of the Constitution was silent on which branch could suspend the writ. A third of the states were in open rebellion, he noted, a fact that was conspicuously absent from Taney's opinion. "It cannot be believed the framers of the instrument intended that in every case, the danger should run its course," Lincoln argued, "until Congress could be called together; the very assembling of which might be prevented, as was intended in this case, by the rebellion." In such an emergency, he contended, the president must have the authority to act.

Lincoln framed the constitutional question raised by the Merryman case differently from Taney: Must a single law, the writ of habeas corpus, be enforced at the cost of sacrificing the government itself? His answer was contained in another question. "[A]re all the laws, *but one*, to go un-executed," he asked, "and the government itself go to pieces, lest that one be violated?" For Lincoln, preservation of the government must be the nation's highest priority.*

A day after Lincoln's address, his Attorney General, Edward Bates, issued a twenty-six-page advisory opinion giving citations and extended arguments in support of the president's position. Despite the Attorney General's best efforts, his opinion did not clear up all of the constitu-tional problems raised by Lincoln's actions. The specter of a president and the U.S. military under his command having an open-ended invita-tion to violate American citizens' individual rights has been a chilling thought since the founding of the republic, and one that the U.S. Supreme Court condemned almost immediately after the Civil War was over. But context has always been important in our constitutional his-tory. Under wartime pressures, the Court has usually deferred to the judg-ment of the president and his generals, willing to sacrifice civil liberties claims in the process.

Postscript: Although Lincoln ignored Taney's opinion, the Chief Justice did not give up on Merryman. The prisoner was released from Fort McHenry in early July 1861 to face charges before a Baltimore grand jury for conspiracy to commit treason. Later, he was indicted and freed on $40,000 bail. Taney's dilatory tactics over the next three years, however, guaranteed that Merryman never came to trial. The Chief Justice ruled that he must preside at Merryman's trial and repeatedly postponed the proceedings because of ill health. At the same time, he refused to allow another federal circuit judge to preside in his absence.

Taney may have ruled as he did because he did not think Merryman

---

* Lincoln, of course, insisted that he had not even broken one law, since he argued that his suspension of the writ of habeas corpus was constitutional. In the same address, he requested that Congress authorize his suspension of the writ of habeas corpus, which it did by statute in 1863.

could receive a fair jury trial in Baltimore, where Union troops had established an intimidating presence. Whatever the explanation, the outcome was ironic. Taney had demanded throughout the habeas corpus proceedings that the Lincoln administration justify Merryman's incarceration before a judge in a civil courtroom. But once the administration had belatedly complied with Taney's judicial directive, the Chief Justice denied the government the opportunity to prove its case.

Chapter Seven

"A PEOPLE'S CONTEST"

A nti-slavery men in the North, cabinet members, and diplomats all agreed that Lincoln was an amiable fellow, described by Ralph Waldo Emerson as a man of "boyish cheerfulness." But no one seemed to think that the president possessed the skills or resolve to lead the nation through the worst crisis in its history. The abolitionist leader Wendell Phillips complained that Lincoln was too timid, "so ignorant as to fear the little near danger more than the danger farther off." Attorney General Edward Bates wrote that he lacked "*will* and *purpose,* and, I greatly fear he, has not *the power to command.*" Charles Francis Adams, who served as U.S. Minister to Great Britain, concluded that the president was "frivolous and uncertain."

The only man who did not appear to underestimate the president was Lincoln himself. He used his genial good humor, when it suited his purposes, to advance his political goals. And those goals were laid out clearly for anyone who listened carefully to his inaugural address. He had pleaded with the rebellious southern states to return to the Union where he promised they would be treated with honor and that their slave societies would continue to have the protection that the Constitution guaranteed. But Lincoln reminded them that they had no right to secede, and that he would take all necessary measures to prevent that illegal act.

The surrender of Fort Sumter to Confederate troops transformed the conciliatory Lincoln into a decisive wartime president who broadly interpreted his constitutional powers to preserve the Union. His proclamation calling for 75,000 militiamen from the states to meet the impending crisis was well within his executive authority, first exercised by President George Washington in 1795. But his orders to blockade southern ports and to suspend the writ of habeas corpus raised serious constitutional questions. Still other actions taken by Lincoln could not, by any reasonable interpretation of the Constitution, fit within his designated powers. He increased the size of the Army and Navy, appropriated money for national defense, and censored the mails, in each instance assuming authority that the framers gave to Congress.

Lincoln was convinced that all of these early decisions were not only necessary but complied with the intention of the framers. The Constitution's authors could not have expected the president to sit idly by, he reasoned, with Congress out of session and one-third of the nation ablaze with insurrection. Lincoln had called for a special congressional session to convene in early July, leaving him three and a half months to act alone to defend the Union. When Congress did convene in the summer, Lincoln reported that he had done nothing that was "beyond the competency of Congress." At his request, Congress then officially ratified virtually all of his actions.

In those desperate early days of the war, Lincoln proved to be a superb politician who knew instinctively how to exercise the broad powers of his office. But he also acted out of deep moral conviction. He believed that he held a sacred trust for the American people to preserve the Union. In language that he would rework to more eloquent effect at Gettysburg two years later, Lincoln told Congress that the rebellion posed the question whether a constitutional republic or democracy, "a government of the people, by the same people—can or cannot maintain its territorial integrity, against its own domestic foes." It was "a People's contest," he said, in which the Union represented the best hope in the world "to elevate the condition of men—to lift artificial weights from all shoulders—to clear the paths of laudable pursuit for all—to afford all, an unfettered start, and a fair chance, in the race of life."

Lincoln's calculated omission of any explicit reference to slavery in his

Fourth of July report was accepted with equanimity by the Republican-controlled Congress as well as northern abolitionists like Horace Greeley, who understood the need for the president's "circumlocutions." They tacitly approved of the president's precarious balancing act—aggressively pursuing a military victory while appealing to the loyalty of southern Unionists, particularly those in the uncommitted slave states of Kentucky, Maryland, and Missouri. Congress followed Lincoln's lead in assuring the slave states that they would be welcomed back in the Union. Almost unanimously, both houses supported a resolution introduced by Kentucky senator John Crittenden that declared the war was not being waged in pursuit of conquest but only to defend the Constitution and preserve the Union.

All that remained was a decisive Union military victory to provide tangible leverage for the president's very public negotiation with the slave states. Toward that end, Lincoln ordered an advance against Confederate troops who were encamped at the Manassas, Virginia, railroad junction, just twenty-five miles southwest of the capital. General of the Army Winfield Scott expressed reservations about the plan, but was overruled by Lincoln and his cabinet. The president put General Irwin McDowell, a veteran of the Mexican War, in charge of the attack. On July 21, McDowell led an army of more than 30,000 Union soldiers, composed mostly of fresh, poorly trained recruits, on their march toward Manassas. They were accompanied by an entourage of congressmen, diplomats, newspaper reporters, and a sampling of Washington's society ladies who brought picnic lunches in their fashionable buggies.

From the hills overlooking Manassas, the eager audience watched the two sides trade fatal volleys of cannon and musket fire. By late afternoon, the Union soldiers were in full retreat, with many of the rawest ninety-day recruits littering the muddy roads with their canteens, overcoats, and rifles. Lincoln and his cabinet received reports of the shocking defeat in General Scott's office throughout the evening. The next day, the president relieved General McDowell of his command and replaced him with the supremely confident thirty-four-year-old General George McClellan.

With the disastrous Union defeat at Manassas,* Lincoln's support among northern abolitionists began to seriously erode. Senators Charles Sumner of Massachusetts and Zachariah Chandler of Michigan urged him to dispense with his single-minded goal of preserving the Union. At its core, the war was about slavery, they said, and it was time for the president to acknowledge publicly that incontrovertible fact. Otherwise, Manassas would be followed by more Confederate victories, aided by the very slaves that they believed should be free. Radical Republicans had already shown their impatience by forcing through Congress the first Confiscation Act, which provided for the freeing of captured slaves who had assisted Confederate forces.

Despite his strong anti-slavery views, Lincoln did not think that public opinion in the North was yet prepared to support a war to free the slaves. Besides, Lincoln believed, a war of emancipation would almost certainly tilt crucial border states, like Kentucky, toward the Confederacy. Kentucky was not only the third most populous slave state but offered vast natural resources that could be used to great military advantage. The Cumberland and Tennessee Rivers that coursed through the state pointed directly toward the midsection of the South. But if the state joined the Confederacy, its east-west axis would provide a buffer for almost half the southern states against invasion by Union troops. The Confederate Congress had already opened recruiting offices in the state and appropriated $1 million to assist Kentucky residents "in repelling any invasion or occupation of their soil."

"I think to lose Kentucky is nearly the same as to lose the whole game," Lincoln wrote Orville Browning, a Quincy, Illinois, attorney who was his long-time friend and political adviser. And that meant he must muffle his, and the Union's, anti-slavery sentiments.

In early August, General John Frémont, commander of Union forces in the West, undermined Lincoln's border state strategy. Short of both supplies and soldiers, Frémont's forces lost a key battle in southwest Missouri and faced spreading guerrilla warfare waged by southern sympathiz-

---

* It would later be known as the First Battle of Bull Run, named for a nearby creek.

ers throughout the state. The general, without consulting with Lincoln, declared that the entire state was under martial law. Any supporter of the rebellion would face military court-martial, and, if found guilty, be shot. Equally troubling to Lincoln was Frémont's order that the slaves of any captured rebels in Missouri would be immediately emancipated, contradicting the Confiscation Act (which required a judicial hearing before a slave could be freed).

Lincoln ordered Frémont to rescind his declaration of martial law but *requested* that he reverse his emancipation order. The embattled general ignored Lincoln's request and, instead, sent his irrepressible wife, Jessie, to Washington to argue his case before the president. Lincoln insisted that Mrs. Frémont meet with him "Now, at once," on the very evening she had completed her arduous journey from St. Louis. When she arrived at the White House, the president did not hide his hostility, refusing to offer her a seat. While both remained standing, Jessie Frémont handed Lincoln a letter from her husband stating that he would not rescind his emancipation proclamation unless openly directed to do so by the president. Mrs. Frémont urged Lincoln to support her husband's order, which, she argued, would bring Great Britain into the war against the Confederacy. "You are quite a female politician," Lincoln replied caustically. He then reminded her that "it was a war for a great national idea, the Union, and . . . General Frémont should not have dragged the Negro into it."

The next day, Lincoln ordered Frémont to modify his emancipation proclamation to conform with the terms of the Confiscation Act and sent copies to the press. His action calmed the frayed nerves of border state Unionists. But it had the opposite effect on indignant abolitionist politicians. The order could only have come from a president "born of 'poor white trash' and educated in a slave state," snarled Senator Ben Wade of Ohio.

By late fall, Lincoln was still looking in vain for the first major Union military victory. For months, the dashing General McClellan, dressed in trim blue uniform astride his magnificent mount, had smartly inspected his troops. An honors graduate of West Point (second in his class), McClellan let no detail of military preparation escape his trained eye. His fortifications around Washington were a model of engineering. Under his demanding drills during the late summer of 1861, the Union soldiers achieved a tight discipline that had been woefully lacking at the Battle of Bull Run. He was also a master of public relations, inviting Lincoln and members of his cabinet and Congress to attend his close-order military drills.

Ever the perfectionist, McClellan refused to send his troops into battle until he was satisfied that conditions guaranteed a victory. When would his Army of the Potomac finally strike a decisive blow for the Union? Not, as it turned out, in the fair weather months of August, September, or October. In November, at McClellan's insistence, Lincoln reluctantly promoted him to lead all of the Union armies (replacing the seventy-five-year-old General Scott). Still, the armies that he had supervised since the summer did not move. To mounting demands from impatient members of Congress, McClellan's refrain was always the same: more trained troops were needed. Senator Chandler, one of the general's early backers, complained, "Fremont's operations were bad enough in all conscience, but as compared with McLellan's they were splendid."

Lincoln attempted to prod McClellan into action, holding strategy sessions with him in the field during the day and making unannounced visits to McClellan's residence at night, much to the general's irritation. One November evening, after being told by a servant that the president was waiting in his parlor, McClellan went directly upstairs to sleep. The general referred to Lincoln as "nothing more than a well meaning baboon."

Lincoln did not respond to the general's crude treatment or barbed insults. He still held out hope that McClellan would yet deliver a crucial military victory. But his support for the general in his report to Congress in December 1861 was notably restrained.

The state of the Union in December was dismal, and General McClellan's failure to deliver a decisive military victory was only part of the problem. Lincoln also faced formidable challenges to his authority in the federal courts, as well as unrelenting pressure to keep the major European powers from aiding the Confederacy. Both challenges, one internal and the other dealing with the administration's foreign policy, stemmed largely from Lincoln's blockade of the southern ports.

When he had announced the blockade, Lincoln chose his words carefully. His action was necessary, he said, because the Union was threatened by "a combination of persons engaged in insurrection." The rebellion was initiated by individual citizens, he insisted, not by the seceding southern states. His denial of the sovereignty of the seceding states was essential to the president's overall war strategy. He wanted to keep open the possibility that the seceding states would soon return to their rightful place in the Union. At the same time, Lincoln was signaling to the European powers, especially Great Britain, that the war was an internal rebellion, not a conflict between two sovereign nations. Lincoln's description of the insurrection and blockade made clear that the administration would object to a foreign nation's diplomatic recognition of the Confederacy or trade with the southern states.

But the blockade also posed problems of both constitutional and international law for Lincoln. A naval blockade was commonly understood to be a military act against a belligerent. By imposing the blockade, Lincoln was implicitly acknowledging that the Union was engaged in a civil war against the Confederate States of America. Under the Constitution, however, only Congress could declare war. At the time that Lincoln issued his orders to blockade the southern ports, Congress was adjourned.

Within months of Lincoln's action, the issue of the constitutionality of the blockade, and the war itself, was raised in federal courts in Florida, Massachusetts, and New York. In each case, a ship was captured and its cargo confiscated by Union naval forces when the vessel was either entering or leaving a southern port. Just days after Lincoln had announced the blockade of Virginia ports, the barque *Hiawatha* was seized sixty miles south of the city of Richmond. A British vessel with a British crew, the *Hiawatha* had sailed from England en route to Richmond with a cargo of salt when it was captured and taken to a prize court in New York. A second ship, the schooner *Crenshaw*, owned by Virginia residents, set sail in May 1861 from Richmond bound for Liverpool, England, with a cargo of tobacco when it was seized and also brought to New York. The brig *Amy Warwick* sailed from Rio de Janeiro to a Virginia port in May carrying a cargo of coffee and was captured in July 1861 and taken to Boston Harbor. A fourth case involved the schooner *Brilliante*, which was owned by the American consul at Campeche, Mexico, and was seized by the USS *Massachusetts* in Biloxi Bay in June with a cargo of six hundred barrels of flour.

In all four cases, the owners claimed that their ships and cargos had been illegally seized by the Union navy. Since Congress had not declared war at the time of the blockade, they argued, there was no constitutional justification for seizing their property. The four lawsuits, known collectively as the Prize Cases, would eventually be decided by the Taney Court. As the test cases slowly wound their way upward to their ultimate judicial destination, lawyers representing the Lincoln administration had reason to be concerned. If the U.S. Supreme Court concluded that the president's blockade was unconstitutional, the decision would undermine the legitimacy of the Union effort to quell the rebellion.

The government's task in the Prize Cases was complicated by the fact that there were three vacancies on the Supreme Court. Two justices, Daniel of Virginia and McLean of Ohio, had died, and Justice Campbell had returned to his native Alabama. Should the Prize Cases come to the Court before the vacancies were filled, six justices would decide the cases. Five of those justices had been in the majority in the *Dred Scott* decision.* Chief Justice Taney, who had only recently lectured the president on his constitutional transgressions in the Merryman case, would preside.

In his December report to Congress, Lincoln addressed the problem presented by the Court vacancies, though he did not mention the Prize

---

* The sixth, Nathan Clifford, a Democrat from Maine, was named by President Buchanan in 1858 to replace Justice Curtis.

Cases. He noted that residents of southern states had traditionally filled two of the vacant seats and presided over federal circuit courts in their section of the country. With the southern states "overrun by revolt," it did not seem feasible to the president to appoint men from that region. "[M]any of the most competent men there," he conceded, "probably would not take the personal hazard of accepting to serve." He suggested that Congress might reorganize and expand the circuits to encompass the previously underrepresented western states. The proposal, if adopted, would allow Lincoln to appoint three new justices from states loyal to the Union. Those three appointees could well shorten the odds for the administration in its effort to make a successful argument in the Prize Cases before a reconstituted Taney Court.

In addition to the president's constitutional problems, his blockade raised formidable obstacles to his administration's determined policy of preventing European nations from formally recognizing the sovereignty of the Confederacy. Under international law, a blockade was interpreted as a militant act by one belligerent against another. By blockading the southern ports, Lincoln seemed to be sending the message to the international legal community that the Union was indeed in a war against the Confederate States of America. If the Union was merely putting down a rebellion of disparate groups of private citizens, as Lincoln maintained, he should have closed the southern ports rather than blockade them. After all, why would the president need to blockade his own ports?

The blockade was "a great blunder and absurdity," groused Pennsylvania's powerful congressman Thaddeus Stevens. "As a lawyer, Mr. Lincoln," he said, "I should have supposed you would have seen the difficulty at once."

The president's response was to strike his best country-lawyer pose. "I'm a good enough lawyer in a Western law court, I suppose," he replied, "but we don't practice the law of nations up there, and I supposed [Secretary of State] Seward knew all about it, and I left it to him." It was a pity, he added, but "it's done now and can't be helped."

• • •

Lincoln surely understood the legal implications of a blockade, as opposed to the closing of southern ports. But he also knew that the weak Union forces had slim chance of enforcing presidential orders in the spring of 1861 to close the southern ports. Besides, both Lincoln and Secretary of State Seward were convinced that a policy of closing the ports would be more offensive to Great Britain than the blockade. The British had consistently taken the position that a country had no right during a rebellion to close its ports to foreign nations.

Shortly after Lincoln had imposed the blockade, Great Britain announced its neutrality in the conflict and extended informal recognition of the Confederacy as a belligerent. Secretary of State Seward was furious, aware that the British might be one short step away from establishing formal diplomatic relations with the southern states. Once Great Britain had established diplomatic relations with the Confederacy, military assistance from the Royal Navy as well as crucial trade between the British textile industry and the cotton-rich South could soon follow.

Seward drafted a letter of protest that was more threat than diplomatic communication. It was addressed to the U.S. Minister to Great Britain, Charles Francis Adams, to be delivered to the British Foreign Office. Before the letter was dispatched, however, Lincoln moderated Seward's harsh language. Where Seward had written that the president "is surprised and grieved" by the unofficial recognition by the British government of the Confederacy, Lincoln inserted "regrets." Seward had said the intercourse between Great Britain and the southern states was "wrongful"; Lincoln substituted "hurtful." Lincoln left intact Seward's grim conclusion that formal British recognition of the Confederacy "would be British intervention to create within our own territory a hostile State by overthrowing this Republic itself."

Lincoln had said that he did not want to fight two wars at once, and his revisions preserved the diplomatic option to resolve differences with Great Britain. He deleted his Secretary of State's sternest warning: "When this act of intervention is distinctly performed, we, from that hour, shall cease to be friends and become once more, as we have twice before been, be forced to become enemies of Great Britain." After making the editorial changes, Lincoln directed Seward to send the letter to Adams, for the minister's eyes only, and not be delivered to the British Foreign Office.

In November 1861, relations between the United States and Great Britain again threatened to rupture. Confederate envoys to Great Britain and France, James Mason of Virginia and John Slidell of Louisiana, escaped through the Union blockade at Charleston Harbor and sailed to Havana, Cuba, where they boarded the British steamer *Trent*. Once at sea, the *Trent* was intercepted by the USS *San Jacinto*, commanded by Captain Charles Wilkes. Without orders from Washington, Wilkes searched the vessel, removed the Confederate envoys, and took them to Fort Warren in Boston Harbor, where they were imprisoned.

The northern press hailed Captain Wilkes as a hero, and the House of Representatives awarded him a gold medal. But on the other side of the Atlantic, the British expressed outrage at the insult to their flag. "You may stand for this, but damned if I will," Prime Minister Palmerston thundered to his cabinet. Palmerston's government charged the United States with a flagrant violation of international law (by forcibly removing passengers from a ship of a neutral nation). More ominous, Great Britain interpreted the capture of Mason and Slidell as a hostile military act by the United States, tantamount to a declaration of war.

At first, Lincoln had been pleased with the capture of Mason and Slidell and refused to believe reports that Great Britain was preparing for war. If only he could meet face-to-face with Lord Lyons, the British Minister to the United States, he was confident he "could show him in five minutes that I am heartily for peace." After his close adviser on foreign affairs, Senator Sumner, told Lincoln that such a conversation would be improper, the senator suggested that the *Trent* affair be submitted to arbitration, perhaps by a disinterested third party such as the king of Prussia. Lincoln seized upon the idea and began drafting a proposal.

But events were moving too fast for arbitration. Her Majesty's Government had already ordered eight thousand troops sent to Canada to protect the nation's interests. And the British Foreign Office had imposed an embargo on saltpeter and other vital military supplies that were headed for New England ports. Lord Lyons presented an ultimatum to the Lincoln administration: The British government demanded an apology and the immediate release of the Confederate envoys. If the terms were not met, the ambassador would close the British Embassy in Washington and return to London.

On Christmas Day, Lincoln called an emergency cabinet meeting to head off the crisis. Seward proposed that the United States concede that Captain Wilkes had violated international law by forcibly removing the Confederate envoys from the *Trent*. But Seward would also tell the British government that Wilkes's action had not been authorized by the Lincoln administration. No apology was then necessary, Seward reasoned, since the U.S. government had not ordered the capture of Mason and Slidell. Seward saved his most politically explosive recommendation for last: the illegally imprisoned Confederate envoys must be released.

Lincoln rejected Seward's solution. It might assuage the Palmerston government, but he feared that the American public would see it as a humiliating capitulation to British demands. The president promised to write a response to Seward's recommendation that evening. But he arrived empty-handed at the cabinet meeting the next morning, and agreed to endorse Seward's proposal.

After the meeting, Seward asked Lincoln why he had not written a response, as he had vowed to do. "I found I could not make an argument that would satisfy my own mind," Lincoln replied, "and that proved to me your ground was the right one."

Lincoln's second thoughts, and better judgment, averted a war with Great Britain that could have spelled disaster for the Union. After the administration had made concessions in the *Trent* affair, relieved diplomats on both sides resumed their traditional roles. The greatest danger that the Civil War would become an international conflict had passed.

While resolution of the *Trent* affair was a diplomatic triumph, the crisis created economic chaos in the North's commercial centers. Fearing war with Great Britain, panicked creditors had rushed to state banks to withdraw gold and then hoarded it. Banks reacted by suspending specie payment for both private and public debts. Meanwhile, the war was costing the federal government $1 million a day. With no federal currency and virtually no specie available, the government was desperately pressed to feed and cloth the 575,000-man Union army, equip them with guns and munitions, and transport them into battle. The Lincoln administration did not have the money to pay soldiers' salaries or government contractors' bills. "The treasury is nearly empty," Secretary of the Treasury Chase told Congress.

"General, what shall I do?" Lincoln asked Quartermaster General Montgomery Meigs on January 10, 1862. "The people are impatient, Chase has no money and he tells me he can raise no more; the General of the Army [McClellan] has typhoid fever. The bottom is out of the tub. What shall I do?"

Congress eased the administration's economic plight in February by passing the Legal Tender Act, which immediately provided $150 million in paper currency. Although Lincoln doubted the constitutionality of the measure (a doubt shared by his nemesis, Chief Justice Taney), he supported the legislation. For the first time, the United States of America printed money that was backed by the government's promise, not specie. The federally issued "greenbacks" eventually supplied $450 million for the administration's financing of the war.

Lincoln knew that additional revenue to support the troops would do no good unless Union forces took the offensive on the battlefield. Increasingly frustrated by McClellan's inertia, the president had begun to read books on military strategy and contemplate, briefly, leading the troops himself. He issued a presidential war order, demanding that Union forces make a general advance by February 22. But the Union's two commanders in the West, Generals Don Carlos Buell and Henry Halleck, appeared to be as risk-averse as McClellan, and balked at the president's order. They awaited better weather conditions and the consolidation of their far-flung troops.

Meanwhile, the president's strained relationship with General Mc-

Clellan further deteriorated. A resentful McClellan had risen from his sickbed in mid-January to meet with Lincoln, cabinet members, and other military commanders to discuss a plan of attack. Expressing his growing impatience, Lincoln wanted to know McClellan's intentions. McClellan replied that he had a plan, but that he was not yet prepared to discuss it. He then whispered to Quartermaster Meigs that Lincoln couldn't be trusted with such confidential information, because he would leak it to the *New York Herald*. In good time, he promised to complete his plans and make them known to the president. Lincoln reluctantly concluded that he had little choice but to defer, once again, to the general.

Lincoln yearned for a military victory that winter, but neither McClellan nor his western commanders, Buell and Halleck, could deliver. The honor belonged to Ulysses S. Grant, an officer of dubious reputation under Halleck's command. Known as a drunk, Grant had quit the Army in 1854, but rejoined shortly after the firing on Fort Sumter. Grant commanded Illinois's 21st Regiment and craved action. He badgered a reluctant Halleck to let him lead an assault on rebel forts in western Kentucky. In February 1862, Halleck granted Grant's request.

In a driving rainstorm, Grant and his foot soldiers trudged through heavy mud to take Fort Henry, which overlooked the Tennessee River. Eleven days later, Grant and his troops confronted Confederate troops at Fort Donelson on the Cumberland River. The Confederate commander, General Simon Bolivar Buckner, sent word to Grant that he wished to discuss terms of surrender. "An unconditional and immediate surrender," Grant gruffly replied, or he would "move immediately on your works." Though Buckner considered Grant "ungenerous and unchivalrous," he nonetheless met his terms. Grant took 13,000 Confederate soldiers as prisoners. His two victories opened the critical channels of the Tennessee and Cumberland Rivers to Union forces that could then push into central Tennessee and farther south to the northern boundary of Alabama. In Grant, Lincoln had finally found a fighting man, not a planner. He immediately promoted him to major general, outranked in the West only by Halleck.

Personal tragedy struck the Lincolns only days after Grant's victories. Their son Willie had been bedridden and treated for typhoid fever since early February. On February 20, he died. Both parents were inconsolable. For weeks, the president wept alone in his room. Mary was so devastated by the loss that she could not bear to attend the funeral, which was held in the White House. She never again entered the bedroom where Willie had died. For nearly a year, she ordered that no social events take place in the Lincolns' official home.

After weeks of mourning, Lincoln forced himself to return to work. He was now served by a new Secretary of War, Edwin Stanton, a rough-edged but effective administrator, who had replaced the incompetent Simon Cameron. The War Department that Stanton inherited was in complete disarray, the result of widespread bureaucratic infighting and rampant corruption in the awarding of military contracts. Stanton's honesty and no-nonsense style soon restored order to the department. But neither he nor the president could fight the war. And by early April 1862, Union forces were again bogged down.

Grant's army had advanced down the Tennessee River to Pittsburgh Landing, near the Mississippi border, and encamped at a little country meetinghouse called Shiloh Church to await reinforcements. At dawn on April 6, Confederate forces struck hard at Grant's army in a surprise attack that almost routed the Union troops. After reinforcements arrived the next day, Grant counterattacked to reclaim lost ground in the savage encounter. The two-day battle at Shiloh Church wreaked unprecedented carnage; 24,000 men, including more than 13,000 Union soldiers, were killed or wounded. The total number of deaths at Shiloh was greater than all American deaths in the Revolutionary War, the War of 1812, and the Mexican War combined. Limited war, Grant concluded, was no longer an option. "I gave up all hope of saving the union except by complete conquest," he wrote.

By this time, McClellan had finally revealed his plan to conquer the South. He would lead more than 100,000 Union troops in an attack on the Confederate capital of Richmond. The troops would first sail down the Potomac River to the Virginia peninsula. Backed by a flotilla of

Union gunboats, McClellan's Army of the Potomac would then begin their methodical ninety-mile march west to Richmond. Lincoln objected to the plan, believing that McClellan should first defeat the large concentration of rebel troops encamped at Manassas. He thought a second battle at Manassas was logistically less risky and of greater strategic importance than McClellan's proposed assault on Richmond. The president was also concerned that McClellan's huge deployment of Union troops to the Virginia peninsula would leave the nation's capital vulnerable to attack. McClellan brushed aside Lincoln's concerns and began preparations for his expedition. But he would not be ready to face the enemy until mid-June.

Lincoln still clung to the hope that he could limit the war's goal to the preservation of the Union, and not enlarge its purpose to include the emancipation of slaves. He nonetheless acted upon his anti-slavery views. He endorsed legislation that prohibited slavery in the national territories, in defiance of the Taney Court's decision in *Dred Scott*. And he supported a treaty with Great Britain that contained stiff provisions prohibiting the international slave trade. He also remained committed to the gradual emancipation of slaves in the southern states and their colonization in another country, positions he had held for more than a decade.

But pressures mounted on the president to reconsider his initial strategy. With no crushing Union victories in the East or West, morale on the front and at home sagged. Recruitment of additional troops in the northern states dwindled at an alarming rate. Lincoln heard ever more insistent demands from Radical Republicans in Congress that the war be declared a moral crusade against slavery.

In March, Lincoln had taken the first tentative step toward making emancipation the war policy of his administration. He asked Congress to pass a joint resolution offering financial assistance to any state that gradually abolished slavery. This measure, which passed overwhelmingly, did not undercut Lincoln's basic belief that slaveowners in the southern states had a right to their human property under the Constitution. The legislation did not force emancipation, only encouraged it. But the border states, the primary focus of Lincoln's initiative, were not enticed by the legislation. No state, not even the almost wholly free state of Delaware, accepted Congress's offer. The only tangible result of the president's action was the passage of a bill for the District of Columbia compensating slaveowners who freed their slaves—an idea that Lincoln had first advocated as a congressman from Illinois in 1849.

He continued to wait in vain for good news from the front. He had stripped McClellan of his overall Union command, replacing him as general in chief with Henry Halleck. When McClellan's Army of the Potomac finally began to march on Richmond, it did so at the rate of only two miles a day. The delays, McClellan reported, were due to bad weather and bad roads. The general then returned to his familiar mantra—that he needed more troops to meet the overwhelming number of rebel soldiers he was certain were poised to destroy his army.

On June 25, troops under the Confederacy's new commander, General Robert E. Lee, battered McClellan's army in the first of a series of weeklong battles that sent the Union soldiers retreating to the lower end of the Virginia peninsula. Lincoln visited McClellan there and, to the general's chagrin, did not ask him for his explanation of the Union's defeats but only whether his troops might be removed safely from the peninsula.

On July 13, Lincoln told two members of his cabinet, Seward and Secretary of the Navy Gideon Welles, that he had come to the conclusion "that we must free the slaves or be ourselves subdued." Even with that startling declaration, Lincoln did not abandon his belief that the southern states had a right under the Constitution to maintain the institution of slavery. If he freed the slaves by presidential proclamation, he would do so as commander in chief of the armed forces to avert a national catastrophe. Unlike his abolitionist critics, he did not justify emancipation on moral grounds, but as a matter of military necessity.

Only four days after Lincoln had confided in Seward and Welles, Radical Republicans pushed through Congress the Second Confiscation Act, which declared all rebels to be traitors and announced the confiscation of all their property and the freeing of slaves within sixty days. The statute had no practical effect, since the confiscation of rebel property required a cumbersome judicial process and, in any event, the act could not be enforced until the South was occupied. The statute nonetheless signaled an unmistakable shift in northern public opinion on the issue of emancipation that focused Lincoln's own thinking on the subject. Lincoln was convinced that a presidential proclamation freeing the slaves was on sounder constitutional grounds than the congressional statute. He believed that only he, not Congress, possessed the war powers to emancipate the slaves. Although he signed the legislation, he placed his objections to the law in the record.

Less than a week after the legislation had been signed into law, Lincoln met with his cabinet to present the first draft of his proposed emancipation proclamation. His statement was a prosaic summary of his views. Unless the rebellious states rejoined the Union, he wrote, the terms of the Second Confiscation Act would take effect in sixty days. He reiterated his support for remuneration for any state, including those in rebellion, that voluntarily and gradually emancipated its slave population. Finally, Lincoln, acting as commander in chief of the armed forces, promised "as a fit and necessary military measure" to declare on January 1, 1863, that "all persons held as slaves within any state . . . wherein the constitutional authority of the United States shall not then be practically recognized . . . shall then, thenceforth, and forever, be free."

Lincoln had not asked for his cabinet's advice, only their attention, but he nonetheless received a cacophony of views on his proposed proclamation. Attorney General Bates applauded the measure, but Secretary of the Treasury Chase feared that such a proclamation would undermine the government's tenuous financial position. Seward warned that the proclamation could push European nations in need of the South's cotton to recognize the Confederacy formally. Even worse, in his opinion, Lincoln's announcement would be viewed as the last gasp of a desperate government. Seward urged the president to wait until the Union forces had produced a significant military victory.

Lincoln first considered making the proclamation public the next day. But Seward's advice lingered in his mind. He decided to keep his draft to himself while he awaited a Union victory. After Horace Greeley complained in print that Lincoln had not emancipated the slaves, as required by the Second Confiscation Act, Lincoln replied: "My paramount object in this struggle *is* to save the Union, and is *not* either to save or to destroy slavery. If I could save the Union without freeing *any* slave I would do it, and if I could save it by freeing *all* the slaves I would do it; and if I could save it by freeing some and leaving others alone I would also do that. What I do about slavery, and the colored race, I do because I believe it helps to save the Union; and what I forbear, I forbear because I do *not* believe it would help to save the Union."

Even though he had drafted the Emancipation Proclamation, Lincoln still held out hope for a frictionless solution to the nation's race problem. In August, he met at the White House with a delegation of freed slaves to ask their cooperation in encouraging fellow blacks to support the colonization of African Americans outside of the United States. "You and we are different races," Lincoln told the delegation. "We have between us a broader difference than exists between almost any other two races." The ideal of equal treatment between the races, he believed, could never be attained. "It is better for us both therefore to be separated." He proposed that a colony of African Americans be settled in central America. If successful, he was confident that the colony would not only be an important step forward for both races but a contribution "for the good of mankind." Members of the delegation promised to discuss the president's proposal with prominent blacks in Philadelphia, New York, and Boston. After further discussions, black leaders emphatically rejected the idea.

During the summer, Lee's troops had delivered a second devastating defeat at Bull Run to the Union army under the command of General John Pope. Emboldened by another Confederate victory in Virginia, Lee pushed his army across the Potomac into western Maryland. McClellan's Army of the Potomac was sent to protect the Union's vulnerable flank. With the daring General James E. B. "Jeb" Stuart's cavalry screening his advance, Lee's forces moved into the Shenandoah Valley and took battle positions on the banks of Antietam Creek near the hamlet of Sharpsburg, Maryland.

On September 17, McClellan's army repeatedly tried to break through Lee's lines, and almost succeeded. But McClellan lost his nerve, and failed to deliver a final, crushing blow to the rebels. He did succeed in forcing Lee's men to retreat across the Potomac. The cost of victory was devastating: nearly 6,000 dead, 17,000 wounded, and thousands of others missing—the largest number of casualties of any single day of the war.

Antietam was not the dramatic victory that Lincoln had hoped for. But it would do. A week later, Lincoln announced his Emancipation Proclamation. On January 1, 1863, "all persons held as slaves" within a state still in rebellion would forever be free.

Lincoln's announcement was naturally welcomed by New England's abolitionists, but was harshly condemned by Democrats throughout the Union. Perhaps more ominously for Lincoln, Republican stalwarts in the western states appeared indifferent to the prospect of fighting the war to free the slaves. "I am satisfied that outside of the New England states, a large majority of the people care nothing about the *moral* aspect of slavery," Lincoln's old friend David Davis observed.

Democrats swept into office in record numbers in the fall elections in the mid-Atlantic and western states, almost doubling their representation in Congress for the December 1862 term. For Lincoln, the Union forces' lack of progress in the field was even worse news than the widespread political setbacks for his party. General McClellan refused to pursue Lee's troops across the Potomac into the Virginia countryside, pleading that his cavalry horses were too exhausted to give chase. "Will you pardon me for asking what the horses of your army have done since the battle of Antietam that fatigue anything?" an exasperated Lincoln asked. Finally, on November 5, Lincoln directed General Halleck to relieve McClellan of his command of the Army of the Potomac.

Faced with the prospect of a long, brutal war of attrition and an increasingly restive electorate, Lincoln returned to his plan of ridding the country of slavery by massive payments to the slave states. He endorsed congressional legislation that would have authorized the issuance of bonds for the payment to states that emancipated their slaves. "Mr. Lincoln's whole soul is absorbed in his plan of remunerative emancipation & he thinks if Congress doesn't fail him, that the problem will be solved," Davis wrote. By the time Lincoln sent his annual message to Congress in December 1862, he had refined his idea, calling for a constitutional amendment that would provide the payment of U.S. bonds to any state that abolished slavery by January 1, 1900. He proposed two additional constitutional amendments. The first moderated his Emancipation Proclamation to the extent of offering payments to individual slaveowners who were loyal to the Union for their freed slaves. He also returned to his long-standing plan of establishing a colony of freed American blacks outside the United States, authorizing congressional appropriations for that purpose.

Lincoln's constitutional proposals revealed a burst of uncharacteristic presidential optimism about ending the war. He was confident, he told Davis, that his latest remunerative emancipation idea would almost certainly be attractive to the border slave states of Delaware, Maryland, Kentucky, and Missouri. He also thought that the prospects were good that the proposal would persuade what he believed to be a moderate majority in the secessionist states, particularly Tennessee and Louisiana, to rejoin the Union. He even held out hope that the Army of the Potomac, now under the command of General Ambrose Burnside, would deliver a devastating defeat to Confederate forces in Virginia before the end of year, making his plans for reconciliation with the Confederacy a matter of military necessity for the rebel states. It would also render his Emancipation Proclamation largely superfluous.

All of Lincoln's bright hopes came crashing to the ground on December 13 on the hill called Marye's Heights behind the town of Fredericksburg, Virginia. There General Burnside ordered his forces to march up the hill to meet the waiting Confederate soldiers and their lethal battery of artillery. Over and over, Burnside sent his brave, doomed soldiers up the hill. By the end of the day, one thousand Union men were dead, nine thousand wounded, and two thousand more missing in action.

Reports of the defeat spread like an epidemic across the nation. "It is thought by every body as if the darkest hour has come," Davis wrote. "Many men are in despair and openly say that they fear there can never be a reunited people. The feeling is increasing that we can't conquer the South."

At the traditional White House reception on New Year's Day, 1863, Lincoln shook hundreds of hands of diplomats, government officers, and private guests. Shortly after noon, he quietly slipped upstairs to his office where Secretary of State Seward had prepared the Emancipation Proclamation for his signature. The president worried that his aching right hand would produce an unsteady signature. But physical fatigue aside, he said, "I never, in my life, felt more certain that I was doing right, than I do in signing this paper." He then clutched the pen firmly and signed his name, not the customary "A. Lincoln," but in bold characters: "Abraham Lincoln."

No sadder figure was to be seen in Washington during the war than the Chief Justice of the United States, Roger B. Taney. The author of *Dred Scott* and *Merryman* was hated by abolitionists in Congress and vilified in the northern press. Even moderates in the Lincoln administration shunned him. Feeble and often incapacitated, Taney spent much of his time in his rooms on Indiana Avenue in the company of his daughter Ellen, who was now a semi-invalid.

Though Taney's body was weak, his mind was as alert as ever. He routinely lay in bed for many hours, puffing on a long black cigar and devouring newspapers and journals that were set out in front of him. He subscribed to several New York and Washington newspapers and *The Times* of London, as well as a variety of literary magazines and Catholic journals. He lamented that his small income did not allow him to purchase more.

Taney's view of the war was starkly different from that of President Lincoln and virtually every other high-ranking member of the federal government. He blamed the conflict on the president and his supporters in the North, who had ignored both the Constitution and the best interests of the nation. The South, by right, should have been allowed to secede peacefully. Had that been done, all of the bloodshed would have been avoided, and each section could have prospered, separately, as an independent and free-standing republic. Instead, the nation was broken into shards of violence.

Taney was convinced that the Lincoln administration had abandoned the rule of law in favor of military domination. The Merryman case was only the first example, in his view, of a president who willingly ignored the Constitution to rule by fiat and the sword. Like John Merryman, many of Taney's friends had been arrested as suspected traitors and sent to military prison. The Chief Justice had no confidence that the defendants could receive a fair trial in Baltimore in the shadow of the menacing presence of Union troops. He therefore became resourceful in finding reasons, usually his bad health, to postpone their trials.

He admired those young men who joined the Confederate army to fight the tyranny of the federal government. When one Confederate recruit, the grandson of a Revolutionary War veteran, came to Taney for a farewell visit, the Chief Justice compared the circumstances under which he was going to war to "those under which your grandfather went into the Revolutionary War." The photograph of Taney's son-in-law, Richard Allison, who served as a major in the Confederate army, hung prominently in his bedroom next to that of Allison's wife, Maria.

Taney's paltry judicial salary, further crimped by wartime inflation, forced him to live in near-penurious circumstances. Adding to his financial woes, his investment of several thousand dollars in Virginia bonds shortly before the war appeared to be worthless. With secession, the Virginia government had passed legislation prohibiting payment of interest to bondholders who resided outside the Confederacy; the law also cast doubt on whether the state was obligated to pay the principal.

Taney's admirers in Richmond (and there were many after publication of his *Merryman* opinion) proposed that an exception be made to the Virginia statute to allow payment of both principal and interest to the Chief Justice. They raised the subject with a close Baltimore friend of Taney's, David M. Perine. When Taney was told of the offer by Perine, he flatly rejected it. If he accepted, he was certain that the offer would be seen as an attempt to influence his judicial opinions. "Malignity would not fail to impute unworthy motives to them and to me," he wrote, "and in the present frenzied state of the public mind, men, who do not know my Virginia friends or me, would be ready to believe it."

Taney did not disguise his disagreements with the president or the policies of his administration. He was the only member of the Supreme Court who was too busy to attend Lincoln's first New Year's Day reception at the White House in 1862. "I expect some friends tomorrow," he wrote his colleague, Justice Wayne, "and as there is no established etiquette which requires the court to wait on the President on the 1st of January, as a matter of official courtesy, I am sure my brethren will excuse me for not joining them tomorrow."

He prepared for the day that the government's paper money, authorized by the Legal Tender Act, would be declared unconstitutional by the Supreme Court. At home, he wrote a long memorandum of law stating the reasons for his conclusions. Congress was given the authority to coin money, he wrote, but not to print it. It could borrow money, he conceded, but it did not have the authority to force unsecured paper currency on private creditors. The Taney opinion was never published, since the issue did not reach the Court for resolution during the war.

Given the opportunity, there is no doubt that Taney would have declared Lincoln's Emancipation Proclamation unconstitutional. He could have documented his conclusion by citing his own judicial opinions in *Strader v. Graham* (1851), *Dred Scott* (1857), and *Merryman* (1861). Like Lincoln, Taney interpreted the Constitution to give exclusive control of the institution of slavery to the states where it existed. The states could maintain it, or abolish it, as their voters wished. The Chief Justice had made that point in *Strader* and repeated it in his opinion in *Dred Scott*. In *Dred Scott*, Taney made the further argument that a slaveowner could not be deprived of his human property without due process of law. Lincoln's Emancipation Proclamation appeared to violate both states' rights and property rights, as Taney interpreted the Constitution.

Had the Taney Court been asked to rule on Lincoln's proclamation, the government would have argued, as did the president, that his war powers authorized his action. Taney's opinion in *Merryman* denied any such broad presidential authority during wartime. And that would have been the end of it, so far as the Chief Justice was concerned.

Neither of these constitutional issues on which the Chief Justice had strong opinions—the Legal Tender Act or Lincoln's Emancipation Proclamation—was decided by the Taney Court. But one constitutional challenge that could have determined the fate of the Union did come before the justices. The Prize Cases, which questioned the legality of Lincoln's blockade of southern ports and, indirectly, the legitimacy of the war itself, were placed on the Court's docket and scheduled for argument in February 1863.

By the time the Supreme Court heard arguments in the Prize Cases, Lincoln had appointed three new justices. Noah Swayne, the first Lincoln appointee, was an outstanding attorney from Columbus, Ohio, who was recognized as an expert in banking law. More important for Lincoln's purposes, Swayne had attended the first national Republican Party convention in 1856 and enthusiastically supported Lincoln's presidential candidacy in 1860. He was a Union man, and opposed to slavery. Swayne was said to be the choice of the man he replaced, Justice John McLean, the most outspoken anti-slavery justice to serve on the Taney Court.

Lincoln's second appointee, Samuel Miller, was born in Richmond, Kentucky, studied medicine at Transylvania University, and practiced as a physician for twelve years. Later, he studied law privately, became a justice of the peace and involved in politics. His opposition to slavery was the major reason that he moved in 1850 to Keokuk, Iowa, where he practiced law and rose to a position of leadership in the state bar. Like Justice Swayne, he was active in the Republican Party and endorsed Lincoln for president in 1860. Miller replaced the ardently pro-slavery Peter Daniel on the Court.

David Davis of Illinois, appointed by the president in December 1862, had been a friend and loyal supporter of Lincoln's for more than two decades, culminating in his service as his campaign manager at the 1860 Republican Convention. Davis had entered Kenyon College in Gambier, Ohio, at the age of thirteen, graduated four years later, and studied briefly at the New Haven Law School. Davis served for many years as an Illinois circuit court judge, presiding at trials in which the state's leading lawyers, including Lincoln, frequently appeared before him. He became a wealthy man by his shrewd purchases of small tracts of land sold for taxes during the depression of the 1840s. With Lincoln, he was active in the Illinois Whig Party before both men joined the Republican Party. Davis succeeded Justice John Campbell of Alabama.

Even with three loyal Lincoln men on the Court, an administration victory in the Prize Cases was by no means a foregone conclusion. Chief Justice Taney, despite his failing health, still commanded respect among his colleagues. His anti-administration views on matters of constitutional law were well known in February 1863. The two other members of the Court from slave states, Justices Catron (Tennessee) and Wayne (Georgia), had voted with the Chief Justice in the Dred Scott decision.

Two additional members of the Court, Justices Grier (Pennsylvania) and Nelson (New York), had also been members of the Dred Scott majority. Since that time, both Grier and Nelson had given the administration reason to worry about their views on the Prize Cases. Robert Grier had angered the administration by refusing to sit in federal circuit court cases in which southern privateers were tried for piracy. As a circuit judge, Samuel Nelson had written one of the lower court opinions in the Prize Cases, but had expressed no view on the merits of the case. He had only affirmed the lower court decision in order to expedite the appeal to the Supreme Court.

The ninth member of the Court, Nathan Clifford of Maine, was an excellent lawyer who had served as his state's attorney general as well as U.S. Attorney General (under President Polk). But after he had been nominated to the Court by his fellow northern Democrat, President Buchanan, Clifford was attacked by abolitionists who considered his political views suspect. Clifford had presided as circuit court judge in one of the Prize Cases, but had sent it to the Supreme Court without giving a clear indication of his views on the merits.

The Prize Cases were argued before the Taney Court for twelve days, beginning on February 10, 1863. The stakes for the Lincoln administration were extraordinarily high. If the justices decided that the Union had illegally seized the ships as prize, the financially strapped government would be liable for huge sums in restitution. Politically, an adverse ruling would be profoundly embarrassing to the administration. Of even greater consequence, such a ruling would undercut the Union's legal authority to put down the rebellion.

A government defeat in the Prize Cases, moreover, would be catastrophic to the administration's foreign policy. For twenty-three months, the Lincoln administration had been exerting every effort to maintain the blockade while, at the same time, preventing foreign nations from extending official recognition to the Confederacy. A decision by the Supreme Court that the blockade was illegal would weaken the Union's standing in the world and encourage cooperation between foreign nations and the Confederacy. Richard Dana, Jr., one of the attorneys defending the government's blockade, described the dire consequences of such a ruling to the U.S. Minister to Great Britain, Charles Francis Adams: "What a position it would put us in before the world whose commerce we have been illegally prohibiting, whom we have unlawfully subjected to a cotton famine, and domestic dangers and distress for two years. It would end the war, and how it would leave us with neutral powers, it is fearful to contemplate!"

But even if the Court decided that the blockade was constitutional, the result could be devastating to the Union cause. A Court decision justifying the blockade under international law would provide the Confederacy with a powerful argument that the conflict was a civil war between two sovereign nations. Once the South could cite a Supreme Court decision in making that argument in European capitals, Great Britain, France, and Spain could be expected to extend formal recognition to the Confederacy and engage in trade essential to the rebellious states' successful prosecution of the war.

To avoid any of these undesirable results, the Lincoln administration needed a Court decision that carefully navigated around the treacherous legal and political shoals posed by the Prize Cases.

The most formidable advocate for the shipowners who challenged the legality of the blockade was James Carlisle, a prominent Washington lawyer and close friend of Chief Justice Taney. In his argument before the justices, Carlisle used Lincoln's and Seward's written statements to dispute the notion that the blockade was a legitimate military measure taken by one belligerent against another under international law. The "so-called blockade," Carlisle said, was by Lincoln's own admission an action "against a combination of persons" who were engaged in an insurrection. Carlisle also quoted Seward's correspondence, which vehemently denied belligerent rights to the Confederacy and insisted that the conflict was an internal rebellion. Taking the president and Secretary of State at their word, he argued that the conflict was a municipal dispute, not a war recognized by international law. The blockade was therefore illegal, and so was the capture of the claimants' ships as prize.

Carlisle conceded that the case ultimately turned on Lincoln's constitutional argument that, as commander in chief, he was authorized to act to preserve the Union. The words of the Constitution betrayed the president's claim, he charged: "It comes to a plea of necessity," but "[t]he Constitution knows no such word." He insisted that the Supreme Court was bound by a literal interpretation of the Constitution, and nowhere in the document did the framers give the president the authority to declare war. That power was entrusted to Congress alone. In imposing the blockade, Lincoln made himself "the impersonation of the country," and invoked "the power and right to use all the force he can command, to 'save the life of the nation.'" But surely that could not have been the framers' intent. "This is to assert that the Constitution contemplated and tacitly provided that the President should be dictator, and all Constitutional Government be at an end, whenever he should think that 'the life of the nation' is in danger."

Justices Catron, Clifford, and Nelson were so impressed with Carlisle's oral argument—as Catron wrote Carlisle—that they wished to have it printed verbatim in the official reports of the Court. Catron agreed with Carlisle that Lincoln's argument from necessity was unworthy of constitutional argument. "Necessity is an old plea—as old as the reign of Tiberias," Catron wrote. "It is the commander's will. The End, we are told is to crush out the Rebellion; that the whole means are at the Presdt's discretion and that he is the sole Judge in the Selection of the means to accomplish the End. That is a rejection of the Constitution with its limitations."

Catron did not include the Chief Justice among the names of his brethren who supported Carlisle's argument. But Taney was surely as pleased with Carlisle's argument as Catron, Clifford, and Nelson. The attorney's relentless assault on Lincoln's constitutional claim was reminiscent of Taney's own attack on the president in his *Merryman* opinion.

Attorney General Bates had originally planned to manage the arguments of the government's lawyers, but ultimately assigned that responsibility to Charles Eames, a Harvard graduate with a national reputation as a maritime lawyer. It was a terrible mistake. After Eames had completed his oral argument, Justice Swayne told Attorney General Bates that all of the justices were thoroughly alienated by Eames's performance. He "did no good, but harm, to the cause," Swayne said, "acting like a harlequin, and turning a solemn trial into a farce." Chief Justice Taney took mischievous note of Eames's failure. He knew that Eames had unsuccessfully defended a Union officer at a court-martial. Taney said that he sympathized with the dishonored officer, who had concluded that "he deserved to be convicted for trusting his case to such a counsel."

The government's cause was not lost, thanks primarily to the argument of Richard Dana, Jr. A graduate of Harvard, Dana had made his literary mark before he entered a courtroom. As a young man, he had sailed as a common seaman on the brig *Pilgrim* from Boston Harbor to California, by way of Cape Horn. When he returned to Boston two years later, he immortalized his adventures (and the wretched treatment of ordinary sailors at sea) in his memoir, *Two Years Before the Mast*. Later, he distinguished himself in private law practice in Boston and as U.S. Attorney for Massachusetts during the Civil War.

At the Prize Cases argument, Dana defended Lincoln's constitutional position with the intensity and passion for which he was well known in New England courtrooms. He argued that Lincoln's extraordinary military measures were fully justified and urged the justices to refrain from second-guessing the president: "If a foreign power springs a war upon us by sea and land, during a recess of Congress, exercising all belligerent rights of capture," shouldn't the president be authorized to repel it? Dana's answer, like Lincoln's, was an emphatic yes.

He dismissed as sophistry Carlisle's contention that Lincoln could impose a blockade of southern ports only if Congress had declared war against the Confederacy. The purpose of a blockade, Dana argued, was to coerce an enemy into submission. It was of no consequence under international law whether war had been officially declared or not. The blockade was justified by the actual state of hostilities between combatants, not by the legislative will. And there could be no doubt that the Union was engaged in a very real and vicious war against the rebellious states.

If blockades were legitimate weapons of war, as Dana contended, then shipowners ran the blockades at their peril. It did not matter whether the ships belonged to citizens of foreign nations or to residents of southern states, even those who professed loyalty to the Union. For purposes of international law, the Union was entitled to seize these shipowners' property on the high seas as prizes of war.

Dana reminded the justices that Lincoln was not the first U.S. president to use his war powers aggressively to protect the nation's security. Polk had sent U.S. troops into battle against Mexico in 1846 without a congressional declaration of war. Congress later ratified the president's action, just as it had done in July 1861 in sanctioning Lincoln's blockade. Without that presidential authority to act in a national emergency, Dana observed, "there is no protection to the State." Both the president and the U.S. Congress had endorsed the blockade, he said. "This is conclusive on the Courts."

Attorney General Bates was overwhelmed with emotion when he congratulated Dana on his presentation, which was described by another observer as "luminous and exquisite." Secretary of State Seward also expressed his admiration. But Dana's most important admirer was Justice Robert Grier. "Well, your little 'Two Years Before the Mast' has settled that question," Grier told one court auditor whom he encountered in the corridor in the rear of the courtroom. Later, Grier extended his congratulations to Dana directly. "I have won Judge Grier's heart," Dana wrote. "He pats me on the shoulder and says I have cleared up all his doubts."

Grier's enthusiasm for Dana's arguments on behalf of the federal government could not have been predicted from a study of his long judicial record. He had been appointed in 1846 by President Polk as a compromise candidate, a conservative northern Democrat who believed in states' rights but did not offend extremists in the North or South. On the issue of slavery, Grier had proved to be true to his earlier states' rights views. He joined Chief Justice Taney's opinions in *Strader v. Graham* and *Dred Scott*, which insisted slave states had the constitutional right to police slavery within their borders. Grier also vigilantly enforced the Fugitive Slave Law. And in the early days of the Civil War, he expressed disapproval of what he often considered to be the Lincoln administration's heavy-handed prosecution of the war.

But Grier, above all else, believed in the Union and deplored the secession of the southern states. After a visit to his son-in-law in Kentucky shortly after the war had begun, he said that he was sorry to learn that his kin "was a secessionist as insane as the others." When he learned of the Union's defeat at the First Battle of Bull Run, he ruefully concluded, "[W]e must conquer this rebellion or declare our republican government a failure." Shortly before the Supreme Court heard arguments in the Prize Cases, Grier presided in a circuit court case in which he rejected the defense of a Confederate privateer who claimed that he had been coerced into the service of the Confederacy. "You might, more justifiably, I think, plead the total insanity of the people in the South altogether," Grier retorted. He labeled all participants in the rebellion, including the defendant, traitors to their country.

On March 20, 1863, Grier announced the decision in the Prize Cases for a narrow Court majority of five justices. He was joined by the three Lincoln appointees, Davis, Miller, and Swayne, as well as by Justice Wayne, a strong nationalist who had chosen to remain on the Court in Washington rather than return to his home in Georgia. In typically robust style, Grier attacked the two major contentions of the shipowners:

first, that Lincoln did not have the constitutional authority to blockade the southern ports before a congressional declaration of war; and, second, that the Union could not legally capture as prizes of war the property of the claimant shipowners, including residents of southern states who were citizens of the United States.

On the first issue, Grier embraced Dana's argument that the Civil War was a fact that did not need the formal imprimatur of a congressional declaration. "The President was bound to meet it [the insurrection] in the shape it presented itself, without waiting for Congress to baptize it with a name," he wrote, "and no name given to it by him or them could change the fact." It was no less a war because it was a rebellion against the lawful authority of the United States. Noting that Great Britain and other European nations had declared their neutrality in the conflict, he wrote that the Court should not be asked "to affect a technical ignorance of the existence of a war, which all the world acknowledges to be the greatest civil war known in the history of the human race."

Under Grier's interpretation of the Constitution, Lincoln possessed ample authority as commander in chief of the armed forces to suppress the rebellion by whatever military means he deemed necessary. Congress had reinforced the president's authority by statutes dating back to 1795 that empowered him to call out the militia to put down an insurrection. In July 1861, Congress had specifically sanctioned the blockade. He concluded, as did Dana in oral argument, that both political branches of government had acted lawfully, and that it was no business of the Supreme Court to interfere.

In answering the second question, Grier repeated Dana's argument that a belligerent had the right to coerce its enemy into submission by all means recognized by international law, including the capture of prize on the high seas. This was a necessary result of a state of war. If the products of agriculture and commerce were "the sinews of war," then the Union was entitled "to cut these sinews of the power of the enemy, by capturing his property on the high seas." He rejected the shipowners' argument that the Union could only seize the property of citizens of foreign nations at war with the United States. By that reasoning, the Confederacy could exercise all rights of belligerents, but the Union could not. Such an argument could not be taken seriously. A legitimate capture under international law, he maintained, depended on the location of the ship, not the citizenship papers of the owner. He concluded that the Union was entitled to all of the property seized on the high seas in the Prize Cases.

Grier's opinion for the Court could not have been more perfectly tailored to the Lincoln administration's specifications. He had described the president's war powers in sweeping terms and put an end, for all practical purposes, to successful legal attacks on the Union's seizures on the high seas. His references to the insurgents were carefully crafted so that nothing in the opinion suggested that the Confederate states could claim sovereignty. They were enemies, to be sure, but he referred to them only as "traitors" and "rebels." Confederate envoys would search in vain for a single sentence in the Court's opinion that lent support to their efforts to gain formal recognition among the European nations.

The Court's dissenting opinion was written by Justice Samuel Nelson, on behalf of himself, Chief Justice Taney, and Associate Justices Catron and Clifford. Like Justice Grier, Nelson resided in a mid-Atlantic state, and his political views were acceptable to moderates on both sides of the Mason-Dixon line. His judicial record was replete with states' rights opinions, including the one that he wrote in Dred Scott. But the comparison with his colleague, Justice Grier, ended there. Whereas Grier was, from the moment that Confederate troops bombarded Fort Sumter, a Union loyalist, Nelson believed that the South had a right to secede. He worked with Justice Campbell in the early days of the Civil War to negotiate an agreement between the Lincoln administration and the Confederacy. He shared Chief Justice Taney's view that necessity would force the Union to make peace with the southern states. As the crisis deepened, he was appalled by what he (and Taney) considered Lincoln's unlawful assumption of broad executive authority.

In his Prize Cases dissent, Nelson conceded that Lincoln was authorized to call out the militia to put down the rebellion, but that did not give him the power to declare war. That was Congress's responsibility, and until the legislature had officially made the conflict a public war, it could only be considered "a personal war" between the Union and the rebels. As such, the conventional methods of warfare between nations, including a blockade, were not recognized under international law. He agreed with Grier that congressional legislation in July 1861 provided constitutional cover for the Union's blockade, but disputed the majority's opinion that the legislation could apply retroactively to Lincoln's April 1861 proclamations. The Union's capture of prize in the cases before the Court, he concluded, was illegal.

Nelson's dissent could not match Grier's majority opinion in muscular prose. There were no memorable phrases, no evidence of the righteous indignation that had characterized Grier's dismissal of the shipowners' arguments. Nelson did not write disparagingly of the president, as Grier had done in describing the rebels. He did not claim that Lincoln had assumed dictatorial powers, as Carlisle had contended, though Nelson agreed with the Washington attorney's argument, as his private correspondence as well as Catron's letter to Carlisle (representing the views of Catron, Clifford, and Nelson) revealed.

Despite its plodding, workmanlike quality, the dissenting opinion would have been compulsory reading on both sides of the Atlantic if Nelson (or Chief Justice Taney) had persuaded one more justice to join them. That reconstructed Court majority would have announced that the Lincoln administration was guilty of reckless and illegal actions. And the president himself would have been presented to the world as a grand scofflaw who had flouted both the Constitution and international law. The Taney Court, with the blessing of the Chief Justice, would then have produced a judicial calamity from which the Union might not have recovered.

Chapter Eight

SILENCING THE AGITATOR

Lincoln's onetime friend and sworn Confederate enemy, Alexander Stephens, derided the president's single-minded determination to save the Union. "The Union with him in sentiment, rose to the sublimity of a religious mysticism," Stephens wrote. He was dead wrong. Lincoln's policies were decidedly earthbound and unerringly pragmatic. Among the president's most controversial policies were his widespread curtailment of civil liberties. He suspended the writ of habeas corpus, first on a limited basis and later throughout the country. He approved the government's censorship of the mails and newspapers critical of the Union's cause. And he backed his military commanders who suppressed free speech and jailed those dissidents they considered to be threats to national security.

As Taney had feared, the arrest and imprisonment of John Merryman in May 1861 signaled the beginning of rough, uncompromising military actions to deal with suspected secessionists in Maryland. In Baltimore, several of Taney's friends followed Merryman to prison, including the city's mayor and the entire board of police commissioners. The editors of seven of the city's newspapers that had been critical of the federal government were jailed, effectively shutting down their publications. Among the imprisoned editors was Francis Key Howard, the grandson of Taney's brother-in-law, Francis Scott Key. Key later wrote of his incarceration, comparing the conditions at Fort Lafayette, where he was imprisoned, to a "slave ship on middle passage."

One of the most sensational arrests in Maryland occurred a year after Merryman's and involved another prominent citizen and friend of the Chief Justice. He was Judge Richard Carmichael, a state circuit judge in the eastern shore town of Easton, Maryland, who had earned a reputation as an outspoken southern sympathizer in the early days of the war. Secretary of State Seward had closely followed Judge Carmichael's words and actions since the early fall of 1861, and had instructed the commanding officer for Maryland's eastern shore, General John Dix, to arrest Carmichael, in his courtroom if necessary. Union leaders on the eastern shore, however, advised the administration to postpone Carmichael's arrest. The judge continued to criticize the federal government, using his grand jury instructions to attack military arrests as "without warrant of law." Like Taney in the Merryman case, Carmichael concluded that Lincoln had no constitutional authority to suspend the writ of habeas corpus. He instructed grand jurors to indict soldiers who made such arrests and private citizens who furnished them with information leading to the arrests.

In May 1862, General Dix learned that a grand jury under Judge Carmichael's supervision was prepared to indict Henry Goldsborough, president of the Maryland Senate, for providing information on suspected local secessionists to Union soldiers. Dix wrote Goldsborough that he was sending four officers who had been summoned as witnesses, as well as a federal marshal and three armed policemen. He advised the Senate leader to ignore the anticipated indictment or, alternatively, to allow the trial to take place immediately. If, however, Goldsborough had incontrovertible proof that Judge Carmichael "has uttered treasonable language in his charge to the grand jury and that the officers of the court have been so biased and are controlled by the disloyalty of the judge as to render a fair trial hopeless," Dix wrote, he would have Carmichael arrested and imprisoned in Fort McHenry.

The federal marshal sent by Dix confirmed in a conversation with Goldborough that Judge Carmichael was indeed guilty of treasonous conduct on the bench. Based on that information, the marshal and his men entered Carmichael's courtroom, where a trial was taking place. They approached the bench and informed the presiding judge that he was under arrest. Carmichael demanded to be shown a warrant and was told that the charges would be made known to him at Fort McHenry. He protested that the officers had no authority to arrest him or to interrupt the proceedings of his court. Ignoring Carmichael, the marshal abruptly announced that the court was adjourned while officers physically restrained the judge.

Carmichael's supporters later charged that General Dix's officers had beaten the judge over the head with a revolver and dragged him, dripping blood, from the courtroom. The general's version of the arrest was more subdued: his officers respectfully informed the judge of his arrest and "unluckily [Carmichael] received a superficial wound on the head before he ceased to resist."

Dix defended the arrest as necessary because Carmichael had used his judicial office to prosecute loyal officers and citizens for doing their duty. Dix further accused the judge of being the author of "a treasonable memorial to the legislature, published and circulated under his own signature while holding a place on the bench."

Petitions of protest poured into the White House, expressing outrage at Carmichael's imprisonment. Lincoln read some of the petitions, but was unmoved. He had reviewed Judge Carmichael's grand jury instructions, he wrote one petitioner, and "was not very favorably impressed toward the Judge." As Lincoln interpreted Carmichael's instructions, the judge's purpose was to prosecute and punish officers attempting to arrest traitors to the Union cause. He wrote, "[T]he Judge was trying to help a little, by giving the protection of law to those who were endeavoring to overthrow the Supreme law—trying if he could to find a safe place for certain men to stand on the constitution, whilst they should stab it in another place."

Lincoln, in consultation with Secretary of War Stanton, agreed that Carmichael should be released if he would take an oath of allegiance to the Union. The judge refused, but nonetheless appealed to the president for his release from military prison. He had not been informed of the charges against him, he wrote Lincoln, but had read in the *Baltimore Sun* that he had been incarcerated for "treason committed in the discharge of official duty." Unaware that Lincoln had already read and disapproved of his grand jury instruction, the judge said that he had only attempted to uphold the Constitution as the supreme law of the land. "If in *this* there be any treason, then indeed I cannot claim to be released," he wrote. "But if the law be as declared in that paper, then is it too much to ask in the *name* of the law, that I be discharged from these bonds?"

There is no record of a reply by Lincoln to the judge's appeal. Carmichael remained in military prison until December 1862. At that time, Union forces, confident that secessionist sentiment in Maryland had crested, released Carmichael and most other prominent Maryland leaders who had been imprisoned on suspicion of aiding the rebellion. Carmichael returned to his courtroom in Easton and resumed his judicial duties.

Harsh military action against suspected southern sympathizers was not confined to border states, like Maryland, whose loyalty to the Union hung precariously in the balance in the early months of the war. The worst abuses of civil liberties occurred in the summer and early fall of 1862 and stretched from New York to the Midwest. At that time, recruitment for the state militias had slowed to a trickle with reports of Confederate battlefield successes and mounting Union fatalities. To meet the crisis, Congress passed the Militia Act on July 17, 1862, which authorized the Lincoln administration to recruit Union soldiers if the states failed to meet their monthly quotas.

Early in August, Secretary of War Stanton put bite into the legislation by issuing a series of executive orders that called for the arrest of any potential conscript between the ages of eighteen and forty-five who left his native state or the country to evade the draft. The writ of habeas corpus was suspended for those arrested "for disloyal practices." On the same day, Stanton issued another order that authorized federal marshals and local chiefs of police to arrest and imprison any person "who may be engaged, by act, speech, or writing, in discouraging volunteer enlistments, or in any way giving aid and comfort to the enemy, or in any other disloyal practice against the United States." The order further provided that the detainees would be tried before a military commission, even though the civil courts were open.

Over the next month, more than 350 civilians in the North were arrested for violating the War Department's orders, the greatest concentration of arrests during the Civil War. Many of the arrests were made on the basis of uncorroborated rumor. One of the most egregious examples occurred in Lincoln's home state on August 24 when Dr. Israel Blanchard of Murphysboro, Illinois, was arrested for disloyalty and sent to the Old Capitol prison in Washington, D.C. The doctor was incarcerated on the basis of an accusation by a Murphysboro man that Blanchard had made traitorous statements at a local meeting of the Knights of the Golden Circle, an organization known to be sympathetic to the Confederacy.

The physician's brother-in-law, John Logan, a twice-wounded Union brigadier, appealed directly to Lincoln to release Blanchard. Logan wrote the president that Dr. Blanchard had twice volunteered for the Union army and had, throughout the conflict, shown an unwavering loyalty to the Union. On the day after Blanchard was accused on making "disloyal remarks," Logan said that the doctor was attending a meeting of the 81st Illinois Volunteers. He further told the president that several local residents could testify that Dr. Blanchard was caring for a sick child at the time he was supposed to have made traitorous remarks at the meeting of the Knights of the Golden Circle.

Lincoln was slow to respond to Logan's appeal, even though the veteran was known to the president as a loyal and valuable citizen. "I strongly incline to discharge Dr. Blanchard," Lincoln finally wrote Secretary of War Stanton on October 9. The doctor was released and returned to Illinois, where he ran successfully for the state senate, as a Democrat, the following year.

Despite receiving scores of letters, like Logan's, reporting widespread abuses of civil liberties, Lincoln did not appear alarmed. In fact, he signed his most expansive suspension of the writ of habeas corpus, applicable throughout the country, on September 24, only two days after he had announced the Emancipation Proclamation. It gave legal cover to Stanton's orders and subjected to martial law "all persons discouraging volunteer enlistments, resisting militia drafts, or guilty of any disloyal practice affording aid and comfort to the rebels." Lincoln did not discuss the suspension of the writ with his cabinet before issuing the proclamation, nor did he appear to ponder the negative effects that it could have on the country. He monitored the arrests more closely only after the Democratic Party registered huge gains in the fall elections, the victories frequently fueled by charges of the administration's abuses of civil liberties. But even then, he intervened sporadically and still deferred to the final judgment of his military commanders, as he did in the case of the Reverend Samuel McPheeters of St. Louis.

McPheeters and his wife had been banished from Missouri by Marshal-Provost Frederick Dick, who acted on reports that the couple was guilty of traitorous activity. Among the charges, Dick accused the minister of failing to pray for the Union. Before his banishment, the minister was ordered to turn his church over to loyal Union men in his congregation. A prominent citizen of St. Louis, Hugh Campbell, complained to David Davis, Lincoln's old friend and recently appointed U.S. Supreme Court Justice, that McPheeters and his wife had not uttered a single disloyal statement, from the pulpit or anywhere else. They had been banished without a trial or hearing. As Campbell expected, his complaint about the handling of the McPheeters case was passed on to Lincoln. The president then directed Major General Samuel Curtis, commander of the Department of Missouri, to suspend the order of banishment.

But that was not the end of the case. General Curtis defended Dick's order, reiterating the charge that Reverend McPheeters had refused to pray for the Union cause. "Rebel priests are dangerous and diabolical in society," he wrote Lincoln. McPheeters traveled to Washington to defend himself and, accompanied by Attorney General Bates, met with the president. He presented a signed oath of his loyalty to the Union. Though Lincoln still had his doubts about McPheeters's loyalty, he accepted the minister at his word and told General Curtis that he considered banishment on mere suspicion to be unjustified. The president nevertheless left McPheeters's ultimate fate to Curtis, who rescinded the order of banishment but refused to allow the minister to return to his pulpit.

Emboldened by his party's gains in the fall elections, Democratic Representative S. S. Cox of Ohio introduced a resolution on the first day of the December congressional session, denouncing the administration's "usurpation of power" and demanding the release of all political prisoners. One of the Democratic Party's rising stars, newly elected New York governor Horatio Seymour, devoted two-thirds of his first annual message to national issues, taking particular aim at the administration's abuse of civil liberties. He had no tolerance, he said, for "this new doctrine . . . that the loyal North lost their constitutional rights when the South rebelled." New Jersey's Democratic governor, Joel Parker, followed Seymour's lead, challenging the federal government's policy of extending martial law "beyond the field of active operations of the commander."

The administration's drive to enlist new recruits in the upper Midwest, meanwhile, had brought agitators to the streets of Port Washington, Wisconsin, and the protests soon led to riots. The state's governor, Edward Salomon, ordered the arrest of some 150 rioters who were delivered to the custody of the U.S. Army for trial by court-martial. Responding to the petition of some of the rioters, the Wisconsin Supreme Court issued a writ of habeas corpus directing the commander in charge of the prisoners, General W. L. Elliot, to justify their incarceration. General Elliot filed a written return explaining the reasons for the detention. But the general also made clear that he would have nothing more to do with the judicial proceeding.

The argument before the Wisconsin Supreme Court in December 1862 was one-sided, since no attorney represented the federal government in the proceeding. One of the lawyers for the prisoners approvingly cited Chief Justice Taney's opinion in the Merryman case and repeated

Taney's argument that the president had no authority to suspend the writ of habeas corpus. The three-judge panel of the court agreed, declaring that the prisoners had been unlawfully imprisoned. But the judges' opinion showed that they were not eager to confront the military authority. They refused to issue the legal order that would have demanded General Elliot's compliance with the decision, and, instead, strongly suggested that the decision should be appealed to the U.S. Supreme Court.

The Wisconsin Supreme Court's decision set off a flurry of letters among Governor Salomon, General Elliot, and members of Lincoln's cabinet. Salomon first wrote to Secretary of War Stanton, urging that the prisoners be released to avert a direct collision between civil and military authorities. Stanton asked Senator Timothy Howe of Wisconsin to go to the state capital, Madison, to report back to him on the crisis. He also wrote General Elliot that the federal government intended to appeal the state supreme court decision to the U.S. Supreme Court.

This was all news to Attorney General Bates, who had responsibility for the administration's appeals to the Supreme Court, and learned of Stanton's plan to appeal the decision two weeks after the War Secretary had communicated with General Elliot. Bates immediately counseled against the appeal. He was not confident that the Taney Court would deliver the anticipated rebuke to the Wisconsin court's decision. Bates noted that the Chief Justice's *Merryman* opinion was consistent with the decision of the state supreme court, and that the other members of the Court were not assuredly pro-administration. Under those unpredictable circumstances, Bates advised that the Lincoln administration not initiate an appeal.

If Lincoln could have pointed to decisive military victories in the winter of 1862–63, the clamor over the curtailment of civil liberties would undoubtedly have receded. After the disaster at Fredericksburg, he waited anxiously for reports of Union successes. Grant's Army of Tennessee had moved overland from Memphis toward Vicksburg, Mississippi, and was bivouacked in Oxford by mid-December. Grant expected to be joined in his attack on Vicksburg by forces under the command of

William Tecumseh Sherman. Together, Grant and Sherman's armies hoped to launch a devastating pincer attack on the Confederate army defending Vicksburg.

But nothing went according to Grant's plan. Daring rebel cavalry raids behind Grant's army destroyed his supplies and cut critical telegraph and railroad lines, leaving his men isolated and vulnerable. Reluctantly, Grant ordered his army to retreat, but he could not communicate his decision to Sherman because of the destroyed telegraph lines. Sherman's troops therefore felt the full brunt of the Confederate forces on Chickasaw Bluffs, north of Vicksburg, where they were thrown back with heavy losses.

Hundreds of miles northeast of Vicksburg, on the eve of the important battle at Stones River in eastern Tennessee, Union and Confederate military bands engaged in an eerie musical duel. The Union musicians struck up "Yankee Doodle" and "Hail, Columbia," and the rebels, only a few hundred yards away, countered with "Dixie" and "The Bonnie Blue Flag." Finally, the bands and armies on both sides collaborated in a soulful rendition of "Home, Sweet Home." The next morning, December 31, 1862, gunfire replaced song as the communicative link between the two armies. The Confederate army, led by General Braxton Bragg, repeatedly charged the Union's Army of the Cumberland. But the Union forces under the command of General William Rosecrans held their ground. After three days of warfare, nearly 13,000 Union soldiers lay dead or wounded on the battlefield, representing 31 percent of Rosecrans's troops. The Confederate army lost nearly 12,000, one-third of the total of Bragg's Army of Tennessee.

"God bless you, and all with you," Lincoln wired Rosecrans. The president knew that the battle at Stones River was no great Union victory, but at least it was not another Fredericksburg. Later, the president reflected on the averted disaster in eastern Tennessee. "You gave us a hard-earned victory," he wrote Rosecrans, "which, if there had been a defeat instead, the nation could hardly have lived over." Such was the nature of the Union "victory" that Rosecrans's depleted army was in no condition to engage in another battle for several months.

Less than a month after the battles at Vicksburg and Stones River,

Ohio congressman Clement Vallandigham, the handsome, charismatic member of the increasingly powerful Peace Democrats, strode purposely to the floor of the House of Representatives to make his farewell speech. That Republicans had gerrymandered him out of his congressional seat in the fall election did not humble Vallandigham or cause him to moderate his criticism of the Lincoln administration's prosecution of the war. In his speech to his House colleagues, he condemned every major policy of the president—his failed decisions as commander in chief, the curtailment of civil liberties, and the Emancipation Proclamation. He blamed Lincoln for making the war a fight for abolition, not for the Union. And at what price? he asked. "Let the dead at Fredericksburg and Vicksburg answer." The president's policies had produced only "defeat, debt, taxation, sepulchres" and a litany of violations of citizens' rights, creating "one of the worst despotisms on earth."

It was obvious to Vallandigham that the North could never defeat the South on the battlefield. The Lincoln administration therefore should initiate discussions for a negotiated peace with the Confederacy, possibly with the help of a neutral European nation. The Ohio congressman was not concerned that an armistice would preserve the institution of slavery in the South. "I see more of barbarism and sin, a thousand times, in the continuance of this war . . . and the enslavement of the white race by debt and taxes and arbitrary power," he said. The Union's negotiators should concentrate on the welfare of the white race "without reference to the effect that settlement may have on the African." After he left Washington, the ambitious Vallandigham promoted his peace message before audiences from New Jersey to his home state of Ohio, where he expected to run for governor and, later, possibly for the presidency.

By early February 1863, the war appeared to have taken an almost unbearable toll on Lincoln. Physically, he was a haggard, ghostly replica of the man who had been elected president in 1860. He slept little and was despondent. Mary offered him little emotional comfort, and he had no intimate friends.

The president nonetheless moved doggedly forward with the prosecution of the war, as did the Republican-controlled Congress. In March, Congress passed the Habeas Corpus Act, providing official sanction for Lincoln's suspension of the writ that had been in operation for almost two years. The statute discouraged an appeal of the Wisconsin Supreme Court's decision to the U.S. Supreme Court as well as other challenges to the president's authority to suspend the writ.

Congress passed a more radical piece of legislation on the same day, the euphemistically titled Enrollment Act. It authorized the federal government to initiate a national draft of young men from twenty to forty-five years old throughout the country to supplement recruitment by state militias. The statute was both desperate and problem-laden. The mandate challenged the ingrained American spirit of volunteerism. It also was patently unfair, allowing wealthy young men of draft age to buy their way out. For $300, a conscript could pay a substitute to serve in his place or purchase his freedom outright from the federal government.

Not surprising, there were widespread protests against the statute, in Ohio and Indiana and the coal-mining districts of Pennsylvania. The worst occurred in New York City, where roving bands of working-class toughs, mainly Irish Americans, rioted for three days in July, resulting in one hundred deaths—the most violent civil disturbance in the nation's history. But the statute served its purpose, in large part, by spurring voluntary enlistments. As a result, tens of thousands of recruits were added to the Union army, guaranteeing that in sheer numbers, the North would eventually overwhelm the South.

Lincoln anticipated a constitutional challenge to the Enrollment Act and prepared a written rebuttal. He argued that the national draft legislation was authorized under Article I of the Constitution, which gave Congress the power to raise and support armies. The draft was known to the framers, he continued, and was used in both the War for Independence and the War of 1812. That the Enrollment Act was imperfect did not make it unconstitutional. It was the result of extensive, open debate in Congress, the democratic process provided for by the Constitution. The president then asked a question that, for him, was rhetorical: Would Americans "shrink from the necessary means to maintain our free government?" He concluded: "It is my purpose to see the draft law faithfully executed."

Everything about wartime Washington infuriated Chief Justice Taney. Life in the nation's capital was "adulterated and corrupt," he wrote, and "truth and honesty is not the general rule but the exception." He complained to his son-in-law, J. Mason Campbell, that his mail was being read and censored by government officials. "I fear the detectives will think themselves hardly paid for their trouble by its contents when they have opened & read & resealed this letter," he wrote contemptuously. The censors were so ignorant that he feared they might seize his precious Cuban cigars as contraband.

He blamed Lincoln for curtailing his selection of newspapers. "Although it may be difficult to say what are the boundaries of the President's *power* at this day—or whether it has any boundaries," he wrote Campbell, "I am not willing to admit that he has a *right* to prescribe what newspapers I shall read—although I know from experience that he has the power to prescribe what I shall not read."

He longed to return to Baltimore to breath "pure Maryland air" and escape "from the foul & corrupt atmosphere of Washington." But his many health problems forced him to remain in the capital. He nonetheless felt fortunate to be alive, he wrote his daughter Anne, on January 4, 1863, and to know that despite "all the horrors that surround us, those most near and dear to me have been spared." And though he considered himself a semi-invalid, he admitted that his health was sufficiently robust to allow him "to discharge my official duties although with pain & by a strong exertion of will."

Alert to Taney's faltering health, the federal district attorney in Baltimore, William Price, suggested that the Chief Justice might relinquish his judicial chair at the circuit court to a Supreme Court colleague, so that the pressing business of prosecuting suspected traitors might go forward. Taney rejected Price's suggestion and asked that circuit court Judge William Giles postpone the next term until May, when he expected that more favorable weather would allow him to travel to Baltimore.

Taney made frequent scathing references to the paper currency that Congress had authorized to help finance the war. As his bills mounted, he lamented that his salary was paid "in the miserable trash which will soon be utterly worthless." His written opinion that the Legal Tender Act was unconstitutional remained in his files, unpublished.

Taney wrote another unofficial opinion, entitled "Thoughts on the Conscription Law of the U. States," in which he charged that the federal government's draft statute, which Lincoln vigorously defended, violated the rights of the states under the Tenth Amendment. The federal and state governments exercised independent authority within their respective constitutional spheres, Taney claimed, reiterating a point that he had made in his 1859 *Booth* decision for the Supreme Court. In *Booth*, he had found that the state of Wisconsin had interfered with the constitutional authority of the federal government to enforce the Fugitive Slave Law. Taney inverted his *Booth* analysis in considering the conscription statute, concluding that the federal government had interfered with the authority of the states to maintain militias. If the federal government could draft young men who were enlisted in state militias, it could ultimately destroy those militias, and that was prohibited by the Constitution.

His unpublished opinions on the Legal Tender and the Enrollment Acts demonstrated that the Chief Justice's mind remained sharp, and that his thoughts never strayed too far from the law. But in those darkest days of the Civil War, when the Court's calendar was noticeably spare, Taney devoted more time than he would have wished to his personal finances. He was very nearly broke and found himself apologizing to David Perine, his old friend who also served as his financial adviser (and benefactor), for his inability to pay his bills. He was appalled, he wrote Perine, that he could not write a check that would cover the full premium owed on his life insurance policy: "All my life I have felt the obligation to pay my debts as a part of my religion & my inability to do so at this time is mortifying." He explained that his rent had been raised from $500 to $800, but that he was prevented from moving to cheaper quarters due to the failing health of his daughter Ellen, who lived with him. This miserable financial situation was maddening to him, he said, because "this city is crowded with men who are growing & have grown rich by the war & they together with depreciated paper run the rents up to a ruinous price for the tenant."

A few months later, Taney wrote nostalgically to Perine about the peaceful bygone days when he had visited his friend on his estate outside Baltimore to enjoy walks in the fresh country air. "But my walking days are over," he wrote, "and I feel that I am sick enough for a hospital." Yet he expected to preside at the next judicial term, although he did not think that the Court could "ever be restored to the authority & rank which the Constitution intended to confer upon it." Ruefully, he concluded: "The supremacy of the military power over the civil seems to be established, & the public mind has acquiesced in it & sanctioned it."

General Ambrose Burnside, who had been relieved of his command of the Army of the Potomac after the disastrous Union defeat at Fredericksburg, approached his new assignment as commander of the Department of the Ohio with fresh resolve. Known for his zealous and impulsive nature, Burnside was immediately alarmed by the widespread criticism of the Union cause expressed in Ohio's Democratic newspapers and at large public meetings around the state. He believed that such criticism undermined government authority and demoralized Union troops in the field. Without Lincoln's knowledge or approval, he declared martial law and issued General Order No. 38, which prohibited treasonous statements in the territory under his command. Civilians violating Order 38 were subject to arrest and trial by a military tribunal. If found guilty, they could be banished or face death by a firing squad.

Burnside's order seemed well timed to boost Clement Vallandigham's flagging campaign to be elected governor of Ohio. On May 1, 1863, less than three weeks after Burnside had issued his order, Vallandigham came to Mount Vernon, Ohio, to deliver his response. He proudly rode into town in a four-mile-long parade of men on horseback, farmers in wagons and buggies, and a six-horse float supporting thirty-four pretty flower girls, each representing one of the states in the Union. A huge crowd, estimated between 15,000 and 20,000, assembled to hear the former congressman make an impassioned plea for voters to reject military rule in favor of an armistice with the South.

For two hours, Vallandigham harangued the crowd, calling the war "wicked, cruel, and unnecessary." He denounced Burnside's order as a "base usurpation of arbitrary authority," and suggested that General Order 38 be replaced with "General Order No. 1—the Constitution of the United States." Once again expressing his opposition to Lincoln's Emancipation Proclamation, he deplored the war fought for "freedom for the blacks and the enslavement of whites." To rousing cheers, he urged voters to knock "King Lincoln from his throne." Union soldiers wearing civilian clothes attended the rally and took notes on the speech.

Four days later, Burnside ordered Vallandigham's arrest. A large squadron of soldiers surrounded Vallandigham's Dayton, Ohio, home at 2:30 a.m., broke down his front door, and dragged him out of his bedroom in his underwear while his wife cried hysterically. He was taken to a prison in Cincinnati to appear before a five-member military commission on charges of violating Order 38 by "publicly expressing . . . sympathy for those in arms against the government of the United States, and declaring disloyal sentiments and opinions with the object and purpose of weakening the power of the government in its efforts to suppress an unlawful rebellion."

Vallandigham's supporters rioted and burned down the office of Dayton's Republican newspaper. The former congressman offered his own protest, refusing to plead before the military tribunal and denying the jurisdiction of the court. Undeterred, the judge advocate entered a plea of not guilty for Vallandigham, and his trial proceeded. The defendant argued that he had been exercising his constitutional right to free speech, and that his criticism of the government was meant to inspire voters to turn the administration out of office. His intention was never to disobey the Constitution or resist the law, he said. At the conclusion of the trial, Vallandigham read aloud a statement objecting to the proceeding as a violation of his constitutional rights to due process.

The military commission rejected all of Vallandigham's arguments, finding him guilty of encouraging his audience at Mount Vernon to distrust their government and to sympathize with "those in arms against it, and a disposition to resist the laws of the land." He was sentenced to "close confinement" in a military prison for the remainder of the war.

Vallandigham immediately filed a petition for a writ of habeas corpus in the U.S. Circuit Court in Cincinnati, repeating his plea that the military tribunal had violated his constitutional rights, including a public trial by an impartial civilian jury. U.S. Circuit Court Judge Humphrey Leavitt was no more sympathetic to Vallandigham's claim than the military commission had been. He rejected his appeal, writing a spirited opinion which adopted the argument of necessity that Lincoln had made in justifying his suspension of the writ of habeas corpus, and that Justice Grier reiterated in his majority opinion in the *Prize Cases*.

"The court cannot shut its eyes to the grave fact that war exists, involving the most imminent public danger, and threatening the subversion and destruction of the constitution itself," Leavitt wrote. "Self preservation is the paramount law," and the judiciary should not "embarrass or thwart the executive in his efforts to deliver the country from the dangers which press so heavily upon it." Under the dire circumstances created by the Civil War, "the president is invested with very high powers." Lincoln's judgment alone in prosecuting the war must be his guide, subject only to Congress's constitutional power of impeachment.

In arresting Vallandigham, the judge said that the military authorities had done their patriotic duty. He characterized Vallandigham as one of those "artful men, disguising their latent treason under hollow pretensions of devotion to the Union," but who are intent on spreading "their pestilent heresies among the masses of people." General Burnside, in issuing General Order No. 38, had recognized the danger of such disloyal efforts and was right to suppress them. Those who criticize the government in time of crisis, he concluded, "must learn that they cannot stab its vitals with impunity."

Democratic newspapers and politicians across the North condemned the judgments of the military tribunal and Judge Leavitt. The *Detroit Free Press* concluded that Vallandigham's conviction and imprisonment left American democratic government in shambles. If a gubernatorial candidate in Ohio could be jailed for opposing the war, the *Free Press* reasoned, then those who would vote for him or other Peace Democrats could to be jailed as well. Democratic congressman Daniel Voorhees of Indiana charged that the Lincoln administration had effectively restored the infamous Sedition Act of 1798, the statute passed by the Federalist-controlled Congress that made it a crime to speak maliciously of the Adams administration.

But the outcry over the Vallandigham conviction was not confined to partisan sniping by Democrats. The *New York Tribune* declared that the Constitution did not prohibit "perverse opinions or unpatriotic speeches." And Lincoln's Republican colleague from Illinois, Senator Lyman Trumbull, denounced Burnside's order as contrary to the Constitution and "all the liberties it guarantees to all citizens."

Lincoln was embarrassed by Vallandigham's arrest but, faced with a worsening military situation for the Union, was not prepared to publicly reprove General Burnside. In the four-day period between Vallandigham's Mount Vernon speech and his arrest, Confederate general Robert E. Lee once again exhibited his superior military skills in the battle at Chancellorsville, Virginia. He divided his force of 60,000 rebel troops and then attacked two wings of the 130,000-man Army of the Potomac under the command of Joseph "Fighting Joe" Hooker. After four days of vicious fighting, Hooker's army retreated, leaving 17,000 Union soldiers dead or wounded, compared to 13,000 of Lee's troops.

This was no time to undermine his generals, Lincoln decided, particularly given the growing sentiment for a peaceful settlement of the conflict among Democrats in the North. He was also concerned that an imprisoned Vallandigham would become an attractive martyr for those opposed to the war. He therefore devised an ingenious alternative punishment for Vallandigham: the prisoner's sentence was commuted in favor of banishment to the Confederacy. On May 25, Vallandigham was delivered by Union cavalry escort under flag of truce to Confederate General Bragg's troops, who were encamped in eastern Tennessee.

As clever as Lincoln's solution was, it did not produce the desired result. The tireless Vallandigham traveled for hundreds of miles unharmed through the Confederacy, finally boarding a blockade runner at Wilmington, North Carolina, eventually arriving in Canada. From the Canadian border city of Windsor, he later resumed his campaign for governor. Ohio Democrats, furious at Lincoln and sympathetic to Vallandigham's plight, made him their party's nominee.

The widespread criticism of Vallandigham's arrest and conviction, meanwhile, continued unabated. Democrats labeled Lincoln a "Caesar" and "tyrant" while praising Vallandigham's nobility and courage. Protest meetings were held throughout the North. A group of New York Democrats meeting in Albany drew up a series of ten resolutions protesting the administration's recent actions. The "Albany Resolves" denounced arbitrary military arrests, in general, and Vallandigham's arrest and conviction by a military tribunal, in particular. They charged that Vallandigham had been convicted for exercising his First Amendment right to criticize the government. The presiding officer at the Albany meeting, Erastus Corning, president of the New York Central Railroad, sent the resolves to Lincoln, requesting his "earnest consideration."

Lincoln's written response to the "Albany Resolves" blended his talent as a skilled trial lawyer with his conviction as commander in chief that he must deal decisively with threats to the nation's security posed by men like Vallandigham. He began, as he often had done in the courtroom, with a concession.* In Vallandigham's case, the Ohio politician had contended that he had done nothing more than criticize the administration at a public meeting. "Now, if there be no mistake about this; if this assertion is the truth and the whole truth; if there was no other reason for the arrest," Lincoln wrote Corning, "then I concede that the arrest was wrong."

This opening gave Lincoln the opportunity to argue that Vallandigham's arrest was made for a different and entirely legitimate rea-

---

* In the Matson case, which Lincoln tried in 1847, for example, he conceded that his client's slaves would be free under the law if, as they claimed, their slaveowner had intended for them to reside permanently in Illinois. But Lincoln had argued that was not his client's intention (see Chapter Two, p. 71).

son: "Mr. Vallandigham avows his hostility to the War on the part of the Union; and his arrest was made because he was laboring, with some effect, to prevent the raising of troops; to encourage desertions from the army, and to leave the Rebellion without an adequate military force to suppress it. He was not arrested because he was damaging the political prospects of the Administration, or the personal interests of the Commanding General, but because he was damaging the Army, upon the existence and vigor of which the life of the Nation depends."

Lincoln maintained that Vallandigham's words were not protected by the Constitution because they undermined the military's ability to prosecute the war. "Must I shoot a simple-minded soldier boy who deserts, while I must not touch a hair of a wily agitator who induces him to desert?" he asked. Vallandigham had done nothing less injurious to the Union cause by suggesting in his Mount Vernon speech that the family of this "soldier boy" should write him "that he is fighting in a bad cause, for a wicked Administration." In such a case, Lincoln continued, "to silence the agitator, and save the boy is not only constitutional, but withal a great mercy."

The president attempted to clinch his argument with another concession—that constitutional norms are different in wartime than when the nation is at peace. He noted that the framers provided for the suspension of the writ of habeas corpus in times of rebellion but not in ordinary times. He had no doubt that "the right to Public Discussion, the Liberty of Speech and the Press" would reign supreme "throughout the indefinite peaceful future." But not in 1863, when the survival of the nation was at stake. It would be the same as suggesting "that a man could contract so strong an appetite for emetics during temporary illness as to persist in feeding upon them during the remainder of his healthful life."

Despite his appealing homely metaphors, Lincoln's constitutional position was less defensible than the one he had made in favor of the imprisonment of another suspected southern sympathizer, John Merryman. Union soldiers had arrested Merryman in his Cockneysville, Maryland, home based on reports that, as an officer in a cavalry unit, he had actively worked to sabotage the Union cause. In Vallandigham's case, there was no evidence in the record that the defendant had undermined the Union's ability to recruit men for military service or caused desertions in the field, as Lincoln charged. Merryman was arrested for his actions, Vallandigham for his words—an important distinction under the Constitution.

Shortly after his reply to Corning, Lincoln elaborated on his argument in a response to resolutions presented by a delegation of Ohio Democrats who condemned Vallandigham's conviction and banishment. "I certainly do not *know* that Mr. V. has specifically, and by direct language, advised against enlistments, and in favor of desertion, and resistance to drafting," he conceded. "I solemnly declare my belief that this hindrance, of the military, including maiming and murder, is due to the course in which Mr. V. has been engaged, in a greater degree than to any other one man." His proof of that sweeping statement was "the whole burthen of his speeches," which, Lincoln said, "has been to stir up men against the prossecution [sic] of the war." Since Vallandigham was not known "in any instance, to counsel against such resistance," he continued, "it is next to impossible to repel the inference that he has counselled directly in favor of it."

Lincoln's charge against Vallandigham, based on the negative inference that he had not counseled *against* resistance to the war, was reminiscent of his 1858 attack on Senator Stephen Douglas for his participation in what he termed the pro-slavery conspiracy of Douglas, Chief Justice Taney, former President Pierce, and President Buchanan. Since Douglas had not denied the charge, Lincoln suggested, it must be true. The conspiracy charge was a clever political ploy, but probably not a winning courtroom argument.

Lincoln was confident that the attacks on Vallandigham contained in his letters to the Albany and Ohio delegations scored impressive political points, so much so that he had both letters reprinted and distributed to leading Republicans. And the charge against Vallandigham, which Lincoln defended, did stand up in a military court. But had a civilian court, unencumbered by wartime pressures, scrupulously reviewed the conviction, it could justifiably have been overturned as a violation of Vallandigham's First Amendment rights.

Lincoln's critics in the Vallandigham case raised the specter of the Sedition Act of 1798, the statute that had been discredited as a blatant violation of an American citizen's right to criticize his government. Without evidence that Vallandigham's words had led to tangible destructive consequences for the Union, his case was not so different from that of Matthew Lyon, the Jeffersonian Republican congressman from Vermont who was convicted under the Sedition Act in 1798 for his outspoken criticism of the Adams administration.

Lyon and Vallandigham had more in common than their vocal opposition to the administrations in power; both campaigned for public office after their convictions. From jail, Lyon successfully ran for reelection to his congressional seat. Vallandigham exhorted his supporters from Windsor, Ontario, but ultimately failed in his bid for the governorship of Ohio. Lincoln did his part to assure Vallandigham's defeat, giving government workers a two-week furlough to return to Ohio to campaign and allowing soldiers from the state to vote in the field, presumably for Vallandigham's Republican opponent.

Vallandigham's conviction was appealed to the U.S. Supreme Court by his attorney, the former Democratic senator from Ohio, George Pugh. On January 22, 1864, Pugh argued before the justices that his client's petition for a writ of habeas corpus had been wrongfully rejected. For purposes of his Supreme Court argument, Pugh characterized the military commission that had convicted Vallandigham as a court, presumably to assure the justices that they could review the judgment. But Pugh quickly added that the military commission was limited to cases concerning land and naval forces and the militia.

The U.S. Judge Advocate, Joseph Holt, responded for the government that the Supreme Court did not have jurisdiction to review the proceedings of a military tribunal, either by writ of error or habeas corpus. Courts-martial and military commissions, he argued, possessed authority to deal with military issues that were not subject to review by the Supreme Court. He quoted from Chief Justice Taney's 1849 opinion in *Luther v. Borden*, which dealt with a civil war in Rhode Island, to reinforce his argument that the military exercised broad power independent of the civilian courts.

Justice Wayne delivered the opinion of the Court on February 15, 1864, agreeing with Holt that the Court did not have the authority to review the judgments of military commissions either on direct appeal or by petition of writ of habeas corpus.* The Court opinion did not discuss the merits of Vallandigham's case. It hinted nonetheless that the justices were not sympathetic to the defendant's argument; the opinion acknowledged that military power was not confined to statutes, but, in part, derived from "the common law of war."

The Court's cautious disposition of the Vallandigham case appeared to corroborate Taney's bitter observation that the wartime Supreme Court was an emasculated version of the powerful tribunal over which he had presided for more than two decades.

Two major Union military victories during the first week in July 1863 proved decisive. At Gettysburg, on the fertile farmland of southern Pennsylvania, more than 50,000 Union and Confederate soldiers were killed or wounded over three days, the most casualties ever recorded in a battle on American soil. In the end, General George Meade, the experienced corps commander who had replaced Joseph Hooker as leader of the Army of the Potomac, claimed victory, though one-fourth of all Union forces lay dead or wounded on the battlefield. Lee's Army of Northern Virginia suffered even greater casualties. A third of Lee's army was killed or wounded at Gettysburg, virtually eliminating any chance that the Confederacy could win the war.

Meade's refusal to chase Lee's retreating troops over the Potomac into Virginia reminded Lincoln of another missed Union opportunity, that of General McClellan at Antietam. The president expressed his frustration in a letter to Meade. "My dear general, I do not believe you appreciate the magnitude of the misfortune involved in Lee's escape," he wrote. "He was within your easy grasp, and to have closed upon him would, in connection with our other late successes, have

---

* Due to illness, Taney did not participate in the justices' *Vallandigham* decision.

ended the war." Lincoln did not sign or send this letter, but allowed the Union's commander, General Halleck, to express his disappointment. Meade immediately offered his resignation, but it was not accepted. After Lincoln calmed down, he realized that Meade's reluctance to pursue Lee's troops into Virginia may have been a wise decision. His troops had suffered enormous losses at Gettysburg and, like Meade himself, were exhausted from the brutal battle. The president later described Meade as "a brave and skillful officer" and gave him credit for the Gettysburg victory.

By this time, the indefatigable General Grant had begun the siege of Vicksburg, the rebel stronghold that overlooked the Mississippi River. On July 4, Confederate general John Pemberton surrendered the city and over 2,000 officers and 27,000 enlisted men. In contrast to his ambivalent opinion of Meade, Lincoln had complete confidence in Grant. The victories at Vicksburg and Gettysburg, Grant wrote, "lifted a great load of anxiety from the minds of the President, his Cabinet and the loyal people all over the North."

By the late summer, Lincoln had begun to reflect on the significance of the war and the reconstruction of the Union after the conflict had ended. Some of his thoughts were contained in a long letter that he wrote to James Conkling, an old Illinois political ally, which he encouraged Conkling to read aloud at a large Springfield rally. In this letter, which was received enthusiastically by a Springfield audience of between 50,000 and 75,000 people, the president aggressively defended his Emancipation Proclamation and the use of black troops to fight the rebels. "If they [black troops] stake their lives for us, they must be prompted by the strongest motive—even the promise of freedom," he said. "And the promise being made, must be kept." He knew that many in the midwestern audience opposed the proclamation and told them to fight exclusively to save the Union. At the same time, he wondered how those critics of the proclamation would be received after the war by returning black troops who had fought bravely to assure recent Union victories. "[T]here will be some black men who can remember that, with silent tongue, and clenched teeth, and steady eye, and well-poised bayonet, they have helped mankind on to this great consummation; while I fear, there will be some white ones, unable to forget that, with malignant heart, and deceitful speech, they have strove to hinder it."

On November 18, Lincoln boarded a special train for Gettysburg, where he was scheduled to make a brief speech at the dedication of the cemetery for the Union soldiers who had died in the critical battle. Though he knew that Edward Everett, the former U.S. senator and president of Harvard, would deliver the major address at the ceremony, Lincoln considered his remarks important and had taken care in composing them before he left Washington. After he had made final edits of the speech early the next morning, Lincoln joined Everett and other officials for the somber procession that moved slowly to the platform overlooking the freshly dug graves.

The 272 words that comprised Lincoln's Gettysburg Address are unsurpassed in force and eloquence in the history of American political oratory. Yet the ideas expressed by the president were not new; indeed, the themes—liberty, equality, and representative democracy—had been familiar staples of his public addresses for almost a decade.

The nation was committed to the ideal of equality written into the Declaration of Independence, he began, striking a theme that he had emphasized in the 1858 Lincoln-Douglas debates (when he challenged Taney's opinion in *Dred Scott*). At Gettysburg, his language soared to lyrical heights: "Four score and seven years ago our fathers brought forth, upon this continent, a new nation, conceived in liberty, and dedicated to the proposition that 'all men are created equal.' " He transformed the sacrifice of the dead Union soldiers into an enduring gift for future generations of Americans. As a result of the cause for which they "gave the full measure of devotion," he said, the nation "shall have a new birth of freedom." His final words, reworked in measured cadence, were reminiscent of a sentence in his earlier address to Congress in July 1861. The dead at Gettysburg, he intoned, had fought for the highest purpose of a constitutional democracy—"that government of the people, by the people, for the people, shall not perish from the earth."

Lincoln's annual report to Congress in December possessed neither the eternal wisdom nor literary brilliance of his Gettysburg Address, but it was a valuable public document nonetheless. When he drafted the report, to which he attached a proclamation presenting his preliminary ideas on postwar reconstruction, he knew that he could not satisfy all of his listeners in Congress, or even in his cabinet. Democrats wanted him to honor his inauguration pledge to welcome the South's return to the Union with its institutions, including slavery, intact. Conservative Republicans, like Secretary of State Seward, conceded that the Emancipation Proclamation was binding but otherwise were prepared to offer the South generous terms to return to the Union. But Radical Republican leaders, including Secretary of the Treasury Chase and Senator Charles Sumner, were determined to exact a very high price on the South for the Civil War. They advocated sweeping political and economic reforms in the postwar South and the exclusion of disloyal officers of the Confederacy from any Reconstruction government. They also insisted that the eradication of slavery not be limited to the terms of the Emancipation Proclamation.

Lincoln had no intention of accepting the *status quo ante*, as the Democrats urged. He no longer believed, as he did at his 1861 Inauguration, that extremists represented a small minority in the South and that responsible moderates would prevail. There would be no return of the South to the Union on the terms that he had presented in those peaceful times. He pleased Conservative Republicans by announcing that most rebels would be granted "full pardon . . . with restoration of all rights of property, except as to slaves." But his proclamation also appealed to Radical Republicans by excepting from that general amnesty high-ranking Confederate officers; they would be required to take an oath of future loyalty to the Constitution and pledge to obey acts of Congress and presidential proclamations relating to slavery. To encourage formal reentry of the southern states into the Union, he promised to honor their prewar boundaries and to recognize their reconstructed governments when a minimum of 10 percent of the voters on their 1860 rolls had taken an oath of allegiance to the federal government. His plan was not final, he said, and he welcomed alternative ideas.

Both Conservative and Radical Republican congressional leaders applauded Lincoln's proclamation, but the president's support remained tenuous among both factions. His willingness to accommodate other proposals suggested to outspoken Conservative and Radical Republicans alike that he lacked decisiveness. At the same time, he appeared to have successfully gauged the public mood. Horace Greeley's *New York Tribune* exulted that no presidential message since George Washington's "had given such general satisfaction." And the editors of the *Chicago Tribune* asked: "Who [is] so fit to carry on what is begun, as he who has so well conducted us . . . thus far?" Almost a year ahead of the presidential election, the *Tribune* informally announced its choice: Abraham Lincoln.

Lincoln aspired to be the first president since Andrew Jackson elected to a second term. But though he seemed to be the choice of Republican voters, restless party leaders quietly searched for a better candidate. In December, shortly after Lincoln had sent his report to Congress, his Treasury Secretary, Salmon P. Chase, let it be known that he was ready and abler than Lincoln to lead the Republican Party.

Before his cabinet appointment, Chase had built his reputation as an ardent champion of the rights of blacks as a trial lawyer, U.S. senator, and governor of Ohio. He was talented and hardworking, but also ponderous and vain (he put his picture on the newly printed one-dollar greenback). He and Lincoln had maintained a correct but distant professional relationship; Chase did not warm to Lincoln's wry humor or approve of his nuanced positions on the issue of slavery. Lincoln recognized Chase's superior grasp of complex economic issues and left his Treasury Secretary alone to do his job. But Chase never felt that he received the attention and credit from Lincoln that he deserved. He was convinced that he was a statesman with a broader postwar vision than Lincoln, and, in contrast to the president, a proven administrator.

While Lincoln's friends were appalled by Chase's maneuvering for the Republican nomination, the president remained outwardly unperturbed. "I suppose he [Chase] will, like the bluebottle fly, lay his eggs in every rotten spot he can find," he joked. He let his supporters, like his former Defense Secretary Simon Cameron, do the necessary work for him. They simply outflanked Chase and his followers, building insurmountable support for Lincoln in the state legislatures and influential Union League organizations throughout the North.

Lincoln's popularity among the masses held steady. "Mr. Chase is trying to get the nomination and he has many politicians here in his favor but the people are for Mr. Lincoln & will elect him," wrote Justice Davis, who again became a key Lincoln campaign strategist. "The general feeling is that it would be disastrous to change this administration as long as these troubles are on the country." By March, Chase's trial balloon had burst, and the Secretary announced that he would not be a candidate for the Republican nomination.

The names of military men, most notably General Grant, were also proposed as possible Republican standard-bearers in 1864. The president adroitly took care of Grant. After the general sent a letter to Lincoln saying that he would not be a candidate for the Republican nomination, Lincoln appointed him general in chief of the Union armies, replacing Halleck. At a brief ceremony at the White House, Lincoln, with Grant at his side, welcomed his new military leader. "As the country herein trusts you," he said, "so, under God, it will sustain you."

When Republicans met at Baltimore in early June under the banner of the National Union Party, Lincoln's nomination was a foregone conclusion. The party platform pledged to restore the Union and endorsed a constitutional amendment abolishing slavery. The only surprise at the convention was the selection of Tennessee's Andrew Johnson to replace the incumbent vice president, Hannibal Hamlin, on the ticket. Though Lincoln did not endorse either man, he was known to admire Johnson's resolute pro-Union stance after his state's secession. Besides, Johnson's presence on the Republican ticket would boost Lincoln's chances in the border states in the upcoming election.

Lincoln's prospects for reelection plummeted soon after the Baltimore convention as the result of a series of Union military setbacks. The euphoria over the victories at Gettysburg and Vicksburg had long since dissipated. In the late spring of 1864, Grant's troops were repelled by Lee's Army of Northern Virginia in the scrub pine thicket of the Wilderness and at Spotsylvania. In June, Grant launched an ill-conceived attack at Cold Harbor and later his Army of the Potomac bogged down in a siege of the well-fortified city of Petersburg. During six weeks of relentless fighting, nearly 100,000 northern troops were killed or wounded. General Sherman was slowly bearing down on Atlanta, but he had been defeated at Kennesaw Mountain, and his final victory was not certain.

The Union's military reversals revived talk of a negotiated peace with the South shortly before the Democratic Convention in Chicago in late August. Peace Democrats, led by the indomitable Clement Vallandigham (who had returned from his Canadian exile), pushed through a party platform that denounced the war, calling for a general amnesty and a restoration of "the Federal Union of the States." The delegates then nominated General George McClellan to be president of the United States.

Lincoln had anticipated McClellan's nomination, and his own defeat in the presidential election. A week before the Democratic Convention, he asked his cabinet to sign, unread, a document that he had prepared. "This morning, as for some days past, it seems exceedingly probable that this Administration will not be reelected," he wrote. "Then it will be my duty to so co-operate with the President elect as to save the Union between the election and the inauguration; as he will have secured his election on such ground that he cannot possibly save it afterwards."

On September 4, General Sherman sent word that "Atlanta is ours and fairly won." That triumphant news came soon after Rear Admiral David Farragut had reported that the Union navy won the Battle of Mobile Bay, the last major Gulf port under Confederate control. Suddenly, the presidential contest had been turned upside down. Even the most stubborn dissidents in the Republican Party now realized that Lincoln would be elected to a second term. One of them, Salmon Chase, whose offer of resignation from the cabinet had been accepted by Lincoln over the summer, asked for a meeting with the president. At the White House, Chase pledged his full support for Lincoln's reelection. He had heard the recurrent rumor that Chief Justice Taney was fatally ill, and did not discourage speculation that he would make an excellent appointment as the next Chief Justice.

Taney had opposed every major policy of Secretary of the Treasury Chase, beginning with Chase's support and implementation of the Legal Tender Act. He referred repeatedly to the paper currency issued by Chase's Treasury Department as "trash" and "worthless." The greenbacks undermined the economic integrity of the government, he believed, and the statute authorizing the currency was unconstitutional.

The Chief Justice had both personal and constitutional reasons to object to a second Chase policy, a tax on the salaries of the justices of the Supreme Court. Congress had passed legislation that provided for a tax of 3 percent on the salaries of all officers of the federal government, and Chase had interpreted the measure to include members of the federal judiciary. Taney was certain that Chase's interpretation was in direct violation of a provision of the Constitution, which guaranteed that the salaries of federal judges could not be reduced during their terms of office. He also knew that the tax would make it impossible for him to pay even his modest day-to-day expenses.

Taney had first discussed his intention to protest the secretary's interpretation of the tax statute with his judicial colleagues, and was told that the matter was under active consideration by Chase. Weeks went by without an official response from Chase, and Taney thought he knew the reason. "[T]he truth, I believe, is that he [Chase] has not a dollar to pay us with even in the trash he daily issues to pay contractors & soldiers arrears," he wrote. "It is impossible that Mr. Chase who is a man of decided talent & firm will could require six weeks to make up his mind on a question like this."

Two weeks later, having received no response from Chase, Taney wrote the Treasury Secretary a long letter challenging his action. The intention of the Constitution was to provide for an independent judiciary, he noted, and that independence would be compromised by giving Congress the power to reduce judicial salaries. He felt obligated to make his objections known even though the issue could not be decided by the Supreme Court, since the justices had an obvious economic interest in the question. "Having been honored with the highest judicial station under the Constitution" he added, "I feel it to be more especially my duty to uphold and maintain the constitutional rights of that department of the government, and not by any act or word of mine have it to be supposed that I acquiesced in a measure that displaces it from the independent position assigned it by the statesmen who framed the Constitution."

Chase ignored Taney's protest, as well as the Chief Justice's request that his letter be placed in the public record at the Treasury Department. Taney then made his letter a part of the public record at the Supreme Court.

Serving as a circuit court judge in Baltimore, Taney declared unconstitutional a regulation issued by Chase that forbade the shipment of goods from Baltimore to southern Maryland without a permit. Chase had issued the regulation in an effort to stop surreptitious trade with the Confederacy, but Taney said that the secretary had intruded on the constitutional rights of Maryland under the Tenth Amendment. Neither Chase, as a member of the executive branch of the federal government, nor Congress could interfere with domestic trade wholly within the state of Maryland, he wrote. Wartime conditions did not alter the constitutional limits of the federal government. "A civil war or any other war does not enlarge the powers of the federal government over the states or the people beyond what the compact has given to it in time of war," he noted. "Nor does a civil war or any other war absolve the judicial department from the duty of maintaining with an even and firm hand the rights and powers of the federal government and of the states and of the citizen, as they are written in the Constitution, which every judge is sworn to support."

In another circuit court opinion, Taney reversed a district court ruling that had supported the government's seizure of dry goods under the trading with the enemy regulation. Taney was so outraged by the elaborate entrapment measures employed by federal officials in confiscating the goods that he ordered the government to pay legal costs and damages. A government detective had posed as an intimate friend of one of the defendant's relatives, urged the defendant to purchase the goods, and then planted incriminating evidence in the defendant's luggage that was seized. The defendant "had been seduced and betrayed" into the purchase of the goods by government agents, Taney wrote, and he "could see no possible benefit to accrue to the Government from such a seizure that would in any way compare with the great evil that would arise from a court of justice countenancing such conduct."

Taney's circuit court colleague, Judge William Giles, informed the Chief Justice that he felt increasing pressure from District Attorney Price to preside at the treason trials of suspected southern sympathizers. Taney had insisted since the early months of the war that Giles alone could not preside and that, due to illness, he could not join him on the bench. But in the spring of 1864, Taney was adamant that the treason trials could not go forward, with or without him in attendance, because the defendants' rights were undermined by the pervasive Union military presence in Baltimore. "The treason cases cannot be tried simply because it is not at present in the power of the court to give the party the rights at the trial which the Constitution requires. Maryland is now under martial law, and the process of the court is obeyed or not at the pleasure of the military authority." He did not understand why, under those intolerable circumstances, Judge Giles would consider acquiescing in the District Attorney's demands. "I am yet to learn that the District Attorney can force the court to do anything that they think illegal or unjust, whatever he may think of it"

At the Supreme Court, Taney had no opportunity during the later stages of the Civil War to record officially his view that major administration policies were unconstitutional. Despite his frustration at the Court's failure to confront these issues, Taney went dutifully about his ordinary business, demonstrating the same courtesy to his colleagues and fastidious attention to detail that had characterized his long career as Chief Justice. In a commercial case involving a small damage claim, Taney wrote his colleague, Justice Davis, a long memorandum explaining his concerns about jurisdictional and other procedural issues. The reason for his delay in presenting his views, he noted, was that "the cold air from the broken pane of glass in the court room did its work so effectually upon my head, that I have been obliged to lie quietly in bed for the last three days." He then proceeded to analyze methodically the issues that concerned him and "respectfully submit these considerations to your judgment." He added, "If you think they are worth anything, show this letter to the other judges."

One of the rare exhilarating moments for Taney in 1864 was writing his grandson, Taney Campbell, to congratulate him on his admission to the bar of the Superior Court of Maryland. His grandson should take advantage of the advice that his father, a lawyer, could give him; but he must do his study of the cases independently in order to develop the judgment necessary to be an outstanding lawyer. "You must study your case yourself & be self reliant," Taney instructed, "but when you have formed an opinion, consult your father, and that conference will show you whether you have fallen into error."

Most of Taney's days were spent in isolation, recuperating from the incessant colds and chronic intestinal illnesses that had plagued him for many years. On his birthday in March 1864, he received good wishes from his friend David Perine. "At the age of eighty seven I cannot hope to see many more birthdays in this world," he replied, "& can hardly hope to live long enough to see more beautiful and happier times."

His debts continued to mount. "Can you lend me three hundred dollars?" he asked Perine. "I must tell you honestly, I do not know when I can repay you." He vowed to "begin a rigid economy & change the habits of my life in that respect—or my family will be literally destitute when I die." By late August, he calculated that he could not pay his bills for more than a few months. He blamed his plight on rampant wartime inflation created by the administration's irresponsible economic policies. A ton of range coal cost $16, twice the amount he had paid before the war; he paid 62 cents for coffee that had previously cost him only 20 cents a pound. "With such prices, which appear to be daily increasing from the depreciated currency & the increasing want of confidence in the ability of the government to meet its engagements, the paper money paid me by the government will not with the strictest economy on my part support me more than six months. I little expected to be placed in this situation in my old age," he added. "But I do not despond & think it must end in some way or other before the end of another year."

On October 12, 1864, Chief Justice Taney lay in his bed close to death, suffering from a severe intestinal infection. He was attended by three physicians. One of them, Taney's old friend the retired Dr. James Hall, reported to the Chief Justice on the vote to be held in Maryland on the adoption of a state constitution under which all slaves in the state would be set free without compensation to their owners. A letter was read aloud to Taney suggesting that he could take an oath of allegiance proposed by President Lincoln and provided for in the new state constitution even though his conscience did not approve. Taney, in the fading moments of his life, rejected the idea. He would not compromise his principles.

The next morning, the clerk of the Supreme Court, D. W. Middleton, informed Taney's brethren that "the great and good Chief Justice is no more." He had died at the age of eighty-seven the previous evening, having served for more than twenty-eight years as the fifth Chief Justice of the United States.

Taney had requested that his funeral service in the nation's capital be brief and private. It was a sensible judgment on his part. He could not have expected a great outpouring of affection in Washington upon his death. Since writing his opinion in the Merryman case, he had been perceived in the North as a traitor to the Union's cause. Nothing he did for the remainder of his life persuaded his enemies to moderate their hostility toward him. "The name of Taney is to be hooted down the page of history," sneered Charles Sumner, the abolitionist senator from Massachusetts.

Lincoln made no public statement acknowledging Taney's death or his contribution to the nation. On October 14, the president met with his cabinet to discuss who should attend the service that was to be held at Taney's home on Indiana Avenue early the next morning. It was decided that it would be left up to the individual cabinet members. Seward said that he considered it his duty to attend the service in Washington, but that he would not go to Frederick, Maryland, for Taney's burial. Lincoln, Seward, Attorney General Bates, and Postmaster General William Dennison agreed to attend the service in Taney's Washington home. Several members of the cabinet refused. One of them, Gideon Welles, Lincoln's Secretary of the Navy, wrote of Taney that "the course pursued in the Dred Scott case and all the attending circumstances forfeited respect for him as a man or a judge."

A few minutes after 6:00 a.m. on October 15, Lincoln and three of his cabinet members sat with Taney's family and friends for the brief service and then joined the cortège for the short distance to the railroad station. There the president waited until a special two-car railroad carriage with Taney's casket, relatives, and close friends had departed for Frederick for the Chief Justice's final funeral service and burial. Edward Bates also traveled to Frederick for Taney's last rites. Bates alone among the members of Lincoln's cabinet had worked closely with the Chief Justice and developed an affection and abiding respect for him. "He was a man of great and varied talents," Bates noted in his diary. "The luster of his fame, as a lawyer and judge, is for the present dimmed by the bitterness of party feeling arising out of his unfortunate judgment in the Dred Scott case. That was a great error; but it ought not and will not, for long, tarnish his otherwise well earned fame."

A requiem mass was sung for Taney in Frederick's tiny St. John's Catholic Church, which sixty years earlier he had helped to build. He was buried across the street in a small cemetery next to his mother, a few blocks away from the graves of his wife and his daughter, Alice, in the town's Presbyterian cemetery.

With the news of the Chief Justice's death, Lincoln was inundated with recommendations for a successor. Bates informed the president that the appointment would be "the crowning, retiring honor of my life." The wife of Secretary of War Stanton, concerned that her husband was exhausted from his cabinet duties, thought the office of Chief Justice would be a fitting and needed sinecure for him. Francis Blair implored Lincoln to name his son, Montgomery Blair, who had represented Dred Scott and later served as Postmaster General. Associate Justice Noah Swayne, Lincoln's first Court appointee, received early support, and so did the senior justice, seventy-four-year-old James Wayne. Leading members of the bar, notably New York's William Evarts, were also urged upon the president.

One name was put forward more insistently than any other: Lincoln's former Secretary of the Treasury, Salmon Chase. Senator Sumner was the most aggressive advocate for Chase. After hearing reports of Taney's death, Sumner wrote the president demanding that he appoint Chase: "Providence has given us a victory in the death of Chief Justice Taney. It is a victory for Liberty and the Constitution." But that victory would not be complete, Sumner suggested, unless Lincoln appointed Chase, whose record as an anti-slavery Radical Republican was as unblemished as Sumner's. The same day, Sumner wrote Francis Lieber that Lincoln had earlier promised him that he would appoint Chase. He also persuaded Chase to write him a letter that he could show to Lincoln: "It is perhaps not exactly *en règle* to say what one will do in regard to an appointment not tendered to him; but it is certainly not wrong to say to you that I should accept."

Lincoln would not be pressured into nominating Chase or anyone else to be the next Chief Justice. There was calculation in his deliberations. He knew that anyone he nominated would offend some segment of the electorate, and he did not want to alienate needlessly any voters before the November presidential election. And after he had handily defeated General McClellan, carrying all but three states in the Union, Lincoln still refused to announce his choice. Chase's name continued to be raised with the president as the best qualified man for the job. Lincoln did not question Chase's intelligence, dedication to public service, or leadership skills. But the president, understandably, had his reservations about the man who had actively sought to replace him at the top of the Republican presidential ticket. "I have only one doubt about his appointment," he told Senator Henry Wilson of Massachusetts. "He is a man of unbounded ambition and has been working all his life to become President. That he can never be; and I fear that if I make him Chief Justice, he will simply become more restless and uneasy, and neglect the place, in his strife and intrigue to make himself President."

Early in December, Lincoln, despite his concerns about Chase's insatiable ambition, concluded finally that he was the best man to lead the Court. His judgment, as usual, was grounded in practical considerations. Chase would be acceptable to both the conservative and radical factions of the Republican Party. The president was also confident that Chase would be on the right side of the issues that mattered most to him. In selecting a member of the Court, Lincoln told Congressman George Boutwell of Massachusetts that "we cannot ask a man what he will do, and if we should, and he should answer us, we should despise him for it. Therefore we must take a man whose opinions are known." In contrast to Taney, Chase was known to be a resolute defender of the Union and an outspoken opponent of slavery. On December 6, Lincoln nominated and the Senate unanimously confirmed the appointment of Salmon P. Chase to serve as the sixth Chief Justice of the United States.

EPILOGUE

Taney's estate was so meager that it did not provide even the basic amenities for his two dependent daughters: Ellen, now chronically ill and a spinster, and Sophia, widowed with a small child. At Taney's death, they were left with a trust fund composed primarily of a $10,000 life insurance policy (whose premiums during the Chief Justice's last years had been paid by David Perine) and a batch of devalued Virginia bonds. The two women were forced to take low-level clerical jobs at the Treasury Department. Years later, Taney's heirs were refunded the amount he had been taxed on his salary by Secretary of the Treasury Chase. One of Chase's successors at the Treasury Department concluded, as did Taney, that the government had illegally taxed the salaries of Supreme Court justices.

Taney was punished by spiteful abolitionists in the Senate even after his death. Early in 1865, after the House of Representatives had passed a bill to appropriate funds for a bust of Taney to be displayed in the courtroom of the Supreme Court, the Senate Judiciary Committee reported the bill to the full Senate for approval. An indignant Senator Sumner rose to oppose the bill, objecting "that now an emancipated country should make a bust to the author of the Dred Scott decision." He added, "[I]f a man has done evil during life, he must not be complimented in marble." Sumner proposed that a vacant space, not a Taney bust, be left in the courtroom to "speak in warning to all who would betray liberty."

Lyman Trumbull, the anti-slavery senator from Illinois who was the bill's sponsor, responded that it was time to heal the wounds created by Taney's *Dred Scott* opinion. No man was infallible, said Trumbull. Taney was a learned and able Chief Justice, who should be recognized for his contributions to the nation as the leader of the Supreme Court for a quarter of a century. He compared Taney to Chief Justice Marshall, stating that both were "great jurists, and each has shed luster upon the judicial tribunal over which he presided."

Sumner roared in rebuttal: "An emancipated country will fasten upon him [Taney] the stigma which he deserves. The Senator says that he for twenty-five years administered justice. He administered justice at last wickedly, and degraded the judiciary of the country, and degraded the age." Sumner vowed that Taney would not be "recognized as a saint by any vote of Congress if I can help it." He was successful; the bill did not pass.*

Another Massachusetts anti-slavery advocate, former Associate Justice Benjamin Curtis, came to Taney's defense. Curtis, as much as Sumner, had reason to resent Taney's *Dred Scott* opinion. He had written a persuasive dissent in the case and became embroiled in an acrimonious exchange of letters with the Chief Justice after he requested a copy of Taney's unpublished opinion. Despite that rancorous episode, which led to Curtis's resignation from the Court, he spoke of the late Chief Justice with deep respect. In judicial conference, he remembered Taney's "dignity, his love of order, his gentleness." He also recalled the Chief Justice's extraordinary command of the facts and law in the cases before the justices. His power of legal analysis, said Curtis, exceeded that of any man he ever knew. Curtis credited Taney and his predecessor, Chief Justice Marshall, with bringing "stability, uniformity, and completeness of our national jurisprudence."

Which portrait of Taney, Sumner's or Curtis's, survives? Both, actually, though Sumner's has proved to be the more enduring image. Certainly Sumner, vitriol aside, accurately forecast that Taney's place in history would be inextricably bound to his disastrous *Dred Scott* opinion. In *Dred Scott*, Taney abandoned the careful, pragmatic approach to con-

---

* In 1874, shortly after Chief Justice Chase had died, Congress passed a bill appropriating funds for busts of both Chase and Taney.

stitutional problems that had been the hallmark of his early judicial tenure in favor of a rigid march to his doctrinaire conclusions. He expected that his opinion would be the final constitutional word on the subject of slavery and that, as a result, the warring factions in North and South would engage in more productive pursuits. He was, of course, wrong, and his tragic miscalculation cost the nation and the Supreme Court dearly.

Though Taney would have denied it, his most controversial judicial opinions, beginning with *Dred Scott*, were influenced by his southern heritage. He was a proud member of his region's landed aristocracy, and when his class was attacked, he vehemently defended it. He bristled at the charge that slavery made the South morally inferior to the North. Although he had freed his own slaves, he joined other southerners in insisting that slaveowners treated blacks more humanely than did northerners. As the North outpaced the South in population and economic power, he shared the fear of most southerners that the terms of the Missouri Compromise would perpetuate the North's dominance. He harbored the prejudices of his region, contrasting the corruption he associated with the North with the pure, refined values of his southern friends. After the southern states seceded, he concluded that it was better that the South be allowed to establish peacefully an independent republic rather than to live under the autocratic rule of the North. Fortunately, his was a doomed reading of American history.

But there is much more to Taney's legacy than his southern perspective or a single ill-fated opinion, even one as momentous as *Dred Scott*. All of the Taney attributes that Curtis eulogized were displayed throughout the twenty-eight years he served as Chief Justice: his acute legal analysis, clarity of expression, sensitivity to the needs of his colleagues, and reverence for the institution he served. He also made significant contributions to constitutional law. As a fervent Jacksonian Democrat, he came to the Court with a profound belief in states' rights—that the best government was closest to the people and that decent agrarian American values were threatened by the crass commercialism of the urban North. If Chief Justice Marshall is justly celebrated for defining the broad perimeters of federal authority, Chief Justice Taney should be recognized for his adroit and subtle trimming of his predecessor's most expansive opinions. It was no coincidence that the published writings of Jefferson, not those of Hamilton or Adams, were prominently displayed on Taney's bookshelf at his death.

Had Taney died before he wrote his *Dred Scott* opinion, he would undoubtedly have secured a prominent place in our constitutional history. But even his post–*Dred Scott* opinions merit a respectful reading. The finely crafted *Booth* opinion declaring the supremacy of federal law when challenged by state judicial authority, for example, could have been written by Chief Justice Marshall. And his opinions written during the Civil War raised basic civil liberties issues in a time of national emergency. To be sure, his sympathy for the South influenced his decisions from *Merryman* to his circuit court opinions striking down Lincoln administration policies and practices. But viewed in the calmer atmosphere of a United States at peace, his commitment to individual liberties has been endorsed by later Supreme Court decisions.

An important constitutional principle articulated in Taney's *Merryman* opinion, which was ignored by Lincoln and pilloried in the northern press, was embraced by the Supreme Court shortly after the South's surrender. Taney had insisted in *Merryman* that neither Lincoln nor Union commander Cadwalader possessed the constitutional authority to prevent John Merryman from challenging his military imprisonment in a civilian court of law. In 1866, Justice David Davis, Lincoln's former campaign manager and Court appointee, declared for the Court that the Constitution did not authorize the military's detention and trial of a U.S. citizen during the war when the civilian courts were open.

In the 1866 decision, the Court considered the rights of an Indiana resident, Lambdin Milligan, who had been convicted of treason and sentenced to death by a military tribunal in 1864. Milligan's military trial had taken place in Indiana, a loyal Union state, not in Merryman's Maryland, where secessionist sentiment in the early days of the war was rampant and the objectivity of the civil courts could reasonably be questioned. Justice Davis's majority opinion nonetheless established the broad principle that "[c]ivil liberty and this kind of martial law cannot endure together; the antagonism is irreconcilable; and, in the conflict, one or the other must perish." He concluded that "[m]artial law can never exist where the [civilian] courts are open."

Sixty-seven years after Taney's death, Chief Justice Charles Evans Hughes traveled to Taney's hometown of Frederick to pay his respects. The occasion was the unveiling of a bust of Taney. The author of the *Dred Scott* decision, said Hughes, "bore his wounds with the fortitude of an invincible spirit." After discussing Taney's opinions in a wide range of fields, including federal-state relations and civil liberties, Hughes concluded that he was "a great Chief Justice."

After his sweeping electoral victory in November 1864, Lincoln moved with renewed confidence to secure a peace with the South on his terms: preservation of the Union and emancipation of the slaves. In his annual address to Congress in December, he reiterated his promise to southerners willing to pledge their loyalty to the federal government that they could return as full-fledged citizens to the Union. At the same time, he pointedly excluded the leadership of the Confederacy from his offer and rejected any suggestion that he should meet with Confederate president Jefferson Davis in an effort to consummate a negotiated settlement. "No attempt at negotiation with the insurgent leader could result in any good," he said. "He would accept nothing short of severance of the Union—precisely what we will not and cannot give."

Lincoln was more determined than ever to enforce his Emancipation Proclamation. He would not retract or modify his proclamation, he told Congress, "nor shall I return to slavery any person who is free by the terms of that proclamation." He also urged congressional Democrats who had voted against the proposed Thirteenth Amendment, which would have abolished slavery throughout the United States, to reconsider their votes. Though the presidential election did not impose a duty on them to change their votes, Lincoln suggested that the people had spoken and undeniably had endorsed the constitutional amendment: "In a great national crisis, like ours, unanimity of action among those seeking a common end is very desirable—almost indispensable."

Lincoln's bold words were backed by Union victories on the battlefield. General Grant's troops had pinned down Lee's army near Richmond. General Sherman ruthlessly spurred his men in their devastating march through southern Georgia. In Tennessee, General George Thomas reported that his troops had repelled the initial Confederate invasion of the state. "You made a magnificent beginning," Lincoln wrote Thomas. "A grand consummation is within your easy reach. Do not let it slip." Thomas did not disappoint the president, routing Confederate troops in the decisive victory at Nashville on December 15 and 16.

While he had promised Congress that he would enforce the Emancipation Proclamation, Lincoln continued to view it as a war measure that would necessarily expire when hostilities ended. He was therefore eager that Congress pass the Thirteenth Amendment. Combining political muscle and venerable Lincolnesque charm, he worked effectively behind the scenes to persuade wavering congressional Democrats to support it. On February 1, 1865, after the 38th Congress voted in favor of the amendment and submitted it to the states for ratification, Lincoln was ecstatic. "[T]his amendment is a King's cure for all the evils [of slavery]," he told an applauding crowd outside the White House. "It winds the whole thing up." And he extended his congratulations to "the country and the whole world upon this great moral victory."

Despite entreaties from the South, Lincoln refused to budge from his demand of an unconditional surrender. In early February 1865, he reiterated his position politely but firmly to three representatives of the Confederacy who had boarded the president's steamer, the *River Queen*, moored at Hampton Roads in northern Virginia. One of the three Confederate envoys, Alexander Stephens (whom Lincoln had last seen sixteen years earlier when both men were Whig members of the House of Representatives), concluded that it was "entirely fruitless" to have further discussions on a peace settlement. A month later, Lincoln sent instructions to General Grant that he was "to have no conference with General Lee unless it be for the capitulation of Gen. Lee's army."

At noon on the gray, gusty day of March 4, Lincoln walked onto the platform at the east front of the Capitol to deliver his second inaugural address. The strain of the war on the president was immediately visible. He appeared weary beyond his fifty-six years, the lines in his gaunt face more deeply furrowed than ever. His mood matched his somber appearance and was eloquently reflected in his brief speech.

He explained the meaning of the war in spare, impersonal terms. "Both parties deprecated war; but one of them would *make* war rather than let the nation survive; and the other would *accept* war rather than let it perish," he said. Slavery was the cause of the war, he contended, but he refused to blame the South beyond observing that "[i]t may seem strange that any men should dare to ask a just God's assistance in wringing their bread from the sweat of other men's faces." And he quickly added, "but let us judge not that we be not judged." God had punished both sides, and He alone would decide when the horrors of the war would end. Despite his fearsome acknowledgment of divine will, Lincoln concluded with inspiring words of hope: "With malice toward none; with charity for all; with firmness in the right, as God gives us to see the right, let us strive on to finish the work we are in; to bind up the nation's wounds; to care for him who shall have borne the battle, and for his widow, and his orphan—to do all which may achieve and cherish a just, and a lasting peace, among ourselves, and with all nations."

For the first time since Andrew Jackson's second inauguration in 1833, Chief Justice Taney was not present to administer the presidential oath. In his place, Chief Justice Chase stepped forward to swear in Lincoln for a second term. At the moment he asked Lincoln to place his hand on a Bible, Chase recalled, the sun suddenly burst through the dark clouds. The Chief Justice interpreted the change in weather as an auspicious omen "of the dispersion of the clouds of war and the restoration of the clear sun light of prosperous peace."

Although Lincoln had spoken of God's will and wrath in his inaugural, he acted afterwards as if the Union's fate was very much in his and his generals' hands. He eagerly received reports of military successes from South Carolina to northern Virginia. General Sherman had turned his army northward from Georgia, wreaking further havoc in South and North Carolina, leaving thousands of dead bodies and miles of burning houses and fields in his wake. Grant's forces, overwhelmingly superior in numbers and equipment, had finally worn down Lee's demoralized Army of Northern Virginia and were moving inexorably south of Petersburg and Richmond. General Philip Sheridan, marching east across the Shenandoah Valley, reported that his troops had routed the Confederate army at Burke's Station, Virginia, and could soon unite with Grant's army for the final assault on Richmond. "If the thing is pressed," Sheridan continued, "I think Lee will surrender." Lincoln immediately wired Grant, "Let the *thing* be pressed."

Lincoln wanted to witness the final scenes of the war. He had accepted an invitation from General Grant to visit his headquarters in City Point, Virginia, in late March. After sailing down the Potomac on the *River Queen* with a small entourage that included Mary and their son Tad, Lincoln felt better than he had in months. At Grant's headquarters, with sounds of Union cannons bombarding Petersburg in the background, the president inspected the battle-toughened troops in the field and visited the wounded in nearby hospital tents. On April 3, he followed Grant's troops into Petersburg, which had been abandoned by Lee's retreating Confederate army. Secretary of War Stanton, who was charged with the president's safety, was appalled. He admonished Lincoln: "Allow me respectfully to ask you to consider whether you ought to expose the nation to the consequences of any disaster to yourself in the pursuit of a treacherous and dangerous enemy like the rebel army." Don't worry, Lincoln assured him. "I will take care of myself."

A day later, after Union troops had taken control of Richmond, Lincoln visited the ravaged capital of the Confederacy. He entered the city wearing his familiar stovepipe hat and long black overcoat. Twelve armed sailors who had rowed him ashore accompanied the president through the streets of Richmond, representing his only protection against a rebel bullet. Lincoln did not seem to notice that white residents peered sullenly through windows at their unwanted visitor. He was hailed as a messiah by awestruck blacks, who clasped his hand and bowed before him, much to the president's discomfort. At the abandoned Vir-

ginia statehouse, he surveyed the chaos—the overturned desks of rebel
legislators and scattered sheets of official documents and worthless Confederate bonds that littered the floor. In the Confederate White House
he sat in Jefferson Davis's chair, and his Union escorts cheered.

Lincoln intended to be more than a conspicuous tourist in Richmond. While at the Confederate White House, he met with former U.S.
Supreme Court Justice John Campbell, one of the southern envoys who
had discussed a peace settlement with the president at Hampton Roads
and the only high-ranking member of the Confederate government remaining in the city. Campbell counseled moderation and magnanimity
on the part of the Union in the anticipated peace settlement with the
defeated South. The next day, Lincoln and Campbell, accompanied by
Richmond attorney Gustavus Myers, resumed their discussions aboard
the USS *Malvern*, anchored on the James River near Richmond. Lincoln
listed three non-negotiable presidential demands: restoration of federal
authority in the South; no retreat from his commitment to former slaves;
and unconditional surrender of Confederate troops. But he also suggested generous terms for the return of confiscated land and the formal
reentry of the secessionist states into the Union.

Lincoln returned to City Point and hoped to remain with Grant for
Lee's surrender. But on April 8, when it appeared that the surrender was
not imminent, he boarded the presidential yacht for the return voyage to
Washington. Shortly after he had arrived the next evening, he was
handed a telegram from Grant reporting Lee's surrender at Appomattox
Courthouse. The news spread quickly through a jubilant capital city the
next day. Cannons boomed, bells rang out, men laughed giddily, and
small children cheered. That night, throngs of celebrants converged on
the White House demanding to hear the president. Appearing in a
second-story window, Lincoln told the crowd that he would have much
to say the next evening and did not want them "to dribble it all out of me
before." He noted the presence of the quartermaster's band and suggested
that the musicians play "Dixie." The Confederate anthem was one of his
favorite tunes, he said, and added wryly that the Attorney General had
informed him that "it is our lawful prize."

Lincoln drafted his written remarks for his April 11 address, which was primarily devoted to the complex problems of Reconstruction, with a lawyer's attention to technical detail. He made no effort to please an audience anticipating a stirring patriotic speech. Nor did he expect to fully satisfy the contentious wings of his party. Conservative Republicans continued to advocate a return of the southern states to the Union on liberal terms—without slavery, to be sure, but with the South's prewar white leadership of planters and businessmen restored to power. Radicals, like Senator Sumner, insisted that freed slaves play a central role in a new South and demanded the complete destruction of the antebellum political and social structure.

Sumner had already indicated his displeasure with the president's earlier expressions of moderation by declining an invitation from Mary Lincoln to view the victory celebration from the White House. His fellow Radical, Chief Justice Chase, sent a letter to Lincoln shortly before he was scheduled to deliver his speech, urging him to accept the total reorganization of southern states "without regard to complexion." It was Chase's way of discouraging the president from persisting in his support for the controversial Reconstruction government in Louisiana, which had not given the vote to blacks.

With the illuminated Capitol visible in the distance, a large, joyful crowd gathered at the north portico of the White House on the evening of the eleventh to hear the president. Lincoln's appearance in an upstairs window was greeted with waves of applause and cheers. As Lincoln methodically read his policy-laden speech, his audience grew restless. By the time he reaffirmed his support for the Louisiana Reconstruction government, many in the crowd had wandered away in disappointment. But the president forged ahead. Though the Louisiana government deprived blacks of the vote, he noted that it had adopted a free constitution, provided public school benefits to blacks and whites equally, and empowered the state legislature to confer the franchise on blacks. For his part, Lincoln wished that intelligent blacks and those who had served in the Union military had been given the vote. But this was not the time to destroy the fledgling effort of Louisiana to return to the Union as a free state. Conceding that "the new government of Louisiana is only to what it should be as the egg to the fowl," Lincoln asked, shouldn't we sooner "have the fowl by hatching the egg than by smashing it?"

The temper of the president's remarks was characteristically moderate, but the remarks were not so interpreted by one disgruntled member of his audience. John Wilkes Booth, a raven-haired, twenty-six-year-old actor, listened with disgust to Lincoln's speech. "That means nigger citizenship," Booth muttered, and vowed that Lincoln's April 11 public address would be his last.

Booth, a native of the slaveholding agricultural community of Bel Air, Maryland, had been stalking Lincoln for months. After contacting the Confederate Secret Service, Booth recruited a small band of southerner sympathizers who had plotted to kidnap the president. The plan called for them to take Lincoln behind Confederate lines in Virginia, where he would be held hostage for the release of thousands of imprisoned Confederate soldiers. But after two aborted attempts at abduction, Booth began to consider assassinating the president rather than kidnapping him. He had been standing in the rotunda of the Capitol when Lincoln walked past him to deliver his second inaugural address a month earlier, and concluded that he could easily come close enough to the president to kill him.

On the evening of April 14, Booth silently slipped into the president's box at Ford Theatre during a performance of the comedy, *Our American Cousin*. At a few minutes after ten o'clock, he pointed his derringer at the back of Lincoln's head and pulled the trigger. The president died nine hours later.

Lincoln's assassination prostrated the nation with grief. Six hundred people crowded into the East Room of the White House for the funeral service, including the cabinet, leaders of Congress, Chief Justice Chase, a tearful General Grant, Mary Lincoln, and her two surviving sons, Tad and Robert. Led by a detachment of black troops, the funeral procession carried Lincoln's body down Pennsylvania Avenue to the rotunda of the Capitol, where thousands of mourners filed past. A nine-car funeral train transported the dead president 1,600 miles across the country. Hundreds of thousands of Americans watched the funeral cortège in silence—in

New York City and Cleveland, Indianapolis and Chicago, until it arrived in Springfield for Lincoln's burial.

If Lincoln had died before Taney wrote his *Dred Scott* opinion, his place in American history, like the Chief Justice's, would be radically different. Without *Dred Scott*, Lincoln might well have been remembered after his death as a good man, a fine lawyer, and a frustrated politician. Having been defeated in 1855 in his first senatorial campaign, Lincoln appeared destined to devote his professional life to the practice of law. But he was outraged by *Dred Scott* and the prospect of slavery spreading across the United States. He challenged Senator Stephen Douglas for his Senate seat in 1858 and very nearly won, in large part because of his effective attack on *Dred Scott* and what he termed the pro-slavery conspiracy comprised of Douglas, Taney, former President Franklin Pierce, and President Buchanan. Even in defeat, Lincoln's political star was ascendant. He was a dark horse candidate for the Republican presidential nomination in 1860, but his victory would surely have been impossible without *Dred Scott* and his superb performance in the Lincoln-Douglas debates.

Lincoln won the presidency in 1860 with less than 40 percent of the vote and almost one-third of the states poised to leave the Union rather than accept his leadership. After the firing on Fort Sumter, he prosecuted the war relentlessly, brusquely dismissing criticism that his policies violated the Constitution. In this regard, Chief Justice Taney was his unwitting foil, challenging Lincoln's assumption of sweeping executive powers. But Lincoln was not to be denied, by Taney or anyone else, in his goal to preserve the Union and, ultimately, to free African Americans from slavery. For those achievements alone, he will always be revered as one of our greatest presidents.

Lincoln's constitutional legacy is more ambiguous. Like every other wartime president from John Adams to George W. Bush, he took measures to protect the nation's security interests at the expense of individual liberties. But in judging Lincoln's actions, it is important to keep in mind that he had taken the presidential oath to see that the laws were "faithfully executed" shortly before the Civil War created the worst crisis in American history.

More than sixty years before the Civil War, President Adams had watched with increasing frustration as both France and Great Britain, who were at war, plundered American shipping on the high seas. The United States had arranged for an uneasy peace with Great Britain by signing the Jay Treaty. But attempts at a peace settlement with France ended in humiliating failure when an American delegation in Paris reported that three French representatives (labeled X, Y, and Z) had demanded a large bribe and loan as preconditions for the negotiation. When the so-called XYZ Affair was made public, Americans were outraged, and the president openly talked of war with France. Adams's Federalist Party inflated the threat of a French invasion of the United States and charged that Jeffersonian Republican critics of the administration posed an immediate danger to national security.

Adams signed the Alien and Sedition Acts, a series of oppressive statutes passed by the Federalist-controlled Congress aimed at intimidating or silencing the administration's Republican critics. The most egregious of those statutes, the Sedition Act of 1798, made it a crime to say or print anything "false, scandalous, and malicious" about the federal government (but made an exception for criticism of Vice President Thomas Jefferson). Within months of the passage of the Sedition Act, federal prosecutors had sent a number of high-profile Republican critics of the administration to jail for violations of the statute.

There was no comparable federal government threat to civil liberties until the Civil War. The Lincoln administration censored the mails and military commanders sporadically shut down newspapers that opposed the war. But Lincoln never proposed, nor did the Republican-controlled Congress pass, a mid-nineteenth-century version of the Alien and Sedition Acts. The opposition press remained robust during the war and continued savagely to attack administration policies.

Lincoln is the only president to have blockaded domestic ports and suspended the writ of habeas corpus. But he is also the only president who faced a rebellion that threatened the very existence of the United

States, He justified his actions as necessary to preserve the Union and authorized by his constitutional power as commander in chief. At his request, Congress immediately endorsed his blockades and later passed a statute authorizing his suspension of the writ. In the Supreme Court's decision in the Prize Cases, a narrow majority of the justices embraced Lincoln's constitutional argument of necessity in imposing the blockades of southern ports. The Court did not rule on his suspension of the writ during the war.

Lincoln's strongest argument for suspension of the writ of habeas corpus was made early in the war after secessionist sympathizers in Maryland had cut the telegraph lines and blown up bridges between Baltimore and the nation's capital, isolating Washington from the northern states. After Chief Justice Taney had condemned the president's action in his *Merryman* opinion, Lincoln issued his famous rejoinder that the framers did not intend for the president to sit idly by (with Congress adjourned) and allow the nation to be torn to pieces by rebellion. Under those circumstances, Lincoln believed that his first constitutional duty was to make certain that the government survived, and it is difficult to challenge his pragmatic judgment. This cannot be said for his later, widespread suspensions of the writ, giving license to local military commanders to arrest and try U.S. civilians before military tribunals. The Supreme Court condemned the president's actions in the *Milligan* decision, but that occurred after the war was over.

By modern constitutional standards, Lincoln's defense of the arrest and conviction of the Peace Democrat Clement Vallandigham is unconvincing. Nothing in the record of Vallandigham's military trial suggested that he did more than criticize the administration's prosecution of the war. That is political speech and should have been protected under the First Amendment. But the civilian courts to which Vallandigham appealed were unresponsive. The federal circuit court judge hearing the appeal emphatically endorsed the military tribunal's judgment, and the U.S. Supreme Court refused to review the case on the merits.

The reluctance of the Supreme Court to declare the government's wartime policies unconstitutional continued through every major war of the twentieth century. During World War I, President Woodrow Wilson's Justice Department aggressively prosecuted outspoken opponents of U.S. involvement in the war under the Espionage Act of 1917, which made it a crime to "willfully cause or attempt to cause . . . disloyalty" or "willfully obstruct" the military draft. The Supreme Court consistently upheld the convictions, including that of Eugene V. Debs, the Socialist Party's frequent presidential candidate, for a speech he delivered to the Ohio Socialist Party convention. Debs's speech was devoted primarily to Socialist principles, but he also assailed the Wilson administration's prosecutions under the Espionage Act and praised those young men who had resisted the draft. Debs appealed his conviction to the Supreme Court, claiming that his speech was protected by the First Amendment. But in *Debs v. United States*, a unanimous Court, speaking through Justice Oliver Wendell Holmes, Jr., rejected Debs's argument, concluding that a jury could have found that his speech had "the natural and intended effect" of obstructing recruiting.

In light of Justice Holmes's *Debs* opinion, Lincoln's constitutional argument in defense of Clement Vallandigham's conviction does not seem unreasonable. After all, Lincoln's argument was made more than fifty years earlier, before the Court had even begun to establish a constitutional shield for political speech. Neither Lincoln's nor Holmes's opinions would prevail under the modern Supreme Court's interpretation of the First Amendment. But the Court's vigilant protection of political speech was not fully developed for more than a century after Lincoln's presidency.

During World War II, the Court again demonstrated extreme solicitude toward the government's wartime policies. One of the modern Supreme Court's most celebrated civil libertarians, Justice Hugo Black, wrote the majority opinion which upheld President Franklin D. Roosevelt's executive order that allowed the military to exclude thousands of Japanese-American citizens from their homes on the West Coast. The Roosevelt administration had argued that military necessity justified the forced exclusion. Although the trial record failed to show that Japanese Americans posed any greater threat to national security than other citizens, the Court rejected the claim of the defendant, Fred Korematsu, a young Japanese-American welder from San Leandro, California, that the government's policy had violated his right to equal protection of the laws.

Recent scholarship has suggested that Congress represents the best check on the growing assumption of executive power in wartime. The problem is that Congress, like the Supreme Court, has been reluctant to curb the president's powers when the nation's security is perceived to be at risk. In 1964, when President Lyndon Johnson was accelerating U.S. military involvement in Vietnam, Congress passed the Gulf of Tonkin Resolution, which gave the president virtual carte blanche power to prosecute the war. After the Vietnam War had ended, Congress passed the War Powers Resolutions of 1973, which imposed explicit restraints on the president's authority to wage war unilaterally. President Richard Nixon declared that the resolutions were an unconstitutional infringement on the president's war powers, a position that has never been tested in the Supreme Court. The resolutions, however, have largely been ignored by every president since their passage.

Shortly after September 11, 2001, Congress passed a joint resolution that effectively gave President George W. Bush open-ended authority to wage the War on Terrorism in the United States and abroad by whatever means he deemed necessary. The Bush administration has prosecuted the War on Terrorism without noticeable attention to constitutional guarantees of individual rights. Suspected enemy combatants have been detained indefinitely without the opportunity for judicial review. And the president has directed the National Security Agency to eavesdrop on Americans' international phone calls without a court warrant.

In two 2004 decisions, the Supreme Court rejected the Bush administration's arguments that the detention of suspected enemy combatants was beyond judicial review. In *Rasul v. Bush*, the Court said that federal courts retained jurisdiction over detainees at Guantánamo Bay, Cuba, a territory that had been leased and controlled by the U.S. military since 1903. More pointed, in *Hamdi v. Rumsfeld*, the Court dismissed the Bush administration's argument that suspected enemy combatants who are

U.S. citizens have no due process rights. "We have long since made clear that a state of war is not a blank check for the president when it comes to the rights of the nation's citizens," Justice Sandra Day O'Connor wrote for the Court. Two years later, in *Hamdan v. Rumsfeld*, the Court again rebuked the Bush administration, declaring that its plan to put Guantánamo detainees on trial before military commissions was unauthorized by federal statute and violated international law.

Compared to the actions of other wartime presidents, Lincoln's broad exercise of executive power during the Civil War does not appear to be extreme. He did not encourage the systematic prosecution of his political critics, as did Adams in 1798. Nor did he uproot thousands of U.S. citizens from their homes, as the Roosevelt administration allowed the military to do to Japanese Americans during World War II. And he did not attempt to escape judicial scrutiny in the name of national security, as the Bush administration has repeatedly done in prosecuting the War on Terrorism, which, unlike the Civil War, has no discernible end.

Throughout the Civil War, Lincoln's moral compass remained steady, and so did his respect for the rule of law. As proud as he was of his Emancipation Proclamation, he only justified it constitutionally as a necessary war measure. His doubts about the proclamations's enduring legality caused him to lobby intensely for the passage of the Thirteenth Amendment. In his prosecution of the war, he wielded his constitutional powers fearlessly, but also with restraint. His purpose was not to seize authority that was unchecked by the other co-equal branches of the federal government.

Although Lincoln's record on the protection of civil liberties was not unblemished, he consciously weighed the legitimate security needs of the nation under siege against the individual rights of its citizens. That is one of the reasons that Justice Felix Frankfurter, a founding member of the American Civil Liberties Union, greatly admired Lincoln. Lincoln's balancing of national security interests against civil liberties also impressed Justice O'Connor, the author of the Court's *Hamdi* opinion. In a lecture delivered less than a year after writing that opinion, she reviewed Lincoln's exercise of executive power, including his suspension of the writ of habeas corpus: "To his immense credit, Lincoln did *not* use this authority to trample on the civil liberties that the writ was meant to protect. . . . He appreciated that the strength of the Union lay not only in force of arms but in the liberties that were guaranteed by the open, and sometimes heated, exchange of ideas."

For Lincoln, the essential goal of the Union in the Civil War was to repair the rupture to the constitutional government established by the framers. He had anticipated that monumental task when he told his friends at Springfield's Great Western Railroad depot on a chilly morning in February 1861 that his presidential challenge was greater than Washington's. He had been elected to preserve what he later described to be "the last best hope" for democratic government in the world. When his body was returned to Springfield in May 1865, the entire nation knew that he had met that challenge with courage and wisdom to become the wartime president indispensable to the future of the United States.

ACKNOWLEDGMENTS

I am grateful to the many people who have helped transform my proposal into a published book. I begin with my agent, Esther Newberg, who offered her usual wise counsel and encouragement. Alice Mayhew, my editor at Simon & Schuster, demonstrated anew her superb talent for bringing clarity and focus to my manuscript. Roger Labrie and Serena Jones at Simon & Schuster moved the manuscript into production with gracious efficiency.

I marveled at the skill and enthusiasm of the many librarians who assisted me with my research, ranging from the professionals overseeing the vast collections in the manuscript division at the Library of Congress to those who helped me at the Calvert County Historical Society in southern Maryland. Singled out for special mention are those scholars at the Abraham Lincoln Presidential Museum and Library in Springfield who extended every courtesy to me: Richard Norton Smith, the executive director; Kim Bauer, Lincoln Curator; Thomas Schwartz, Illinois State Historian; and Chris Schnell, assistant editor, Lincoln Legal Papers. I also wish to thank the staff at the New York Law School Library, particularly Bill Mills, my longtime library liaison, who never seems to tire of responding to endless requests for more material, and reference librarian Rosalie Sanderson. My thanks also go to my fine student research assistants at New York Law School: Helena Lynch, Diana Raynes, Katherine Smith, and Lauren Young. My assistant, Cathy Jenkins, completed a myriad of tasks with unwavering good cheer and competence. Dean Richard Matasar and Associate Dean Stephen Ellmann at New York Law School encouraged me and approved generous summer research grants to support my work. I also benefitted from comments from my colleagues at New York Law School at a faculty seminar in which I presented a chapter of the manuscript.

I was fortunate to be able to call on a number of outstanding scholars to read the manuscript and offer critical commentary, although, of course, I alone am responsible for the published work. They are: my colleagues at New York Law School, Professor Annette Gordon-Reed, and Edward Purcell, Jr., Joseph Solomon Distinguished Professor of Law; Philip Shaw Paludan, Naomi B. Lynn Distinguished Chair of Lincoln Studies at the University of Illinois at Springfield; Thomas Schwartz, Illinois State Historian; G. Edward White, David and Mary Harrison Distinguished Professor of Law at the University of Virginia School of Law; and Douglas L. Wilson, George A. Lawrence Distinguished Service Professor Emeritus of English and Co-Director of The Lincoln Studies Center, Knox College.

Finally, my wife, Marcia, served as expert editor and supportive spouse throughout the process. She has been essential to the successful completion of this book.

NOTES

The source notes are limited to primary materials and the basic secondary works that I have used. The bibliography of Lincoln is immense and too great to reproduce here. The bibliographic task is much easier for Taney, since a comparatively sparse literature is available. I have relied primarily on the published writings of Lincoln found in eight volumes: *The Collected Works of Abraham Lincoln*, edited by Roy P. Basler, et al. I have also reviewed materials in the Abraham Lincoln Papers and the Herndon-Weik Collection in the Library of Congress and Lincoln's papers in the collection of the Illinois State Historical Library in Springfield. I have studied Taney's letters in the Taney Papers and the Andrew Jackson Papers at the Library of Congress and in several collections at the Maryland Historical Society in Baltimore. I also found copies of Taney letters in the Frederick County (Maryland) Historical Society.

There are many important biographies of Lincoln, including the following multivolume works: *Abraham Lincoln: A History* (1890) by John G. Nicolay and John Hay; *Herndon's Lincoln: The True Story of the Great Life* (1889) by William Herndon and Jesse Weik; *The Life of Abraham Lincoln* (1917) by Ida M. Tarbell; *Abraham Lincoln: The Prairie Years* (1926) and *Abraham Lincoln: The War Years* (1939) by Carl Sandburg; *Abraham Lincoln* (1928) by Albert J. Beveridge; and *Lincoln the President* (1945–55) by J. G. Randall. Notable one-volume works include *Abraham Lincoln: A Biography* (1952) by Benjamin P. Thomas; *With Malice Toward None: The Life of Abraham Lincoln* (1977) by Stephen B. Oates; *The Last Best Hope of Earth: Abraham Lincoln and the Promise of America* (1993) by Mark E. Neely, Jr; *The Presidency of Abraham Lincoln* (1994) by

Phillip Shaw Paludin; *Abraham Lincoln: Redeemer President* (1999) by Allen C. Guelzo; *Abraham Lincoln and Civil War America* (2002) by William E. Gienapp; *Lincoln* (2003) by Richard J. Carwardine; and *Team of Rivals: The Political Genius of Abraham Lincoln* (2005) by Doris Kearns Goodwin. I found David Herbert Donald's fine biography, *Lincoln* (1995), especially valuable. Biographical works on Taney include *Memoir of Roger Brooke Taney* (1872) by Samuel Tyler; *Life of Roger Taney* (1922) by Bernard C. Steiner; *Roger B. Taney: Jacksonian Jurist* (1936) by Charles W. Smith, Jr.; and *Without Fear or Favor: A Biography of Roger Brooke Taney* (1964) by Walker Lewis. Carl Brent Swisher's *Roger B. Taney* (1935) is particularly insightful and remains the standard Taney biography.

My study of the decisions of the Taney Court is based on the opinions in the U.S. Reports, the official record of the decisions of the Supreme Court of the United States. *History of the Supreme Court of the United States: The Taney Period, 1836–64*, Vol. 5 (1974), by Carl Brent Swisher, was also valuable, as was *The Supreme Court in United States History, 1836–1918*, Vol. 2 (1926), by Charles Warren.

The notes are, for the most part, self-explanatory. I have used acronyms to identify frequently cited sources. Thus, a citation from p. 178 of Vol. 7 of *The Collected Letters of Abraham Lincoln*, ed. Basler, et al., becomes CWAL7, p. 178. U.S. Supreme Court decisions follow legal methods of citation: *Dred Scott v. Sandford*, 19 How. 393 (1857) means that the Supreme Court decided the case in 1857 and that it is reported at p. 393 of the 19th volume of decisions reported by Benjamin Howard. Later Supreme Court decisions are simply reported by the official volume number of the U.S. Reports, e.g., the citation for *Debs v. U.S.* is 249 U.S. 211 (1919).

Abbreviations

AJPLC—Andrew Jackson Papers, Library of Congress
AL—Abraham Lincoln
ALPLC—Abraham Lincoln Papers, Library of Congress
CPMHS—J. Mason Campbell Papers, Maryland Historical Society

CWAL-*The Collected Works of Abraham Lincoln*, 8 vols., ed. Roy P. Basler, et al.

DPISHL-David Davis Papers, Illinois State Historical Library

HPMHS—Benjamin Howard Papers, Maryland Historical Society

HWC-Herndon-Weik Collection, Library of Congress

LOC—Library of Congress

PPMHS—David M. Perine Papers, Maryland Historical Society

RBT—Roger B. Taney

RBTPLC-Roger B. Taney Papers, Library of Congress

Introduction

1 Taney's anti-slavery pronouncement: John D. Lawson, ed., *American State Trials*, Vol. 1 (1914), p. 88.

1 Lincoln's view of slavery: AL to A. Hodges, April 4, 1864, CWAL7, p. 281.

2 Taney Court decisions on slavery in the 1840s: See *U.S. v. Schooner Amistad*, 15 Pet. 518 (1841); *Groves v. Slaughter*, 15 Pet. 449 (1841); and *Prigg v. Pennsylvania*, 16 Pet. 539 (1842).

2 AL's proposal for DC, January 10, 1849: CWAL2, pp. 20–22.

3 *Dred Scott v. Sandford:* 19 How. 393 (1857).

3 AL's accusation of a pro-slavery conspiracy: AL speech, Aug. 21, 1858, CWAL3, p. 22.

3 AL's opposition to secession: AL inaugural address, March 4, 1861, CWAL4, p. 264.

3 RBT's support for secession: RBT to Franklin Pierce, June 12, 1861, Franklin Pierce Papers, New Hampshire Historical Society, Concord, NH.

Chapter One: "A Moonlight Mind"

5 "Michael Taney, Gentleman": Swisher, *Taney*, p. 4.

6 "She was pious": Tyler, p. 26.

6 Nisbet's influence on RBT: Tyler, pp. 38–42; RBT's copy of Nisbet's book on moral philosophy, HPMHS.

7 RBT's first trial: Tyler, pp. 76–78.

7 "[M]y system": Ibid., p. 80.

8 RBT's interruption of priest: Steiner, p. 45.

8 RBT's support for War of 1812: Swisher, *Taney*, pp. 54–68.

9 RBT's position on slaves and free blacks: Swisher, *Taney*, pp. 93–100; Tyler, pp. 124–32.

9 Gruber preached: Lawson, pp. 80–89; William P. Strickland, *The Life of Jacob Gruber* (1860), pp. 136–38.

10 "Lawyer Taney": Strickland, p. 140.

10 Gruber trial: See Lawson, pp. 69–106; David Martin, *Trial of the Rev. Jacob Gruber* (1819); Strickland, pp. 155–70; and Tyler, pp. 127–31.

12 RBT's position on Missouri Compromise: Swisher, *Taney*, pp. 99, 100.

12 Etting case: *Etting v. Bank of the United States*, 11 Wheaton 59 (1826).

13 "have had but little": *Life and Letters of Joseph Story*, Vol. 1, p. 493.

13 "a positive deceit": *Etting*, 11 Wheaton 59 (1826), p. 67.

13 "that infernal apostolic": John E. Semmes, *John H. B. Latrobe and His Times* (1917), p. 203.

13 "a moonlight mind": Quoted in George Van Santvoord, *Lives of the Chief Justices* (1854), pp. 477, 478.

14 Jackson impressed Taney: Swisher, *Taney*, pp. 121–29.

15 Taney's opinion on states' rights and slavery: *Official Opinions of the Attorneys General* (1831), Vol. 2, p. 475.

17 Hamilton-Jefferson debate on National Bank: James F. Simon, *What Kind of Nation: Thomas Jefferson, John Marshall, and the Epic Struggle to Create a United States* (2002), pp. 29–31.

18 *McCulloch v. Maryland*: 4 Wheaton 316 (1819).

19 known as the Bank War: For background on the Bank War, see Arthur M. Schlesinger, Jr., *The Age of Jackson* (1953), pp. 74–114; Swisher, *Taney*, pp. 160–285; and Taney, Bank War manuscript (1849), RBT-PLC.

19 Jackson's proposal for a new Bank, December 1830: James D. Richardson, ed., *Messages and Papers of the Presidents*, Vol. 2, p. 529.

19 Biddle's opposition: See, e.g., Nicholas Biddle to J. Hemphill, Dec. 14, 1830, Nicholas Biddle Papers, LOC.

19 RBT's opposition to the bank: See Taney, Bank War manuscript.

20 RBT memo to Jackson: June 27, 1832, AJPLC.

20 "The veto works well": Schlesinger, *The Age of Jackson*, p. 91.

21 "wantonly attacks": *Cong. Globe*, 22nd Cong., 1st Sess. (1832), p. 1240.

21 Webster's denunciation of Taney's "trash": Daniel Webster to Joseph Story, July 21, 1832, Joseph Story Papers, Massachusetts Historical Society, Boston.

22 RBT's memo opposing rechartering the bank: RBT to Andrew Jackson, April 3, 1833, AJPLC.

23 "unites with me": Andrew Jackson to M. Van Buren, Sept. 23, 1833, AJPLC.

23 "We have a fiery contest": RBT to A. Stevenson, Nov. 16, 1833, Andrew Stevenson Papers, LOC.

23 "We are in the midst": *Cong. Globe*, 23rd Cong., 1st Sess. (1833), p. 59.

24 "Nicholas Biddle now rules": Andrew Jackson to E. Livingston, June 27, 1834, AJPLC.

25 RBT speech responding to Webster: Tyler, pp. 233, 234.

26 "[t]here was hardly": Recalled in speech of Reverdy Johnson, *Cong. Globe*, 38th Cong., 1st Sess. (1864), p. 1363.

26 "I confess": J. Story to F. Lieber, Nov. 28, 1836, Francis Lieber Papers, Huntington Library, San Marino, CA.

26 "The pure ermine": *New York American*, March 17, 1836.

26 "The accomplished Taney": *Richmond Enquirer*, March 19, 1836.

26 "I owe this honor": RBT to Andrew Jackson, March 17, 1836, AJPLC.

27 *Marbury v. Madison:* 1 Cranch 137 (1803).

29 the Charles River Bridge case: *Charles River Bridge v. Warren Bridge*, 11 Pet. 420 (1837); summary of oral arguments, 11 Pet., pp. 428–536; for background, see Stanley I. Kutler, *Privilege and Creative Destruction: The Charles River Bridge Case* (1971); Swisher, *History*, pp. 73–97; and Warren, *Supreme Court History*, pp. 21–25.

32 "a little too much": J. Story to C. Sumner, January 25, 1837, *Life and Letters of Joseph Story*, Vol. 2, p. 266.

32 "Taney is smooth and plausible": Daniel Webster to J. Mason, Feb. 3, 1837, Swisher, *History*, p. 86.

33 "The millions of property": 11 Pet. 420 (1837), p. 552.

34 "A case of grosser injustice": J. Story to Mrs. Story, Feb. 14, 1837, William W. Story, ed., *Life and Letters of Joseph Story*, Vol. 2, p. 268.

34 *New York v. Miln:* 11 Pet. 102 (1837).

34 *Gibbons v. Ogden:* 9 Wheat. 1 (1824).

35 Kentucky bank decision: *Briscoe v. Bank of the Commonwealth of Kentucky*, 11 Pet. 257 (1837).

36 1839 out-of-state banking corporation decision: *Bank of Augusta v. Earle*, 13 Pet. 519 (1839).

36 "frightened half the lawyers": J. Story to C. Sumner, June 17, 1838, Charles Sumner Papers, Harvard University, Cambridge.

37 "has given very general": J. Story to RBT, April 19, 1839, Tyler, p. 288.

38 the *Amistad* case: *U. S. v. Schooner Amistad*, 15 Pet. 518 (1841); summary of oral arguments, 15 Pet., pp. 538–87; see also Charles F. Adams, ed., *Memoirs of John Quincy Adams*, Vol. 10, pp. 398–431; for background, see Swisher, *History*, pp. 189–95; and Warren, *Supreme Court History*, pp. 73–76.

39 *Courier* view of *Amistad* case: *Charleston Courier*, Jan. 13, 1841.

39 "extraordinary, I say": J. Story to Mrs. Story, Feb. 28, 1841, Story, Vol. 2, p. 348.

39 "upon the eternal principles": *U.S. v. Schooner Amistad*, 15 Pet. 518 (1841), p. 595.

40 Taney opinion in second 1841 slavery case: *Groves v. Slaughter*, 15 Pet. 449 (1841).

40 *Prigg v. Pennyslvania:* 16 Pet. 539 (1842); summary of oral arguments, 16 Pet., pp. 557–606; for background, see Paul Finkelman, "*Prigg v. Pennsylvania* and Northern State Courts Anti-Slavery Use of a Pro-Slavery Decision," 25 *Civil War History* 5 (1979); Swisher, *History*, pp. 535–47; and Warren, *History*, pp. 83–87.

42 "become an open pathway": 16 Pet. 539 (1842), p. 632.

42 "Mr. Chief Justice": Recalled in speech of Reverdy Johnson, *Cong. Globe*, 38th Cong., 1st Sess. (1864), p. 1363.

43 "The Bank of the United States": RBT to Andrew Jackson, July 3, 1837, AJPLC.

43 "disgraceful buffoonery": RBT to Andrew Jackson, Oct. 24, 1842, AJPLC.

43 "We have passed through": RBT to J. K. Polk, Nov. 20, 1844, James K. Polk Papers, LOC.

43 RBT's 1849 Court opinion: *Passenger Cases—Norris v. City of Boston*; *Smith v. Turner*, 7 How. 283 (1849).

44 "For all the great purposes": *Passenger Cases*, 7 How. 283 (1849), p. 492.

Chapter Two: "My Politics Are Short and Sweet"

45 "My parents were both": AL's campaign autobiography, AL to J. Fell, Dec. 20, 1859, CWAL3, p. 511.

46 "Uncle Mord had run off": Francis F. Brown, *The Every-Day Life of Abraham Lincoln* (1913), Vol. 1, p. 4.

47 was "naturally anti-slavery": AL to A. Hodges, April 4, 1864, CWAL7, p. 281.

47 "I cannot remember": Ibid.

47 "she had been his best Friend": A. Chapman to W. Herndon, Oct. 8, 1865, HWCLC.

47 "did not amount": AL autobiography written for J. Scripps, June 1860, CWAL4, p. 62.

49 who "was born and": AL speech, March 9, 1832, CWAL1, pp. 8, 9.

49 "My politics are short": Herndon and Weik, *Herndon's Lincoln*, Vol. 1, p. 104.

51 "I believed he was thoroughly": Ibid., p. 107.

51 "winked out": AL autobiography, June 1860, CWAL4, p. 65.

51 was "too insignificant": Ibid.

52 "Mr. Lincoln had the monopoly": R. Wilson to W. Herndon, Feb. 10, 1866, HWCLC.

53 "Boys if that is all": J. Herndon to W. Herndon, May 28, 1865, ibid.

53 "make a decent appearance": C. Smoot to W. Herndon, May 7, 1866, ibid.

53 "in good earnest": AL autobiography, June 1860, CWAL4, p. 65.

53 "to build a toll bridge": AL's bill, Dec. 9, 1834, CWAL1, p. 28.

54 to "show their hands": AL letter to *Sangamo Journal*, June 13, 1836, ibid., p. 48.

55 AL confrontation with Forquer: Joshua F. Speed, *Reminiscences of Abraham Lincoln and Notes of a Visit to California: Two Lectures* (1884), pp. 17, 18.

55 Governor Duncan's address: Illinois *House Journal*, Sess. 1836–37, pp. 19–26.

56 "the sinking fortunes": Frank E. Stevens, "Life of Stephen A. Douglas," *Ill. State Hist. Soc. Journal*, 16 (1924), p. 300.

57 The governor informed the legislators: See *House Journal*, Sess. 1836–37, p. 134.

58 "The Congress of": AL and Dan Stone protest, March 3, 1837, CWAL1, p. 75.

60 AL's address to the Young Men's Lyceum, Jan. 27, 1838: Ibid., pp. 108–15; quotes at pp. 109, 111, 112.

62 "If we do our duty": AL to Jesse Fell, July 23, 1838, CWAL1, p. 120.

62 "unnaturalized foreigners": AL letter to *Chicago American*, June 24, 1839, ibid., p. 151.

62 "we had heard": AL to J. Stuart, Nov. 14, 1839, ibid., p. 154.

63 AL's major speech on Dec. 26, 1839: Ibid., pp. 159–79, quotes at pp. 171, 175.

64 "in the main": *Illinois State Register*, Feb. 14, 1840.

64 "I am the most unfortunate": Quoted in Merrill Peterson, *The Great Triumvirate* (1987), pp. 1291, 1292.

65 "[t]o see each man": AL's campaign plan, January 1840, CWAL1, p. 180.

65 "The chance to do so": AL to JS, Jan. 20, 1840, ibid., p. 184.

65 AL and colleagues' rebuttal: *Sangamo Journal*, Feb. 28, 1840, ibid., pp. 203–05.

65 AL's Tremont speech, May 2, 1840: Ibid., pp. 209, 210.

66 "in the worst way": W. Herndon interview with Mrs. N. Edwards, Jan. 10, 1866, HWCLC.

67 "a reception as shall be worthy": AL et al. to HC, Aug. 29, 1842, CWAL1, p. 297.

68 "If the Whig abolitionists": AL to W. Durley, Oct. 3, 1845, ibid., p. 347.

69 Matson case: See *Matson v. Rutherford* (1847), Lincoln Legal Papers, Illinois State Historical Library, Springfield, IL; circuit court opinion, *In the Matter of Jane, A Woman of Color*, 5 *Western Law Journal* 202; Anton-Hermann Chroust, "Abraham Lincoln Argues a Pro-Slavery Case," 5 *American Journal of Legal History* 299 (October 1961); O. B. Ficklin, "A Pioneer Lawyer," *Tuscola Review*, Sept. 7, 1922, Illinois State Historical Library; Duncan T. McIntyre, "Lincoln and the Matson Slave Case," 1 *Illinois L.R.* 386 (1907); and Jesse W. Weik, "Lincoln and the Matson Negroes," 17 *Arena* 752 (April 1897).

72 "trenchant blows": Chroust, p. 304; Ficklin, note 1.

73 "an open scoffer": AL handbill replying to charges, July 31, 1846, CWAL1, p. 382.

73 "That reminds me . . .": Tarbell, *Lincoln*, Vol. 1, p. 208.

73 AL aggressively attacked Polk: Dec. 22, 1847, CWAL1, pp. 420–22.

75 AL's proposal for DC: Jan. 10, 1849, CWAL2, pp. 20–22.

75 "that slave hound": Beveridge, Vol. 2, p. 185.

Chapter Three: "The Monstrous Injustice of Slavery"

77 "Old Zack is a good old soul": Glyndon G. Van Deusen, *Horace Greeley, Nineteenth Century Crusader* (1953), p. 137.

77 "and will march up": *Cong. Globe*, 31st Cong., 1st Sess. (1850), p. 137.

77 William H. Seward rejected: Ibid., appendix, p. 265.

78 "furious . . . bloody . . .": Ibid., p. 127.

78 "If you are unwilling": Ibid., p. 455.

78 Webster's view: Ibid., pp. 274, 275.

79 "Why did all manly gifts": Ralph Waldo Emerson, *Collected Works* (1904), Vol. 9, p. 399.

79 AL's Clay eulogy, July 6, 1852: CWAL2, pp. 121–32.

80 "He ever was, on principle": Ibid., p. 130.

80 "settled forever": Ibid., p. 232.

81 "will raise a hell": Gerald M. Capers, *Stephen Douglas, Defender of the Union* (1959), p. 95.

81 "a gross violation": John Niven, *Salmon P. Chase: A Biography* (1995), p. 150.

82 AL's criticism at Scott County Whig meeting: *Illinois Journal*, Aug. 26, Sept. 2, 1854, CWAL2, p. 227.

82 Douglas defense: Robert W. Johannsen, *Stephen A. Douglas* (1973), pp. 453–57.

83 AL's Springfield speech, Oct. 4, 1854: *Illinois Journal*, Oct. 5, 1854, CWAL2, pp. 240–47; quotes at pp. 241, 242, 244, 245.

86 his "lifeless remains": *Illinois State Register*, Oct. 9, 1854.

86 AL's Peoria speech, Oct. 16, 1854: CWAL2, pp. 247–83; "I felt confident," p. 248; AL's view on colonization, p. 255; "I hate it," ibid.; "When the white man," p. 266; "Judge Douglas," ibid.; "It shows," pp. 281, 282.

88 "You used to express": AL to Charles Hoyt, Nov. 10, 1854, ibid., p. 286.

88 "It has come round": AL to Thomas Henderson, Nov. 27, 1854, ibid., p. 288.

88 "he slept, like Napoleon": Herndon and Weik, Vol. 2, p. 375.

89 "Not too disappointed": Horace White, *The Life of Lyman Trumbull* (1913), p. 45.

90 denounced their action as "revolutionary": Richardson, Vol. 6, p. 2891.

90 "Our political problem": AL to G. Robertson, Aug. 15, 1855, CWAL2, p. 318.

91 "the high regard which": William Seward to RBT, Jan. 31, 1851, Tyler, p. 318.

91 "Who doubts": *Cong. Globe*, 30th Cong., 1st Sess., (1848), p.1155.

91 "If the decision": Ibid., p. 1081.

91 Curtis's view of RBT: Curtis's eulogy, Oct. 15, 1864, Benjamin Robbins Curtis, *Memoir and Writings of Benjamin Robbins Curtis* (1879), Vol. 2, pp. 336–42.

92 "It is the unmitigable": Peter Daniel to Martin Van Buren, Nov. 1, 1847, Van Buren Papers, LOC.

92 McLean's ambitions: Francis P. Weisenberger. *The Life of John McLean* (1937), pp. 139–52.

94 "unhappy agitators": *Oliver v. Kauffman*, 18 Fed. Cas. 657, 661 (No. 10497) (C.C.E.D. Pa. 1850).

94 "very unwilling": RBT to William Seward, Jan. 31, 1851, Tyler, p. 318.

96 "I have not the slightest": RBT to J. Mason Campbell, June 26, 1855, CPMHS.

96 "[I]t has pleased God": RBT to B. Curtis, Nov. 3, 1855, Tyler, pp. 327, 328.

Chapter Four: Dred Scott

99 Seward's proposal: *Cong. Globe,* 34th Cong., 2nd Sess. (1856), p. 365.

99 "He is a noble": *Cong. Globe*, 33rd Cong., 2nd Sess. (1854), p. 41.

99 Chase's praise: Ibid., p. 217.

99 "For one": *New York Tribune*, Dec. 19, 1855.

100 "there has been no assumption": *Cong. Globe,* 33rd Cong., 2nd Sess. (1854), p. 347.

100 the *Dred Scott* case: For background, the best study is Don E. Fehrenbacher's *The Dred Scott Case: Its Significance in American Law and Politics* (1978); also useful are Paul Finkelman, *Dred Scott v. Sandford: A Brief History with Documents* (1997); Stanley I. Kutler, ed., *The Dred Scott Decision, Law or Politics?* (1967); Robert L. Stern, "Chief Justice Taney and the Shadow of Dred Scott," *Journal of Supreme Court History* (1992), pp. 39–52; Swisher, *History*, pp. 592–630; and Warren, *History*, pp. 279–319.

101 the lawsuit of *Scott, Man of Color v. Emerson:* 15 Mo. 577 (1852).

102 "have been possessed with a dark": Ibid., p. 586.

103 "because he is a negro": Lawson, Vol. 13, pp. 247, 248.

104 "The judge said that according": Ibid. p. 244.

105 McLean's letter: John McLean to J. Teesdale, Nov. 2, 1855, Weisenburger, p. 190.

105 Harvey's report: *New York Tribune*, April 10, 1856.

105 justices' initial deliberations: B. Curtis to G. Ticknor, April 8, 1856, Curtis, *Memoir*, Vol. 1, p. 180.

106 *Tribune's* report on RBT: *New York Tribune*, May 14, 1856.

107 AL's remarks at meeting, Feb. 22, 1856: CWAL2, p. 333.

108 Sumner speech: *Cong. Globe*, 34th Cong., 1st Sess. (1856), p. 530.

109 The assault confirmed: Emerson, *Collected Works*, Vol. 9, p. 247.

109 Report of AL's Bloomington speech, May 29, 1856: CWAL2, p. 341.

109 "in the inspiration": Herndon and Weik, Vol. 2, p. 384.

109 "It must be": CWAL2, p. 341.

110 Curtis's private opinion of McLean: B. Curtis to G. Ticknor, April 8, 1856, Curtis, Vol. 1, p. 180.

110 McLean's political views: Weisenberger, pp. 148, 149.

110 AL supports McLean: AL to L. Trumbull, June 7, 1856, CWAL2, p. 342.

110 "I reckon that": Henry C. Whitney, *Life on the Circuit with Lincoln*, ed. Paul M. Angle (1940), p. 80.

111 RBT's sense of foreboding: RBT to J. Mason Campbell, Oct. 2, 1856, CPMHS.

112 "The South is doomed": Ibid.

113 "With the Fremont and Fillmore men": AL to H. Wells, Aug. 4, 1856, CWAL2, p. 358.

113 AL's speech at Chicago banquet, Dec. 10, 1856: Ibid., pp. 383–85, quote at p. 385.

113 "The great object": James Buchanan to R. Grier, Nov. 14, 1856, James Buchanan Papers, Pennsylvania Historical Society, Philadelphia, Pa.

113 Pierce's last annual address: Richardson, Vol. 5, pp. 399–401.

114 the Taney Court convened: For *Dred Scott* legal briefs and oral arguments, see Philip B. Kurland and Gerhard Casper, eds., *Landmark Briefs and Arguments of the Supreme Court of the United States* (1978), Vol.3, pp. 167–283.

114 press reaction to case: See Warren, pp. 285–89.

115 "[t]rue blacks are not": Geyer brief, Kurland and Casper, p. 232.

116 "Slavery promises to exist": Bernard C. Steiner, *Life of Reverdy Johnson* (1914), p. 38.

116 Alexander Stephens's report: Richard M. Johnson and William H. Browne, *Life of Alexander H. Stephens* (1883), p. 318.

116 "Judicial tyranny": *New York Tribune*, Jan. 5, 1857.

116 Benjamin Stanton proposal: *Cong. Globe*, 34th Cong., 3rd Sess., (1857), p. 300.

117 Curtis's report on Daniel: BC to G. Ticknor, Feb. 27, 1857, Curtis, Vol. 1, p. 193.

117 "Our aged Chief Justice": Ibid., pp. 193, 194.

117 the Court's compromise unraveled: for the Justices' deliberations, see J. Catron to J. Buchanan, Feb. 10, Feb. 19, Feb. 23, 1857; R. Grier to J. Buchanan, Feb. 23, 1857, Buchanan Papers; Curtis, Vol. 1, pp. 206, 207, 234–37; Fehrenbacher, pp. 305–21; Warren, pp. 293–97; and Swisher, *History*, pp. 615–19.

118 he "became convinced": Curtis, Vol. 1, p. 206.

119 "With the best of intentions": Ibid.

119 "drop Grier a line": JC to James Buchanan, Feb. 19, 1857, Buchanan Papers.

120 Buchanan's inaugural address: Richardson, Vol. 5, p. 431.

121 Taney asserted that: *Dred Scott v. Sandford*, 19 How. 393 (1857), pp. 399–454.

121 "too plain to be": Ibid., p. 407.

122 "cruel war against": Julian P. Boyd, ed., *Papers of Thomas Jefferson*, Vol. 1, p. 426.

124 "it is a constitution": *McCulloch v. Maryland*, 4 Wheat. 316 (1819).

125 Marshall had drawn broad perimeters: *Gibbons v. Ogden*, 9 Wheat. 1 (1824); *McCulloch v. Maryland*, 4 Wheat. 316 (1819); *American Insurance Co. v. Center*, 1 Peters 511 (1828).

127 Campbell and Catron's earlier opinions: See Swisher, *History*, p. 626; Campbell's opinion, 19 How. 393 (1857), pp. 493–518; Catron's opinion, ibid., pp. 518–29; Daniel's opinion, pp. 469–93; McLean's dissent, pp. 529–64; Curtis's dissent, pp. 564–633; "has its origin," p. 538.

129 "wicked," *New York Tribune*, March 7, 1857; "feeling of": Chicago *Democratic-Press*, March 13, 1857.

130 RBT-Curtis exchange of letters: See Curtis, Vol. 1, pp. 212–25, quote at p. 221.

131 "Every intelligent person": RBT to Rev. S. Nott, August 19, 1857, *Massachusetts Historical Society Proceedings* (1873), pp. 445–47.

131 "the war is waged": RBT to Franklin Pierce, Aug. 29, 1857, Pierce Papers, LOC.

Chapter Five: "The Better Angels of Our Nature"

133 AL's Galena speech, July 23, 1856: CWAL2, pp. 353–55, quote at p. 355.

133 "Having devoted the most": AL to Charles Gilfillan, May 9, 1857, CWAL2, p. 395.

133 One of his clients: AL's declaration against Illinois Central Railroad, April 1857, ibid., p. 392.

134 AL's speech to jury in drawbridge case, Sept. 22, 1857, Sept. 23, 1857: Ibid., pp. 415–22.

134 Douglas's Springfield speech, June 1857: Johannsen, pp. 567–71.

136 AL's Springfield speech, June 26, 1857: CWAL2, pp. 398–410.

139 the Democratic press reaction to AL's Springfield speech: Beveridge, Vol. 4, pp. 156,157.

139 Douglas's reaction: Johannsen, p. 574.

140 "Mr. Douglas": Allan Nevins, *The Emergence of Lincoln: Douglas, Buchanan, and Party Chaos, 1857–1859* (1950), Vol. 1, p. 253.

141 Douglas's Senate speech: *Cong. Globe*, 35th Cong., 1st Sess. (1857), p. 14.

142 "What does": AL to Lyman Trumbull, Dec. 28, 1857, CWAL2, p. 430.

142 "There seems to be": *Chicago Tribune*, April 21, 1858.

142 "first and only": Beveridge, Vol. 4, p. 211.

142 AL's "House Divided" speech, June 16, 1858: CWAL2, pp. 461–69; "A house divided," p. 461; "We can not," pp. 465, 466; "another nice," p. 467; "[H]e *cares* not," p. 463.

146 were "fairly headed off": AL to John L. Scripps, June 23, 1858, ibid., p. 471.

146 Douglas's Chicago speech: Paul. M. Angle, ed., *Created Equal? The Complete Lincoln-Douglas Debates* (1958), pp. 12–25.

146 AL's Chicago speech, July 10, 1858: CWAL2, pp. 484–502; "a hundred times," p. 492; "as an exceedingly," p. 494.

147 "was a party to that conspiracy": AL speech, Springfield, July 17, 1858, ibid., p. 521.

147 From late summer: For background on the Lincoln-Douglas debates, see Beveridge, Vol. 4, pp. 280–333; Donald, pp. 209–24; Don E. Fehrenbacher, *Prelude to Greatness: Lincoln in the 1850s* (1962), pp. 96–142; Johannsen, pp. 662–77; Nevins, pp. 374–99; and David M.

Potter, *The Impending Crisis, 1848–1861*, ed. Don E. Fehrenbacher (1976), pp. 328–55.

148 "the fair young ladies": Beveridge, Vol. 4, p. 284.

148 "some mighty champion": *Philadelphia Press*, Aug. 23, 1858.

148 the Ottawa debate, Aug. 21, 1858: CWAL3, pp. 1–37: "For my part," p. 10; "physical differences," p. 16; "took a default," p. 2; "I do not say," ibid.

149 the Freeport debate, Aug. 27, 1858: Ibid., pp. 38–76; "most extraordinary," p. 41; "exceedingly sorry," p. 41; "an act of moral," p. 54; "the people have," p. 51.

152 "He cares nothing": AL to H. Asbury, July 31, 1858, CWAL2, p. 530.

153 "[I]f you, Black Republicans": CWAL3, p. 56.

153 the Jonesboro debate, Sept. 15, 1858: Ibid., pp. 102–144.

153 the Charleston debate, Sept. 18, 1858: Ibid., pp.145–201.

153 the Galesburg debate, Oct. 7, 1858: Ibid., pp. 207–44; quote at p. 220.

153 the Quincy debate, Oct. 13, 1858: Ibid., pp. 245–83; quote at p. 267.

153 the Alton debate, Oct. 15, 1858: Ibid., pp. 283–325; "I care more," p. 322; "the eternal," p. 315.

155 "I am glad I made": AL to Dr. Anson Henry, Nov. 19, 1858, ibid., p. 339.

155 "that judicial usurpation": *Cong. Globe*, 35th Cong. 1st Sess. (1858), p. 943.

155 RBT's reaction to Seward's attack: Tyler, p. 391.

156 RBT's thirty-page *Dred Scott* addendum: Ibid., pp. 578–608; "ignorant, degraded," pp. 599, 600; "founded upon," pp. 607, 608.

157 named Sherman Booth: For background on the Booth cases, see A. Beitzinger, "Federal Law Enforcement and the Booth Cases," 41 *Marq. L. Rev.* 7 (1957); Vroman Mason, "The Fugitive Slave Law in Wisconsin," *State Historical Society of Wisconsin Proceedings* (1896); Swisher, *History*, pp. 654–73; and Warren, pp. 258–65, 332–44.

158 "Freemen!": Mason, p. 124.

158 "Glory! Hallelujah!": Ibid., p. 125.

159 "prefer to see": Ibid., p. 129.

159 "I solemnly believe": *In re Booth*, 3 Wis. I, 48 (1848).

159 "the virus of a National Bench": *New York Tribune*, Feb. 2, 1855.

160 "moral perjury": Miller's charge, *Milwaukee Daily Wisconsin*, Jan. 26, 1855.

160 scathing criticism of Miller: Mason, p. 136.

160 When the Booth cases: For legal briefs and Supreme Court oral arguments in Booth cases, see Kurland and Casper, Vol. 3, pp. 287–334.

161 RBT's opinion in Booth cases: *Ableman v. Booth, U.S. v. Booth*, 21 How. 506 (1858). For the Wisconsin legislature resolutions, see Warren, p. 341.

163 "the deformity of Nullification": *National Intelligencer*, April 1, 1859.

164 "I have been on expences": AL to Norman Judd, Nov. 16, 1858, CWAL3, p. 377.

164 "I have no doubt": AL to Salmon P. Chase, June 9, 1859, ibid., p. 384.

165 "*white men*, even": AL to T. Canisius, May 17, 1859, ibid., p. 380.

165 Douglas published an article: *Harper's Magazine*, Vol. 19, (September 1859), pp. 521–26.

165 AL's Ohio speeches: CWAL3, pp. 400–62.

167 "glittering generalities": AL to H. Pierce, April 6, 1859, ibid., p. 375.

167 After he was informed: For background on AL's Cooper Union speech, see Harold Holzer, *Lincoln at Cooper Union: The Speech That Made Abraham Lincoln President* (2004).

167 AL's speech at Cooper Union, Feb. 27, 1860: CWAL3, pp. 522–50.

168 "LET US HAVE": Ibid., p. 550.

168 "Mr. Lincoln is one": Holzer, p. 146.

168 "went off passably": AL to Mary Lincoln, March 4, 1860, CWAL3, p. 555.

168 Robert's "homely" father: Holzer, p. 187.

168 "The taste *is* in my mouth": AL to Lyman Trumbull, April 29, 1860, CWAL4, p. 45.

170 "I hesitate to say it": AL to Simeon Francis, Aug. 4, 1860, ibid., p. 90.

170 "Honest Abe of the West": Tarbell, Vol. 1, p. 371.

171 "a blood-thirsty tyrant": Oates, p. 187.

171 "Mr. President": Donald, p. 255.

172 AL's insertion in Trumbull's speech, Nov. 20, 1860: CWAL4, pp. 141,142.

172 "This is just as": AL to H. Raymond Nov. 28, 1860, ibid., p. 146.

172 "THE UNION IS": *Charleston Mercury*, Dec. 20, 1860.

173 "Do the people": AL to Alexander Stephens, Dec. 22, 1860, CWAL4, p. 160.

173 "Stand firm": AL to Lyman Trumbull, Dec. 10, 1860, ibid., p. 150.

173 Lincoln bid farewell: Ibid., pp. 190, 191.

173 "that I may see": Ibid., p. 218.

174 "every star and stripe": Ibid., p. 192.

174 "[i]t may be necessary": Ibid., p. 237.

174 Lincoln concentrated on completing: For AL's cabinet, see Doris Kearns Goodwin, *Team of Rivals: The Political Genius of Abraham Lincoln* (2005).

175 Draft and final text of AL's first inaugural address: CWAL4, pp. 249–71; quotes at pp. 268, 271.

Chapter Six: "All the Laws But One"

177 RBT's gloomy prediction: RBT to J. Campbell, July 11, 1860, Oct. 19, 1860, HPMHS.

179 "on the brink": *National Intelligencer*, Dec. 29, 1860.

179 the unanimous Court decision: for Supreme Court arguments in *Kentucky v. Dennison*, see 24 How. (1861), pp. 70–95.

180 "the Constitution was the work": Swisher, *History*, p. 687.

180 RBT opinion in *Dennison*: 24 How. (1861), pp. 95–110.

180 "that he may be coerced": Ibid., p. 108.

180 John Marshall had performed: *Marbury v. Madison*, 1 Cranch 137 (1803).

181 "judicial twaddle": *New York Evening Post*, March 16, 1861.

182 AL's cabinet split, March 15, 1861: CWAL4, pp. 284, 285.

182 to "vindicate the hardy": Montgomery Blair to AL, March 15, 1861, ALPLC.

183 AL's proclamation, April 15, 1861: CWAL4, pp. 331, 332.

183 "without seriously repressing": James M. McPherson, *Battle Cry of Freedom: The Civil War Era* (1988), p. 275.

184 "Kentucky will furnish": Nicolay and Hay, Vol. 4, p. 90.

185 AL reply to Baltimore committee, April 22, 1861. CWAL4, pp. 341, 342.

185 "Why don't they come?": McPherson, p. 286.

186 "the bombardment of": AL to Gen. Scott, April 25, 1861, CWAL4, p. 344.

186 AL's suspension of the writ: AL to Gen. Scott, April 27, 1861, ibid., p. 347.

186 Merryman was seized: For background on the Merryman case, see George W. Brown, *Baltimore and the 19th of April 1861* (1887); William H. Rehnquist, *All the Laws But One: Civil Liberties in Wartime* (1998), pp. 11–39; Steiner, *Taney*, pp. 490–503; Swisher, *Taney*, pp. 547–56;

Swisher, *History*, pp. 844–54; and Tyler, pp. 419–31, 640–59. For background on Lincoln and civil liberties, see Dàniel Farber, *Lincoln's Constitution* (2003); Paul Finkelman, "Civil Liberties and the Civil War: The Great Emancipator as Civil Libertarian," 91 *Mich. L.R.* 1353 (1993); Mark E. Neely, Jr., *The Fate of Liberty: Abraham Lincoln and Civil Liberties* (1991); J. G. Randall, *Constitutional Problems Under Lincoln* (1951); and Geoffrey R. Stone, *Perilous Times: Free Speech in Wartime* (2004), pp. 79–134.

187 "charged with various": Tyler, p. 643.

187 "He [Cadwalader] most respectfully": Ibid.

188 "General Cadwalader was commanded": Ibid., p. 644.

189 "[t]he President, under the Constitution": Ibid., p. 645.

189 "Sensation": *Baltimore American*, May 29, 1861.

189 "Mr. Brown": Brown, p. 90.

190 "rebuke to the hoary": *New York Tribune*, May 29, 1861.

190 "to bring on a collision": *New York Times*, May 29, 1861.

190 At the outset: RBT opinion, *Ex parte Merryman*, 17 Federal Cases, 144, No. 9487 (C.C.D. Md. 1861).

190 "I certainly listened": Ibid., p. 149.

191 Marshall's opinion, *Ex parte Bollman*, 4 Cranch 95 (1807).

191 "But there is not": *Ex parte Merryman*, p. 150.

192 "that the laws shall be": Ibid., p. 151.

192 "upon any pretext": Ibid., p. 155.

193 "is essential to the existence": *Luther v. Borden*, 7 How. 1 (1849) at p. 45.

194 "The paroxysm of passion": RBT to Franklin Pierce, June 12, 1861, Pierce Papers.

195 AL's address to Congress, July 4, 1861: CWAL4, pp. 421–41; "so-called," p. 427; "the attention of," p. 429; "[A]re all the laws," p. 430.

197 Bates's advisory opinion: *Official Opinions of the Attorneys General* (1831–864), Vol. 10, p.74.

Chapter Seven: "A People's Contest"

199 "boyish cheerfulness": Ralph L. Rusk, *The Life of Ralph Waldo Emerson* (1949), p. 414.

199 "so ignorant": T. Harry Williams, ed., *The Union Sundered: The Life History of the United States*, Vol. 5: 1849–1865 (1963), p. 112.

199 "*will* and *purpose*": Howard K. Beale, ed., "The Diary of Edward Bates,"

Annual Report of the American Historical Association . . . 1930, Vol. 4, p. 220.

199 "frivolous and uncertain": Williams, p. 111.

200 "beyond the competency": CWAL4, p. 429.

200 "a government of": Ibid., p. 426.

200 "a People's contest": Ibid., p. 438.

201 "circumlocutions": *New York Tribune*, July 10, 1861.

202 "in repelling any invasion": Paludan, p. 87.

202 "I think to lose": AL to O. Browning, Sept. 22, 1861, CWAL4, p. 532.

203 AL's original order to Frémont: AL to John Frémont Sept. 2, 1861, ibid., p. 506.

203 AL's invitation to Mrs. Frémont ("Now, at once"): Sept.10, 1861, ibid., p. 515.

203 "You are quite a female": Allan Nevins, *Frémont: Pathmarker of the West* (1955), p. 516.

203 AL's second order to Frémont, Sept. 11, 1861: CWAL4, pp. 517, 518.

203 "born of": B. Wade to Z. Chandler, Sept. 23, 1861, Zachariah Chandler Papers, LOC.

204 "Fremont's operations": A. Chandler, to L. Chandler, Oct. 27, 1861, Chandler Papers, LOC.

204 as "nothing more than": Stephen W. Sears, ed., *The Civil War Papers of George B. McClellan: Selected Correspondence, 1860–1865* (1989), pp. 85, 86.

205 AL's blockade proclamation, April 19, 1861: CWAL4, pp. 338, 339.

205 In each case, a ship: For background on the Prize Cases, see *The Hiawatha* (*Crenshaw* and *Hiawatha* cases argued together), 12 Fed. Cas. 95 (No. 6451) (D.C.S.D.N.Y.); *The Amy Warwick*, 1 Fed. Cas. 808 (No. 342) (D.C.d. Mass. 1862); the *Brilliante* case was unreported in the lower court; see H.R. Exec. Doc. No.73, 37th Cong. 3rd Sess. (1863), p. 115; Swisher, *History*, pp. 877–85; Warren, pp. 380–84.

206 In his December report to Congress, Dec. 3, 1861: CWAL5, pp. 35–53.

207 "overrun by revolt": Ibid., p. 41.

207 AL–Thaddeus Stevens conversation: Charles M. Segal, ed., *Conversations with Lincoln* (1961), pp. 113, 114.

208 Lincoln moderated Seward's harsh: CWAL4, pp. 376–80.

208 "regrets": Ibid. p. 377.

208 "When this act": Ibid. p. 379.

209 "You may stand": Allan Nevins, *The War for the Union: The Improvised War, 1861–1862*, Vol. 1 (1959), p. 388.

209 "could show him in five minutes": Theodore Peace and James G. Randall, eds., *The Diary of Orville Hickman Browning* (1925–33), Vol. 1, p. 516.

210 "I found I could not": Frederick W. Seward, *Seward at Washington as Senator and Secretary of State* (1891), pp. 25, 26.

211 "The treasury is": Paludan, p. 109.

211 "General, what shall I do?": "General M. C. Meigs on the Conduct of the War," 26 *American Historical Review* 292 (1921).

211 He issued a presidential war order, Jan. 27, 1862: CWAL5, pp. 111, 112.

212 A resentful McClellan: Donald, p. 330.

212 "An unconditional and immediate surrender": McPherson, p. 402.

213 "I gave up all hope": Ulysses S. Grant, *Personal Memoirs* (1952), pp. 29, 30.

214 AL's message to Congress on slavery, March 6, 1862: CWAL5, pp. 144–46.

215 "that we must free": Howard K. Beale, ed., *Diary of Gideon Welles* (1960), Vol. 1, pp. 70, 71.

216 he placed his objections to the law, July 17, 1862: CWAL5, pp. 328–31.

216 the first draft of his proposed emancipation proclamation, July 22, 1862: Ibid., pp. 336–38.

216 "as a fit and necessary": Ibid., pp. 336, 337.

216 Lincoln had not asked: Goodwin, pp. 463–68.

217 "My paramount object": AL to Horace Greeley, Aug. 22, 1862, CWAL5, p. 388.

217 AL's meeting with freed slaves, Aug. 14, 1862: Ibid., pp. 370–75.

217 "You and we are": Ibid., p. 371.

218 AL's preliminary Emancipation Proclamation, Sept. 22, 1862: Ibid., pp. 433–36; quote at p. 434.

218 "I am satisfied": David Davis to L. Sweatt, Nov. 26, 1862, DPISHL.

218 "Will you pardon": AL to Gen. McCellan, Oct 24, 1862, CWAL5, p. 474.

219 "Mr. Lincoln's whole": David Davis to L. Sweatt, Nov. 26, 1862, DPISHL.

219 AL's annual message to Congress, Dec. 1, 1862: CWAL5, pp. 518–37.

219 "It is thought": David Davis to L. Sweatt, Dec. 22, 1862, DPISHL.

220 "I never, in my life": Seward, p. 151.

221 "those under which": Steiner, *Taney*, p. 503.

222 "Malignity would not fail": RBT to D. Perine, July 18, 1861, PPMHS.

222 "I expect some": RBT to Justice Wayne, Dec. 31, 1861, 13 *Maryland Historical Magazine* 167.

222 At home, he wrote: RBT's unpublished Legal Tender Act opinion, copy of manuscript, New York Public Library, New York.

223 By the time the Supreme Court heard: For background on Prize Cases before Supreme Court, legal briefs, see Kurland and Casper, Vol. 3, pp. 337–565; oral arguments, ibid., pp. 567–678; see also Charles Francis Adams, *Richard H. Dana*, Vol. 2, (1890), pp. 266–277; Swisher, *History*, pp. 877–900; and Warren, *History*, pp. 380–84.

225 "What a position": Adams, p. 266.

226 The "so-called blockade": Kurland and Casper, p. 572.

226 "It comes to": Ibid., p. 578.

226 "Necessity is an old plea": J. Catron to J. Carlisle, Feb. 26, 1863, 1 *Legal Historian* 51,52 (1958).

227 He "did no good": Howard Beale, ed., "The Diary of Edward Bates," 4 *Annual Report of the American Historical Association* 281 (1933).

227 "he deserved to be convicted": Ibid.

227 At the Prize Cases argument: 2 Black 635 (1863); "If a foreign power," p. 659; "there is no protection," p. 660; "This is conclusive," p. 664.

228 as "luminous and exquisite": Adams, p. 269.

228 "Well, your little": Ibid.

229 "I have won": Ibid., p. 270.

229 "was a secessionist": R. Grier to N. Clifford, July 24, 1861, Nathan Clifford Papers, Maine Historical Society, Portland, ME.

229 "[W]e must conquer": Ibid.

229 "You might": William D. Kelley, *Report of the Trial of William Smith, Piracy* (1861), p. 46.

230 "The President was bound": 2 Black at p. 669.

230 "the sinews of war": Ibid., p. 672.

231 Justice Nelson's concerns about the war: W. Nelson to N. Clifford, Sept. 25, 1862, Clifford Papers.

232 "a personal war": 2 Black at p. 695.

Chapter Eight: Silencing the Agitator

233 "The Union with him": Alexander H. Stephens, *A Constitutional View of the Late War between the States* (1868–70), Vol. 2, p. 448.

234 a "slave ship": Francis Key Howard, *Fourteen Months in American Bastiles* (1863), p. 29.

234 "without warrant of law": a printed copy of one of Carmichael's charges is filed with a letter from Carmichael to AL, July 22, 1862, ALPLC.

234 "has uttered treasonable language": J. Dix to H. Goldsborough, May 23, 1862, *Official Records of the Union and Confederate Armies, The War of the Rebellion* (cited hereafter as O.R.), 2nd (1880–1901), Vol. 3, pp. 576, 577.

235 "unluckily [Carmichael] received": J. Dix to E. Stanton, June 25, 1862, ALPLC.

235 "a treasonable memorial": J. Dix to A. Bradford, Feb. 10, 1862, O.R., 2nd, Vol. 2, p. 213.

235 "was not very favorably": AL to J. Crisfield, June 26, 1862, CWAL5, p. 285.

236 "treason committed": R. Carmichael to AL, July 22, 1862, ALPLC.

236 "for disloyal practices": AL's proclamation, Sept. 24, 1862, CWAL5, pp. 436, 437.

236 "who may be engaged": O.R., 3rd, Vol. 3, pp. 321, 322.

237 John Logan appealed directly: J. Logan to AL, Aug. 30, 1862, in Neely, p. 55.

237 "I strongly incline": AL to E. Stanton, Oct. 9, 1862, ibid.

238 "all persons discouraging": AL proclamation, Sept. 24, 1862, CWAL5, p. 437.

238 Hugh Campbell's complaint: Campbell to David Davis, Dec. 20, 1862, ALPLC.

238 AL's suspension of McPheeter order: AL to S. Curtis, Dec. 27, 1862, CWAL6, p. 20.

238 "Rebel priests": S. Curtis to AL, Dec. 28, 1862, ALPLC.

239 "usurpation of power": *Cong. Globe*, 37th Cong., 3rd Sess. (1862), p. 99.

239 "this new doctrine": [Indianapolis] *Daily State Sentinel*, Jan. 13, 1863.

239 "beyond the field": Stewart Mitchell, *Horatio Seymour of New York* (1938), p. 270.

239	the Wisconsin Supreme Court issued: *In re Kemp,* 16 Wis. 359 (1863).

240	Bates immediately counseled: E. Bates to E. Stanton, Jan. 31, 1863, Edwin Stanton Papers, LOC.

241	military serenades at Stones River: See McPherson, p. 588.

241	"God bless you": AL to Gen. Rosencrans, Jan. 5, 1863, CWAL6, p. 39.

241	"You gave us": AL to Gen. Rosencrans, Aug. 31, 1863, ibid., p. 424.

242	Vallandigham speech: *Cong. Globe,* 37th Cong., 3rd Sess. (1863), pp. 53–60; quotes at p. 54.

243	Lincoln anticipated: Enrollment Act, draft opinion, Sept. 14, 1863, CWAL6, pp. 444–49; quotes at pp. 448, 449.

244	"adulterated and corrupt": RBT to J. Mason Campbell, June 29, 1862, HPMHS.

244	"Although it may be": RBT to J. Mason Campbell, Sept. 13, 1861, ibid.

244	"pure Maryland air": RBT to B. Howard, July 29, 1862, ibid.

244	"all the horrors": RBT to Anne Campbell, Jan. 4, 1863, ibid.

244	Taney rejected Price's suggestion: RBT to J. Mason Campbell, March 18, 1863, ibid.

245	"in the miserable trash": RBT to D. Perine, Feb. 1, 1863, PPMHS.

245	RBT unpublished opinion on conscription law: Copy in New York Public Library, NY.

245	"All my life": RBT to David Perine, April 4, 1863, PPMHS.

246	"But my walking days": RBT to David Perine, Aug. 6, 1863, ibid.

247	"wicked, cruel": *Trial,* pp. 11, 12.

247	Burnside ordered Vallandigham's arrest: For background on the Vallandigham case, see *The Trial of Hon. Clement L. Vallandigham by a Military Commission* (1863); Farber, pp. 63–74; Frank L. Klement, *The Limits of Dissent: Clement L. Vallandigham and the Civil War* (1970), pp. 149–89; Rehnquist, pp. 59–74; Stone, pp. 94–120; and James L. Vallandigham, *A Life of Clement L. Vallandigham* (1872) pp. 262–95.

247	by "publicly expressing": *Ex parte Vallandigham,* 28 F Cases 874, 875 (C.C.O. 1863).

248	"those in arms": *Trial,* p. 264.

248	"The court cannot shut its eyes": *Ex parte Vallandigham,* 28 F. Cases, 874, 921, 922.

248	"artful men": Ibid., p. 923.

249	"perverse opinions": *New York Tribune,* May 16, 1863.

249	"all the liberties": Trumbull speech reported in *Cincinnati Daily Commercial,* June 11, 1863.

250 a "Caesar" and "tyrant": Klement, p. 109.

250 his "earnest consideration": Erastus Corning to AL, May 19, 1863, ibid., p. 181.

250 AL's defense of Vallandigham's arrest and conviction: AL to Erastus Corning, June 12, 1863, CWAL6, pp. 260–69: "Now, if there be," p. 266; "Mr. Vallandigham avows," "Must I shoot," Ibid.; "throughout the indefinite," p. 267.

252 AL's response to Ohio Democrats, June 29, 1863: CWAL6, pp. 300–06.

253 Matthew Lyon's case: Simon, pp. 53, 54; Stone, pp. 17–20.

253 Vallandigham's conviction: For the legal briefs, see Kurland and Casper, Vol. 4, pp. 167–89.

254 Supreme Court decision: *Ex parte Vallandigham*, 1 Wall 243 (1864).

254 "the common law": Ibid., p. 249

254 "My dear general": AL to Gen. McClellan, July 14, 1863, CWAL6, p. 328.

255 "a brave and skillful officer": AL to O. Howard, July 21, 1863, ibid., p. 341.

255 "lifted a great load": Grant, p. 381.

255 AL's long letter to James Conkling, Aug. 26, 1863: CWAL6, pp. 406–10; quotes at pp. 409, 410.

256 On November 18, Lincoln boarded: For background and brilliant analysis of AL's Gettysburg Address, see Garry Wills, *Lincoln at Gettysburg: The Words That Remade America* (1992). For drafts of AL's Gettysburg address, see CWAL7, pp. 17–23. For the final draft, ibid., p. 23.

256 Lincoln's annual report to Congress and proclamation, Dec. 8, 1863: Ibid., pp. 36–56; quote at p. 54.

258 "had given such": *New York Tribune*, Dec. 10, 1863.

258 "Who [is] so fit": *Chicago Tribune*, Dec. 14, 1863.

258 "I suppose he [Chase]": Tyler Bennett, ed., *Lincoln and the Civil War in the Diaries and Letters of John Hay* (1939), p. 110.

259 "Mr. Chase is": David Davis to G. Davis, Feb. 7, 1864, DPISHL.

259 "As the country": AL speech, March 9, 1864, CWAL7, p. 234.

260 "the Federal Union": Edward McPherson, *The Political History of the United States of America During the Great Rebellion* (1865), p. 420.

260 "This morning, as": AL memorandum, Aug. 23, 1864, CWAL7, p. 514.

260 "Atlanta is ours": McPherson, p. 774.

261 as "trash" and "worthless": RBT to J. Campbell, Jan. 14, 1863, CPMHS; RBT to D. Perine, Feb. 1, 1863, PPMHS.

261 "[T]he truth, I believe": RBT to J. Campbell, Jan. 14, 1863, CPMHS.

262 "Having been honored": RBT to Salmon P. Chase, Feb. 16, 1863, Tyler, p. 434.

262 "A civil war": *Carpenter v. U.S.* (RBT's opinion was omitted from the official volume of circuit court decisions but was reported in the *Baltimore Sun*, June 20, 1863.)

263 "had been seduced and betrayed": *Claimants of Merchandise v. U.S.* (Again, RBT's opinion was omitted from the official volume of circuit court decisions but was reported in the *Baltimore Daily Gazette*, June 4, 1863.)

263 "The treason cases": RBT to J. Campbell, May 14, 1864, HPMHS.

264 "the cold air": RBT to David Davis, Dec. 16, 1863, DPISHL.

264 "You must study": RBT to Taney Campbell, June 4, 1864, HPMHS.

264 "At the age of": RBT to David Perine, March 18, 1864, PPMHS.

264 "Can you lend": RBT to David Perine, May 25, 1864, ibid.

264 "With such prices": RBT to David Perine, Aug. 21, 1864, ibid.

265 Taney, in the fading moments: *Baltimore Sun*, Oct. 15, 1864.

265 "the great and good": D. W. Middleton to David Davis, Oct. 13, 1864, DPISHL.

265 "The name of Taney": *Cong. Globe*, 38th Cong., 2nd Sess. (1865), p. 1012.

266 "the course pursued": Beale, ed., *Welles Diary*, Vol. 2, pp. 176, 177.

266 "He was a man": Beale, ed. *Bates Diary*, p. 418.

266 "the crowning, retiring honor": E. Bates to AL, Oct. 13, 1864, ALPLC.

267 "Providence has given": Charles Sumner to AL, Oct. 12, 1864, ALPLC.

267 "It is perhaps": Salmon P. Chase to Charles Sumner, Oct. 19, 1864, ALPLC.

267 "I have only one doubt": Nicolay and Hay, Vol. 9, p. 394.

268 "we cannot ask": David M. Silver, *Lincoln's Supreme Court* (1956), p. 208.

Epilogue

269 Taney's estate: See Swisher, *Taney*, pp. 579, 580.

269 "that now an emancipated": *Cong. Globe*, 38th Cong., 2nd Sess. (1865), pp. 1013, 1017.

270 "dignity, his love of order": Tyler, p. 512.

270 "stability, uniformity": Ibid., p. 516.

272 In the 1866 decision: *Ex parte Milligan*, 4 Wall. 2 (1866).

273 "[c]ivil liberty": Ibid., pp. 124, 125.

273 "bore his wounds": 17 *American Bar Assoc. Journal* 790 (1931).

273 AL's annual address to Congress, Dec. 6, 1864: CWAL8, pp. 136–53; quotes at pp. 151, 152, 149.

274 "You made a magnificent": AL to Gen. Thomas, Dec. 16, 1864, ibid., p. 169.

274 "[T]his amendment": AL's response to crowd, ibid., pp. 254, 255.

274 it was "entirely fruitless": Stephens, Vol. 2, pp. 599–619.

274 "to have no": AL to Gen. Grant, March 3, 1865, CWAL8, p.330.

275 AL's second inaugural address, March 4, 1865: Ibid., pp. 332, 333.

275 "of the dispersion": Salmon P. Chase to Mary Lincoln, March 4, 1865, ALPLC.

276 "Let the *thing* be pressed": AL to Gen. Grant, April 7, 1865, CWAL8, p.392.

276 "Allow me respectfully": E. Stanton to AL, April 3, 1865, ALPLC.

276 "I will take care": AL to E. Stanton April 3, 1865, CWAL8, p. 385.

277 Lincoln listed three: AL to J. Campbell, April 5, 1865, ibid., pp. 386, 387.

277 "to dribble it": AL's response to crowd, April 10, 1865, ibid., p. 393.

278 "without regard": Salmon P. Chase to AL, April 11, 1865, ibid., p. 399.

278 AL's address, April 11, 1865: Ibid., pp. 399–405; quote at p. 404.

279 "That means": William Hanchette, *The Lincoln Murder Conspiracies* (1983), p. 37.

281 "false, scandalous, and malicious": *Cong. Globe*, 5th Cong., 2nd Sess. (1798), ch. 74.

283 The Espionage Act of 1917: 40 Stat. 217, 219.

283 Supreme Court's *Debs* decision: *Debs v. U.S.*, 249 U.S. 211 (1919).

283 "the natural and intended": Ibid., p. 216.

283 Court's vigilant protection of political speech: See *Brandenburg v. Ohio*, 395 U.S. 444 (1969).

284 The Court rejected: *Korematsu v. U.S.*, 323 U.S. 214 (1944).

284 Recent scholarship has suggested: See, e.g., John H. Ely, *War and Responsibility: Constitutional Lessons of Vietnam and Its Aftermath* (1993).

284 The War Powers Resolutions of 1973: 87 Stat. 555.

284 In *Rasul v. Bush*: 124 S. Ct. 2686 (2004).

284 in *Hamdi v. Rumsfeld*: 124 S. Ct. 2633 (2004).

285 In *Hamden v. Rumsfeld*, No. 05–184, decided June 29, 2006.

285 "We have long": Ibid., p. 2650.

285 Frankfurter's admiration for AL: See James F. Simon, *The Antagonists: Hugo Black, Felix Frankfurter and Civil Liberties in Modern America* (1989), p. 38; *Minersville School Dist. v. Gobitis*, 310 U.S.586 (1940), p. 596.

285 "To his immense credit": Trachtman lecture, Feb. 26, 2005, delivered to the American College of Trust and Estate Counsel, Orlando, FL.

286 "the last best hope": AL's annual message to Congress, Dec. 1, 1862, CWAL5, p. 537.

INDEX